ST. MARY'S UNIVERSITY COLLEGE

ST.MARY'S UNIVERSITY COLLEGE LIBRARY
7 DAY

ST. MARY'S UNIVERSITY COLLEGE LIBRARY
A COLLEGE OF THE UNIVERSITY OF BELFAST

68237

Web: rys-belfast.ac.uk
email: marys-belfast.ac.uk

7 DAY LOAN

Fines will be charged for overdue and recalled books not returned by stated date.

Date Due	Date Due	Date Due
- 2 DEC 2008	0 4 DEC 2012	
19 OCT 2009	19 NOV 2013	
26 OCT 2009	26 OCT 2015	
0 7 JAN 2010	30 NOV 2017	
18 JAN 2010	12 NOV 2018	
- 5 DEC 2011		
14 DEC 2011		
23 MAY 2012		
2 OCT 2012		

LINDISFARNE
BOOKS

First published 1999 by
Lindisfarne Books
7-8 Lower Abbey Street
Dublin 1

Available in the UK from:
Veritas Co. (UK) Ltd
Lower Avenue
Leamington Spa
Warwickshire CV31 3NP

Lindisfarne is an imprint of Veritas Publications

ISBN 1 85390 463 5

Cover design by Bill Bolger
Printed in the Republic of Ireland by Betaprint Ltd, Dublin

You can take the man out of Armagh, but you may ask
yourself,
can you take the Armagh out of the man in the big Armani suit?

Paul Muldoon, 'Talking Heads: *True Stories*', in *Hay (1998)*

ACKNOWLEDGEMENTS

This volume began life as a series of annual lectures hosted by St Andrew's College to mark Education Week in the Scottish Catholic Church. Over the years these lectures have been supported by the Roman Catholic Bishops' conference of Scotland and I am grateful, in particular, to Cardinal T. J. Winning and Archbishop K. P. O'Brien. In recent years Veritas Publications has played a prominent role in the development of the lectures and I am grateful to Maura Hyland, Bríd Healy and Fiona Biggs for their support for both this volume and the public lectures. It has been a privilege to have been able to host these lectures and so invite thoughtful and challenging scholars of international reputation to St Andrew's. Earlier versions of the essays by J. Day, V. Duminuco, J. Haldane, J. Hull, A. Price and J. O'Keefe were published in the St Andrew's College Occasional Papers in Education series edited by Conroy.

Finally, I am grateful to colleagues in the Department of Religious Education and the Library at St Andrew's College for their support. Honor Hania, Deputy Librarian, deserves particular mention for her willingness to assist with the proofing and referencing of this text.

CONTENTS

FROM CLICHÉ TO CRITIQUE:
AN INTRODUCTION

James C. Conroy

It was only serendipity which would have enabled a Catholic teacher or student of education to encounter a serious study of Catholic education originating in Britain in the 1970s. Certainly there were books and papers on religious education in a Catholic context, notably in the work of Kevin Nichols (1979, 1980), though most of these were generated by local conferences of bishops or their education officers, or had their roots in Conciliar and post-Conciliar documents. So too, there were some sociological studies about Catholicism or the Catholic community by Hornsby-Smith (1979) and others. Studies about, or philo-theological reflections on the system of Catholic education were, however, rare indeed. Any public discussion tended to be negative with scholars such as Paul Hirst (1974) regarding education within a religious tradition as coercive and indoctrinatory, and consequently unable or unfitted to make a proper contribution to a genuinely democratic polity. Where there was positive scholarship it was largely historical, dealing with the development and evolution of the separate Catholic school system. Teachers and others interested in Catholic education tended to look to North America and Continental Europe for new and challenging perspectives.

By way of contrast the 1990s have seen a rash of studies about Catholic education in the British Isles. Many of these studies have their origins in the work of Nichols, in the publication by the Bishops' Conference of England & Wales of *Signposts and Homecomings* (1980), in the visit of Pope John Paul II to Britain with his many exhortations to both reflect upon and nurture Catholic education, and in a growing self-confidence of Catholics as 'fully paid up' members of British society. This last point is

nteresting in as much as such self-confidence
an index of integration into the polity. In the
e then Secretary of State for Education, himself
n to be increasingly relying on the advice of
other Catholics in or on the margins of education; when the leader
of Her Majesty's Opposition, subsequently Prime Minister, chose
to send his children to a Catholic school it might be argued that
Catholic schools have come of age. Yet further corroboration of this
new-found 'importance' is to be had in the many press reports
which have accompanied recent Ofsted studies, suggesting that
Catholic schools were academically and socially more effective than
other schools located in similar catchments and drawing upon the
same or similar socio-economic groups. On one interpretation
these events may be seen as a sign of the maturity of the Catholic
community and, as such, are to be welcomed.

It is equally possible to interpret such developments as the final
steps in the submerging of a distinctive Catholic culture – for a
coming generation, attachment to Catholicism is likely to be a
cultural rather than an epistemic or an ontological phenomenon.
In such circumstances it becomes urgent that Catholics interested
in education continue to reflect meaningfully on whether or not
there is a continuing role for Catholic schooling and, if there is,
what shape this should take.

Previous collections about Catholic education have tended to
focus on Catholic educationalists talking to other Catholic
educationalists with the occasional intervention by a bishop. This
volume represents something of a departure in so far as it attempts
to invite others, who operate outside Catholic education, to enter
into a dialogue with those of us who work from within. In this
sense it is both an open-ended conversation about and a study in
the politics of Catholic education. Part One focuses on the
reflections of Catholics within the tradition whereas Part Two
provides the opportunity for a number of reflective friends to offer
comment on Catholic education from without. Part One is further

divided into two sections, the first being concerned with generic and political issues to do with Catholic education; the second to interrogate what is or might be the forms and content of Catholic education.

In Part One, Section One, essays by O'Keefe and Duminuco focus on the development of a structural understanding of Catholic education; drawing on the traditions of the Church as heuristic devices they ask, 'can we legitimately defend our rhetorical claims as to the purposes of Catholic education by reference to actual practice and the pupils' lived experiences?' My own chapter offers a distinctive, but I hope not unreasonable, set of spectacles with which to view Catholic education. To ask whether or not Catholic schools should continue to exist is to ask, 'how are they different from other schools?' Just as City Technology Colleges or Magnet schools for the gifted, talented or more able, or special schools exist because of the distinctiveness of their actual provision, the manner in which resources are deployed and so on, so too Catholic schools should be required to justify their continued existence in terms of their distinctiveness. In parenthesis, it is worth observing that public and political discourse about the 'able' is on the increase while conversations about other individuals and groups of children is on the slide.

John Brick returns us to our roots through the provision of an expansive interrogation of the Conciliar and post-Conciliar documents on education. In doing so he opens up fresh approaches to some of the very real and immediate challenges of our contemporary culture. These are taken up by Price, who charts a pathway through the political and religious turbulence which has sought to redefine the historic premises and presuppositions upon which Catholic education has built its system since 1870. In this he makes us aware of the emergence of an important distinction between those who have regarded Catholic education as representing a coherent and cohesive system of education and those who now see Catholic schools as discrete, with the focus on their particularity. Here, more than anywhere, we may see the impact of the neo-liberal political and economic view of the world which, by its very nature, breaks down traditional, if informal, allegiances and identities.

In the second section of Part One, Davis lucidly opens up a central, if frequently avoided, question as to what might count as the underlying principles of a Catholic curriculum. In his essay he manages to trace the ways in which we have enslaved ourselves by a too close allegiance to the particular forms of knowing offered us by the Enlightenment. In their different ways Haldane and Carr take up this theme, suggesting that there are coherent alternatives to the subjectivism currently offered in the exploration of truth and value. In Haldane's case the reduction of spirituality to a 'warm feeling' is robustly challenged. For both, there is a cogent and important argument to be made for the resurrection of authoritative tradition as a counterpoint to the collapse into individual preferences.

MacMillan, not an educationalist but a gifted artist with a real concern for Catholic education, offers a refreshing perspective on the place of inspiration in both the curriculum and the culture of the school. His is a timely reminder that all is not vested in the system or the management but in the openness to the spirit which nurtures our creativity and our imagination. The writers in this section, either implicitly or explicitly, expose the weakness of current trends towards 'quick fix' education which is generally represented by the triumph of glossy presentation over substance.

In Part Two, MacKenzie advances a phenomenological view of Catholic education in Scotland. His incisiveness enables us to explore Catholic education by drawing upon a range of sociological and cultural perspectives as heuristic devices. While, like some others in this section, he looks at the particularity of the Scottish experience, the importance and usefulness of his observations are not limited to Scotland. Also, like others, including McCreath, Day and Rodgers, he offers a glimpse at what is probably a widely held perception: that the institution of the Catholic Church has yet to clarify, for itself, the distinctions between authority and authoritarianism and that this failure continues to bedevil the practice in Catholic schools and the Catholic system. This also finds interesting echoes in Haldane's essay.

Day and Hull, coming from very different perspectives, provide profound insights into the place of relationality in Catholic education. Theirs is a stark warning that a failure to have right relationships, whether they be with others or with money, open our schools and system to a form of self-mutilation which fails to allow our real potential to emerge. The particular attitudes to money take us back to the heart of O'Keefe's anxieties that Catholic schools are in danger of becoming 'life-style' enclaves. The forms of idolatry which they hint at also resonate with McCreath's analysis of management and its implications for the inner life of the Catholic school. Too often we delude ourselves into one of two false positions: that we have a thing called Catholic management which is *sui generis,* or that we just have to adopt the techniques and strategies of the latest guru uncritically. Neither of these, he suggests, will do.

As citizenship moves up the political agenda, McGettrick's Epilogue concludes with some reflections pointing us towards new and creative ways of engaging with the polity. Indeed this volume has at its very heart the attempt to open up an honest, intellectually satisfying and provocative debate about how Catholic education and, by implication, Catholics should relate to the polity. It does not provide a single focus or a party line but sets out a substantial and wide-ranging debate about both the enormous gift of Catholic education to the polity and its current limitations. As Catholic educators we are concerned to engage in a cutting-edge debate which makes new and interesting dissonances and connections; the better to see the whole.

Glasgow 1999

PART ONE
Catholic Education – Inside-Out/Outside-In

SECTION ONE
Structural Issues in Catholic Education

1

VISIONARY LEADERSHIP IN CATHOLIC SCHOOLS

Joseph O'Keefe

The contemporary social context

At the centre of every New England town, there exists an open green space that we call the commons. Originally, when these towns were founded by Puritans in the seventeenth century, a common space provided pasture as well as a venue for civic and religious events. It was surrounded by houses, stores and churches, a vibrant incarnation of the community that called itself a commonwealth. Today these commons are often dangerous as a result of crime and are overrun with weeds because of taxpayers' refusal to commit themselves to public services. The wealthy most often remain in fenced communities, behind high walls, protected by sophisticated security devices. The poor, by contrast, are often condemned to the treeless and grey world of urban blight.

What has happened to the commons? In their study of 145 people who lead lives of commitment in a complex world, Laurent Daloz and his colleagues discovered the challenge of the contemporary scene:

> For most, our common gathering places are increasingly restaurants, where our association is primarily one of anonymity; the video arcade, where the young are mesmerised into single-syllable conversation by neon violence; the mall, where consumer thirst and adolescent drift are the primary agenda; the high-rise office building, where we meet briefly in elevators; the TV screen, where we feel both engaged and

removed; and, for some, the Internet, where we meet fleetingly – and often anonymously – in cyberspace (1996, pp. 2-3)

Daloz and his colleagues are not the first to describe the culture of anonymity and depersonalisation.

In the early 1980s, Robert Bellah and his associates conducted interviews with a nation-wide sample of white middle-class Americans in an attempt to provide a broad-scale observation of American culture. Alarmed by the anomie that emerged so powerfully in their data, they called for a renewal of the best of the past, a recollection which could become the linch-pin of what they called a 'community of memory... a group of people who are different yet interdependent, who are bound together by mutual responsibilities arising out of a common history constituted by their past' (1985, p. 246). Such communities are indeed rare, especially given the uncritical assumption of a philosophy of free-market individualism. In contemporary culture, human gatherings are often ersatz communities, 'lifestyle enclaves', where 'history and hope are forgotten and community means only a gathering of the similar' (Bellah, 1985, p. 154).

American culture today suffers from ethical anomie, a societal 'rudderlessness' with respect to values, a lack of clarity about what constitutes an ethical 'common ground' (Purpel, 1989). Two frequent and unsatisfactory responses to this condition are nostalgia and narcissism. In contrast to the thoughtful recollection of the past that constitutes a 'community of memory', nostalgia is an uncritical longing for things as they once were. In this vein, the past was a better time with more caring and intact families, less bureaucratic government, safety on the streets, a greater sense of personal responsibility and clear consensus concerning values. Ironically, nostalgia 'does not entail the exercise of memory at all, since the past it idealises stands outside time, frozen in unchanging perfection' (Lasch, 1991, p. 83). It involves a longing 'for the way we never were' (Coontz, 1992) and therefore fails to solve the problem of anomie.

If nostalgia involves a looking to the past for simplistic answers to an ethical crisis, another response, narcissism, involves looking within. Narcissism is the obsession with oneself and one's own well-being. The flood of books, magazines, groups and seminars pertaining to self-help, self-realisation, self-actualisation and finding oneself confirms the existence of such an obsession. An outgrowth of narcissism is the 'therapeutic self' which is 'defined by its own wants and satisfactions, coordinated by cost-benefit calculation' (Bellah, 1985, p. 127).

Whether referred to as 'the culture of contentment' (Galbraith, 1992), 'the culture of procurement' (Delattre, 1988) or 'the culture of narcissism' (Lasch, 1979), excessive focus on one's individual well-being ultimately produces a chillingly cold new world. Lasch explains: 'Now that private life has been largely absorbed by the market, a new school of economic thought offers what amounts to a new moral vision: a society wholly dominated by the market, in which economic relations are no longer softened by ties of trust and solidarity' (1995, p. 102).

Very many thoughtful and cautious commentators echo this line of argument. While some intact communities do in fact exist and thrive, nostalgia and narcissism erode any sense of a broader commonwealth. Jean Beth comments:

> No doubt a distinction should be made between the dominant rhetoric of individualism and the culture of cynicism, on the one hand, and how we actually behave as members of families, communities, churches, and neighbourhoods, on the other hand. But surely it is true that our social practices are under extraordinary pressure and thus that democracy itself is being squeezed. In America today, fearful people rush to arm themselves, believing safety to be a matter of aggressive self-help. Angry people want all the politicians to be kicked out of office, but they believe new ones will be no better. Anxious people fear that their neighbours' children may get some unfair

advantage over their own. Despairing people destroy their own lives and the lives of those around them. Careless people ignore their children and then blast the teachers and social workers who must tend to the mess they have made, screaming all the while that folks ought to 'mind their own business'. Many human ills cannot be cured, of course. All human lives are lived on the edge of quiet desperation. We must all be rescued from time to time from fear and sorrow. But I read the palpable despair and cynicism and violence as dark signs of the times, as warnings that democracy may not be up to the task of satisfying the yearnings it unleashes for freedom and fairness and equality (1995, pp. 20-21).

An assimilated Church

Since the publication of the 1971 Catholic document *Justice in the World*, the notion of 'reading the signs of the times' has entered the lexicon of the Church community (Synod of Roman Catholic Bishops, 1971, § 2). Catholics in the United States are by no means immune from the dark signs of contemporary culture. This marks a change; from the nation's founding to the recent past, Catholics constituted an immigrant subculture that was often impervious to larger trends. Recent sociological inquiry confirms that by every standard, the 25% of American citizens who call themselves Catholics resemble the other 75% of the nation's population.

American Catholics today are more highly educated than ever, more at ease as full participants in the exercise of social and political power from Congress to boardroom, more often in contact with other Christian religious groups, and more in tune with American ideas of individual freedom, personal autonomy, politically, socially, and economically. The situation today is a culmination of a half century of constant change (D'Antonio, Davidson, Hoge & Wallace, 1996, p. 160).

The election of John F. Kennedy as President of the United States was emblematic of the assimilation and upward mobility of the Catholic population, an event roughly concurrent with the Second Vatican Council. Assimilation, upward mobility and internal ecclesial renewal together changed the face of the American Church, for good and for ill.

In a recently published comprehensive history of the Church in the United States, Charles Morris describes the impact of these changes on the laity:

> To a remarkable degree they run the parishes, plan liturgies, carry out works of mercy, supervise the budget. They treat their priests with respect as sacramental ministers but don't hesitate to pass judgment on them as leaders and teachers. They still look to the Church for moral guidance, but they are searching for principles not rulers. The traditional Catholic code of behaviour was perfect for peasants fighting their way out of the bogs, and it worked well enough for second-generation immigrants on the first rungs of middle-class respectability. But except for the newest wave of Hispanic immigrants, American Catholics have long since made it in America. As much as any other religious body, they are middle-class, suburban, educated and affluent. They exercise control over their own lives in a way their grandparents never did (Morris, 1997, pp. 430-31).

A challenge for Catholic schools

Schools are a microcosm of society, reflecting the larger environment. Broader changes in American Catholicism have altered the philosophy and practice of education. Heightened lay responsibility for institutional commitments, religious belief based more on critical reflection than docility, engagement in politics and commerce on the highest levels – these have brought great benefit to the Church's educational endeavours. Along with these benefits, however, comes crass and short-sighted secularism that characterises the Era of the Market in which we now live. In his history of parochial schools, Timothy Walch comments that 'The principal concern of all parents – Catholic as well as non-Catholic – is the future careers and economic security of their children. Unlike their parents and grandparents, Catholic parents today do not value the spiritual development of their children as highly as their career development' (Walch, 1996, p. 245).

The metaphor of the marketplace reflects the narcissism that afflicts contemporary society. Advocates of consumer-oriented education want to create a 'market' of schools wherein parents and students choose what is best for them; this choosing a school on the basis of self-interest will supposedly create a competitive environment between schools where none exists now, thereby pressuring schools to improve. The fundamental unit of consideration in the education marketplace is the individual, however, and not the well-being of the whole. Some have questioned the wisdom of such a movement:

> With all these developments has come the new educational vocabulary of 'customers' and 'service delivery'; of 'marketing' and 'promotion'; of 'the chief executive' and the 'business plan'; of 'cost control' and 'quality assurance'. What are we to make of all this – we parents, we governors, we teachers and headteachers, we citizens and taxpayers, we pupils and students, the citizens of tomorrow? Has the education system at last been brought to sanity and the real world? Will it be reinvigorated and made more effective by the application of market principles? Or is all this an ideologically-led perversion of a system which needs to be governed by quite different economic and social principles? (Bridges & McLaughlin, 1994, p. 3).

Sadly, many Catholic educators uncritically embrace these principles, in practice and on the level of public policy. Gerald Grace's assessment of the English scene is appropriate for the United States as well:

> Catholic schools in many societies are working in social, political and ideological conditions which challenge fundamentally their distinctive educational mission and their historical educational commitments. In these present contexts, a Catholic conception of education as primarily moral and spiritual, concerned with principled behaviour and focused upon community and public good outcomes faces a major challenge from New Right conceptions of education which are aggressively market oriented and individualistic in approach (Grace, 1996, p. 70).

A challenge for all schools   *Positive of Cshouls*

The demise of the commons has placed new challenges on the school. Increasingly, a social service provider in isolation cannot respond effectively to the needs of today's young people. In dramatic contrast to the dominant ethos of nostalgia and narcissism, these times demand novel collaborative structures, especially in communities that experience gang violence, drug selling, family violence, child abuse and poverty. Clearly, 'the complexity of problems facing communities requires a comprehensive approach' (Perkins, Borden & Hogue, 1998).

Nostalgia is not a proper response to the detrimental effects of narcissism. Rather, the challenges of the present can be met through the recovery of the best of the past, the community of memory to which Bellah refers, a group of people, 'bound together by mutual responsibilities arising out of a common history constituted by their past'.

The informal but powerful family and community connections that existed in Catholic parish schools do not appear to be as strong as they once had been. This change in Catholic schooling has occurred at the same time that society has begun to recognise the necessity and power of the school-family-community link, not only for the academic development of the child as a learner, but, more fundamentally, for the overall development of the whole child as human being and future citizen. As public schools begin to shift in the direction of stronger school-family-community links, Catholic schools must also seek ways to recover or maintain the strength in this area that they have known in past decades (Walsh, Buckley & Howard, 1998).

A strength of Catholic schools has always been its emphasis on the education of the whole person, exercised within a web of integrated services. Although the social context and ecclesial self-understanding is not the same as it was for the immigrant Church, the need for such a communal ethos has never been as great. According to its charter document, the contemporary Catholic school

is designed not only to develop with special care the intellectual faculties but also to form the ability to judge rightly, to hand on the cultural legacy of previous generations, to foster a sense of values, to prepare for professional life. Between pupils of different talents and backgrounds it promotes friendly relations and fosters a spirit of mutual understanding; and it establishes as it were a center whose work and progress must be shared together by families, teachers, associations of various types that foster cultural, civic, and religious life, as well as by civil society and the entire human community (*Gravissimum educationis*, 1965, § 5).

Creating a formative Catholic school culture

The joys and hopes, the griefs and anxieties (*Gaudium et spes*, §1) of the contemporary world demand a revitalised role for Catholic schools. In a recent articulation of a Catholic philosophy of education, Thomas Groome (1998) delineates eight features of Catholicism that undergird the educational response to the current social context:

1. A positive anthropology (a good people, in God's own image and likeness);
2. A gracious world (seeing God in all things);
3. A community for life (made for each other);
4. A tradition to inherit (a family heirloom);
5. A reasonable wisdom (thinking for life);
6. A spirituality for everyone (our hearts are restless until they rest in you);
7. A faith that does justice (beyond the scales);
8. A Catholic openness (here come everybody).

In similar fashion, I present for consideration my articulation of eight characteristics of the contemporary Catholic school.

Eight characteristics of the contemporary Catholic school

1. Lex orandi, lex credendi

Beliefs are shaped by the experience of communal prayer; faith is more than intellectual assent to formal propositions. Catholicism has a rich tradition of ritual. In the realm of faith, the eloquence of words is often surpassed by bread, wine, water, oil and fire. Catholic schools should immerse students in a living Catholic culture that permeates all aspects of school life. They should experience the traditions of prayer that mark the passage of hours, understand the rhythm of the liturgical year from fasts to feasts and experience in sound, sight, taste, touch and smell the living tradition which they inherit. Young people come to faith through invitation and attraction, not coercion. Catholic educators have a host of symbols to sustain strong school communities in this post-positivistic age, when the secular world is discovering the importance of culture, meaning, metaphor, ritual, ceremony, stories and heroes (Bolman & Deal, 1997).

2. *Et Verbum caro factum est*

At the heart of a Catholic sensibility is the mystery of the Incarnation; the word was made flesh. This Christological tenet is the basis of an anthropology of hope. While recognising the nature of sin and facing honestly the brokenness that is constitutive of the human experience, Catholics see in the Incarnation the nearness of God and the possibilities of authentic existence. Even in a world filled with cynicism, it is indeed possible to have the courage of one's convictions.

In an era of narcissism, Catholic anthropology stands as a challenge to the relativism of the contemporary age. The dignity of the human person and the importance of respect for self and others can offer a compelling alternative to the disrespect for life that manifests itself in dehumanising sexual mores, expedient medical decisions that affect the lives of the unborn and the dying, indifference to the needs of poor children, neglect of the disabled and disregard for the elderly.

Catholicism offers to the young the lives of Mary and other saints who, through the centuries, followed the way of Christ. A panoply of saints, officially canonised or popularly acclaimed, demonstrates that holiness is neither abstract nor unattainable, but incarnated in the real world.

3. *The school is a community of memory*

Catholicism honours a tradition that is centuries old. In a world plagued by anomie students must learn the stories told in a way that is compelling for the present. Students should be exposed to Catholic culture: literature, history, music and art. Likewise, students should learn the rich and complex history of the Church, read developmentally appropriate original sources in theology and philosophy and learn about the controversies and councils that chronicle a pilgrim Church, a community. Education is the passing of sacred stories from one generation to the next.

In confronting the challenges of the present, Catholic educators can turn to the past to find elements of a creative response to the present. For example, Jesuit schools in the United States look to their Ignatian tradition. A key principle of Ignatian spirituality is *simul contemplivus in actione* (contemplation in action). Not only did the Spiritual Exercises (developed by Ignatius) call for reflection on experience in the world; in founding his community Ignatius explicitly avoided the isolation of monastic life. It is only through reflection on experience that one can come to see 'God in all things'. The instruction to teachers in the document on Ignatian pedagogy (International Commission on the Apostolate of Jesuit Education, 1994) specifies a five-step process, based on principles of the Spiritual Exercises of St Ignatius, to 'develop men and women of competence, conscience and compassion'. The following represents a summary of those five steps:

1) *Context* – Recognise family, peers, social situations, the school itself, politics, economics, cultural climate, religion, media and other realities that affect the learning process.
2) *Experience* – Foster a broad base of experience that goes beyond memorisation and requires application, analysis, synthesis and evaluation so that learners are attentive to the human reality that confronts them.

3) *Reflection* – Reconsider subject matter so that students raise the questions, 'Who am I?' and 'Who might I be in relation to others?' Broadening students' awareness through discussion, journaling, reaction/reflection papers, or in simply considering the viewpoints of others.

4) *Action* – For Ignatius, love is shown in deeds not words. Through experience that has been reflected upon, students make the truth their own and serve others. Educators help students to consider their experience from a personal, human point of view while, at the same time, remaining open to where the truth might lead. Ignatian education also strives to convince students to act upon their convictions for the welfare of society.

5) *Evaluation* – Educators evaluate the whole person, physical, intellectual, religious, social and cultural. Effective methods of evaluation include assessment, peer tutoring, journal reflection, and critical skill application. Educators congratulate and encourage students for their progress.

The five pedagogical principles above concern learning; they are complemented by the five characteristics articulated by Jesuit educators concerning the graduate at graduation. These latter five characteristics have more to do with the kind of person one becomes, with the practice of life. At the end of secondary studies, young men and women should be competent in five domains: open to growth; intellectually competent; religious; loving; and, committed to doing justice. These five characteristics might be viewed as the outcome of the five-step educational process already described, the life's practice which is the aim of Ignatian pedagogy. A summary word on each:

1) *Open to growth* – The student should have matured to a level that reflects intentional responsibility for growth as opposed to a passive drifting or a laissez-faire attitude. He/she

is beginning to reach out in his/her development, seeking opportunities to stretch his/her mind, imagination, feelings and religious consciousness.

2) *Intellectually competent* – The graduate should demonstrate mastery of fundamental tools of learning and will be well on the way to advanced levels of learning in skills and attitudes. He/she should possess a literate, scientific, critical consciousness as well as a basic knowledge of intellectual history, global perspectives and the formation of public policy.

3) *Religious* – The graduate must have a basic knowledge of major doctrines and practices of the Catholic faith as well as an articulation of personal feelings and beliefs with a view toward choosing a fundamental orientation toward God and relationship with a religious tradition and community. He/she should have exposure to non-Catholic and non-Christian traditions. The graduate should have a well-formed conscience to evaluate moral choices. He/she is beginning to understand the relationship between faith in Jesus and being a person for others, has had some satisfying experiences of serving others in need and has come to a sympathetic appreciation of their need for respect, justice and love.

4) *Loving* – The graduate will have established his/her own identity beyond self-interest. He/she will have integrated sexuality and developed deeper levels of relationship in which the self has been disclosed and the mystery of another person accepted. The graduate trusts the fidelity of significant others, has come to grips with prejudices and stereotypes, and has the potential to show empathy toward a wide range of people.

5) *Committed to doing justice* – The graduate knows the needs of local and wider communities and prepares to take a place in these communities as a competent, concerned and responsible member. He/she sees the potential for complicity with unjust structures and recognises selfish attitudes. Since Christian faith implies a commitment to a just society, the graduate is

beginning to understand the structural roots of injustice in social institutions, attitudes and customs, has compassion for victims of injustice and concern for those social changes that will assist them in gaining their rights and increased human dignity. He/she is beginning to see the importance of voter influence on public policy in local, regional, national and international arenas, beginning to understand the complexity of many social issues and the need for critical reading of diverse sources of information about them. He/she is beginning to realise that the values of a consumer society are often in conflict with the demands of a just society, and indeed with the Gospel (Commission on Research and Development of the Jesuit Secondary Education Association, 1992).

4. The best decisions are made at local level

A cornerstone of a Catholic view of society is the principle of subsidiarity: while all structures must be judged according to the common good, especially the good of disadvantaged members of the global human family, the preferable arena of decision-making and action is local. Human dignity is served better by families, neighbourhoods and local communities than by large, impersonal, bureaucratic structures. The Church has reaffirmed this conviction: in concert with solidarity one must oppose all forms of collectivism (*CCC* 1886, 1988); larger entities must exercise restraint, especially in order to protect the integrity of the family (*CCC* 2209). Like many others, Bryk (1996, pp. 30-31) attributes much of the success of Catholic schools to this sensibility: 'Rather than regulating human activity under the homogenising norms of a central bureaucracy, the role of external governance is to facilitate and stimulate collective local action.' Bureaucracy and centralisation are alien to a Catholic sensibility.

5. *Everyone is my brother or sister*

The principle of subsidiarity can be followed to a fault; it must exist in creative tension with the principle of solidarity. David Hollenbach explains that 'the stress on the importance of the local, the small-scale, and the particular must be complemented by a kind of solidarity that is more universal in scope. This wider solidarity is essential if the quest for community is to avoid becoming a source of increased conflict in a world already driven by narrowness of vision' (1996, p. 94).

Mary Beth Elshtain points out that Catholic social thought '...begins from a fundamentally different ontology from that assumed and required by individualism and statist collectivism on the other' (1994, p. 160).

In his encyclical on the organising principles of social entities, Pope John Paul II describes the theological underpinning of solidarity:

> One's neighbour is then not only a human being with his or her own rights and a fundamental equality with everyone else, but becomes the living image of God the Father, redeemed by the blood of Jesus Christ and placed under the permanent action of the Holy Spirit. One's neighbour must therefore be loved, even if an enemy, with the same love with which the Lord loves him or her; and for that person's sake one must be ready for sacrifice, even the ultimate one: to lay down one's life for the brethren.

He then distinguishes solidarity from sentimentality:

> This then is not a feeling of vague compassion or shallow distress at the misfortunes of so many people, both near and far. On the contrary, it is a firm and persevering determination to commit oneself to the common good; that is to say to the

good of all and of each individual, because we are all really responsible for all (Pope John Paul II, 1987, §38).

The ramifications of this commitment to the common good is that 'those who are oppressed by poverty are the object of a preferential love on the part of the Church' (*CCC* 2448). In both personal and communal commitments, Catholics must

be convinced of the seriousness of the present moment and of each one's individual responsibility, and to implement – by the way [we] live as individuals and as families, by the use of [our] resources, by [our] civic activity, by contributing to economic and political decisions and by personal commitment to national and international undertakings – the measures inspired by solidarity and love of preference for the poor (Pope John Paul II, 1987, §47).

Solidarity calls Catholic educators out of narrowness of vision and short-term thinking. For example, in regard to refugees and immigrants 'solidarity helps to reverse the tendency to see the world solely from one's own point of view' (Pontifical Council for the Pastoral Care of Migrants and Itinerant People, 1992, p. 10).

6. The Catholic Church is Catholic

In June 1992, members of the Black Clergy Caucus wrote: 'Catholic social teachings have been bold and uncompromising.' The sad problem, it added, is that these teachings 'are all too often unknown, unpreached, untaught, and unbelieved' (Gibson, 1996, p. 8). In light of a history of outright discrimination or complicit silence in the face of racial discrimination, Catholics in the United States must be committed to the welfare of African-Americans. Catholics believe that, wherever possible, remission of sin requires retribution. Cyprian Davis writes that 'the Catholic Church in the

South before the Civil War owed its physical and material development to the labor of men and women who were never paid for their services and were degraded and demeaned as persons'. He continues:

> Some Church leaders went so far as to justify slavery. Others sought to ameliorate it. Almost no Catholic leader in America took a public stand against it or joined the ranks of the Abolitionists until just before the Civil War. And in 1839 when Pope Gregory XVI condemned the slave trade in his papal brief *In Supremo Apostolatus*, Bishop John England of Charleston published a series of articles in his diocesan newspaper to deny that the pope was criticising or condemning slavery as it existed in the United States (1996, p. 11).

One hundred and fifty three years after Pope Gregory's statement, Pope John Paul II visited the Slave House on the Senegalese Island of Gorée. He said:

> Throughout a whole period of history of the African continent, Black men, women, and children were torn from their land, separated from their relatives, to be sold as merchandise. How can one forget the enormous suffering inflicted – ignoring the most basic human rights – on the populations deported from the African continent. How can one forget the human lives destroyed by slavery?

He is quoted in Gibson as saying that he went to Gorée to 'implore heaven's forgiveness' and to 'pray that in the future Christ's disciples may show themselves absolutely faithful to the observance of the commandment of brotherly love left them by their master' (Gibson, 1996, p. 7). The following year the Pope told a group of US bishops: 'Racism is an intolerable injustice by reason of the social conflicts which it provokes, but even more so by reason of the way in which it dishonors the inalienable dignity of all human beings, irrespective of their race or ethnic identity' (ibid., p. 8).

In *The Church and Racism: Towards a More Fraternal Society*, the Vatican has articulated the moral grounding of its teaching on race: respect for differences, fraternity, and solidarity built on the dignity of every human being (Pontifical Commission for Peace and Justice, 1988, p. 33). In the document the Church eschews a model of assimilation to European cultural patterns and adopts a philosophy of cultural pluralism that is reflective of its global character. Solidarity and communion do not demand uniformity, but a positive appreciation of the complementary diversity of peoples. Catholic institutions must enhance a 'well-understood pluralism' that can resolve 'the problem of closed racism' (ibid., p. 45).

The Church has also addressed racial injustice through statements of the US Bishops. In *Brothers and Sisters to Us*, they call for an honest appraisal of history, one freed from the cultural lens that 'obscures the evil of the past and denies the burdens that history has placed on the shoulders of our Black, Hispanic, Native American and Asian brothers and sisters' (National Catholic Conference of Bishops, 1979, p. 5). The bishops see clearly that racism is a fundamental sin, a primary pathology in human society, 'a radical evil dividing the human family and denying the new creation of a redeemed world. To struggle against it demands an equal radical transformation in our own minds and hearts as well as the structure of society' (ibid., p. 10). Although their pastoral letter is nineteen years old, that analysis of subtle and covert racism that permeates capitalist culture is more salient today than when it was written:

> Crude and blatant expressions of racist sentiment, though they occasionally exist, are today considered bad form. Yet racism itself persists in covert ways. Under the guise of other motives, it is manifest in the tendency to stereotype and marginalize

whole segments of the population whose presence is perceived as a threat. It is manifest also in the indifference that replaces open hatred. The minority poor are seen as the dross of post-industrial society – without skills, without motivation, without incentive. They are expendable. Many times the new face of racism is the computer print-out, the graph of profits and losses, the pink slip, the nameless statistic. Today's racism flourishes in the triumph of private concern over public commitment and personal fulfilment over authentic compassion. It is Christ's face that is the composite of all persons, but in a most significant way of today's poor, today's marginal people, today's minorities (ibid., p. 12).

The bishops found that scarcity of spending-power among the middle class by these groups further fragments society and

reveals an unresolved racism that permeates our society's structures and resides in the hearts of many among the majority. Because it is less blatant, this subtle form of racism is in some respects even more dangerous – harder to combat and easier to ignore. Major segments of the population are being pushed to the margins of society in our nation. As economic pressures tighten, those people who are often Black, Hispanic, Native American and Asian – and always poor – slip further into the unending cycle of poverty, deprivation, ignorance, disease and crime. Racial identity is for them an iron curtain barring the way to a decent life and livelihood (ibid., p. 13).

The bishops made explicit recommendations to their own flock. The pastoral letter calls for the conversion of Catholics from this social sin, recruitment of people of colour to ministry within the Church, social programmes for migrant workers and undocumented aliens, fair employment practices in Catholic institutions and responsible investment of the assets of those institutions, financial support of groups advancing the cause of racial minorities, and the continuation and expansion of Catholic schools in the inner cities and other disadvantaged areas because 'no sacrifice can be so great, no price can be so high, no short-range goals can be so important as to warrant the lessening of our commitment to Catholic education in minority neighborhoods' (ibid., p. 13).

In 1983 the bishops wrote another letter on racism, this time focused on Latinos. In *The Hispanic Presence: Challenge and Commitment* they made an argument from history to demand that Catholics take positive steps to enhance the welfare of this rapidly growing ethnic minority:

> Historically, the Church in the United States has been an 'immigrant Church' whose outstanding record of care for countless European immigrants remains unmatched Today that same tradition must inspire in the Church's approach to recent Hispanic immigrants a similar authority, compassion and decisiveness (National Catholic Conference of Bishops, 1983, p. 4).

7. Pluralism does not necessarily dilute particularism

As a community of memory, the Church cherishes its particularity, manifest in its worship, teachings, polity, art, literature and music. One can uphold particularism without denigrating the beliefs and customs of others in today's pluralistic world.

In the wake of the Second Vatican Council, Catholics embarked on a number of ecumenical ventures, from theological dialogue at the Vatican to shared pulpits in local parishes. Many would argue that ecumenical fervour has waned over the past thirty years. In the United States it seems that the Spirit has transformed many schools, once fortresses to protect beleaguered Catholic immigrants from a hostile Protestant majority, into places of dialogue and cooperation among Christians of many denominations. Survey data point to this ecumenical reality. Anecdotal evidence indicates that many schools function as 'ecumenical churches' in which Catholics, Baptists and other Protestants share prayer and service in recognition of their common baptismal vocation.

In the encyclical *Ut Unum Sint* (1995), Pope John Paul II largely addressed himself to the Churches of the East but he also called for enhanced relationships with Protestants. He wrote:

> I wish to address especially those who, through the sacrament of Baptism and the profession of the same Creed, share a real, though imperfect, communion with us. I am certain that the concern expressed in this Encyclical as well as the motives inspiring it will be familiar to them, for these motives are inspired by the Gospel of Jesus Christ. We can find here a new invitation to bear witness together to our common convictions concerning the dignity of man, created by God, redeemed by Christ, made holy by the Spirit and called upon in this world to live a life in conformity with this dignity (§47).

While the Pope described important ecumenical initiatives at the highest levels, he also stated that 'the Church's commitment to ecumenical dialogue, as it has clearly appeared since the Council, far from being the responsibility of the Apostolic See alone, is also the duty of individual, local or particular Churches' (§31). He exhorted all Catholics to engage in 'ecumenical cooperation [which] is a true school of ecumenism, a dynamic road to unity' (§40). In the United States these figurative 'schools of ecumenism' are quite literally schools.

The late Sister Thea Bowman describes the positive dimensions of religious diversity that extend beyond Christian ecumenism:

> When we as Catholic students, parents, faculty, staff and administrators, approach believers in other religious traditions

with appreciation and reverence, we realise their faith and faithfulness. We are inspired by their convictions. We are broadened by their perspectives and challenged by their questions. We learn from their religious experience. And as we work with them for peace and justice, as we cooperate with them in feeding the hungry, clothing the naked, teaching the ignorant, empowering the oppressed, we truly share the Good News of the Kingdom (1984, p. 21).

In the United States, the number of non-Christians is growing. The longstanding Jewish community is being joined by Muslims, Buddhists and other religions though immigration. The presence of these groups in a pluralistic society can be seen as an opportunity for dialogue and growth, not viewed defensively as a threat to particularism.

8. *Always keep in mind the end for which something is created*

The Catholic tradition is teleological: human structures are means to an end, used only insofar as they serve their original purpose. As a result, they are always probationary and stand in need of constant revision. Institutional stability, predictability and longevity should give way to the values of experimentation, risk and change. In an Ignatian worldview, for example, all things must be judged according to the criteria for which they were created: the glory of God and the salvation of souls. Insofar as these created things foster the end for which they were created, they are to be embraced. Otherwise, they are to be modified or abandoned. Through lived example, students should be invited to this spirit of keen insight and courageous freedom.

The implication for administrators and teachers is not to be overlooked. Creative school leadership, especially for principals, is like trying to redesign a 747 while it is in flight. Roland Barth (1990, pp. 72-3), describes the situation thus:

Like most who work in schools these days, principals walk a narrow edge between being able and not being able to fulfil their complex job. Exhaustion and discouragement are high; discretionary time and energy are low. In such a climate, opportunities to participate in a new activity, even one addressed to the principal's own renewal, entail risks and demand that the principal give up something to make room for the new activity or else risk becoming further over extended and depleted. A major paradox confronting any who would assist principals as well as teachers in becoming learners in their schools, then, is that professional development is energy and time depleting as well as energy and time replenishing.

Despite the best of intentions, practitioners often find themselves saying, 'Let me just get through the day.' In contrast to the culture of narcissism and nostalgia, the view *sub specie aeternitatis* can lift educators out of the tyranny of the immediate to a larger view of reality.

Conclusion

Young people in the United States today and, I would venture, in other similar national contexts, face a world in which dehumanisation is rampant. For those excluded from 'the common', the dehumanisation is palpable; the plight of the affluent is less readily evident but just as potent. Doloz and his colleagues vividly articulate this reality:

At the extreme but increasingly visible edge, our youth are shooting themselves up with needles, and down with guns. We try to teach our young people to be careful, but many also learn to be fearful. We cannot give them a safe society, so we seek to protect them as individuals. Yet even as we try to shelter our children within the home, the protective membrane wears thin. Increasingly, market-driven television and computer programs threaten to turn some children into passive consumers, pawns on the economic chess board, while others sink into poverty, locked out of the mainstream economy with little hope of ever having the nurture, education and skills to enable them to prosper in the twenty-first century. These young adults still in the economic mainstream are encouraged to hone their competitive edge at all costs, to capture their niche in a world prepared to shunt them aside (Daloz *et. al.*, p. 10).

It is in the signs of these times that the contemporary Catholic school finds its vocation.

In the culture of narcissism and nostalgia, the task for Catholic educators is daunting. But they have a store of resources from the past and the promise of the creative Spirit of God in the present, a Spirit that casts out all fear. Catholic schools are well poised to form the basis of a good society, institutions 'that are functioning well, that give the individuals within them a purpose and an identity, not through moulding them into conformity but through challenging them to become active, innovative, responsible, and thus happy persons because they understand what they are doing and why it is important' (Bellah, 1991, p. 51).

Crises of context, identity and diversity will not be met by an unthinking return to the past because 'Our capacity to construct communities of hope depends on the quality and vitality of our imagination' (Wallis, 1995, p. 257). Nor will crises be met by a turning in on oneself individually or collectively. Only through visionary leadership on the part of all concerned, teachers, parents, administrators and clergy, can Catholic schools engage in the task God has set before them: To build a new commons for themselves and for all.

'THE LONG JOHNS' AND CATHOLIC EDUCATION

James C. Conroy

Introduction

In Britain[1] Catholic education has attracted increasing interest in recent years. Such interest has focused on two essentially conflicting discourses. One conversation may be construed as applauding the advantages of Catholic education as more academically effective than parallel schools in the state-maintained sector (Morris, 1998). The other suggests that Catholic schools should be abandoned as sectarian and unhelpful if not antithetical to the establishment of a cohesive democratic forum (Little, 1998). This essay proposes that the central arguments of these contesting accounts of the 'social' efficacy of Catholic education are each misplaced precisely because they share a similarly limited view of the possible nature and purposes of Catholic education at this time in history and in this particular polity. The essay goes on to suggest (perhaps unexpectedly) that the rehabilitation of *laughter* as a central characteristic of Christian education offers the possibility of creatively critiquing what is to count as engaging in or 'doing' Catholic education and, concomitantly, provides a distinctive grounding for the continued existence of Catholic schools in a 'liberal' polity.

In order to establish a reasonable grounding for the ongoing growth and development of Catholic schools it is important to clear up some basic confusions perpetrated by both the pro- and anti-Catholic school lobbies. At least in their confusion they share a common ground!

Clearing the ground

In recent years Catholics have increasingly justified the continuance of their schools to the wider community in terms of their contribution to the social and political capital of the nation (McCann, 1998). Catholics are not, and certainly do not wish to be perceived as, other than good citizens who contribute to the commonwealth as paid up members of British society. They are as respectable as any other British citizen and this respectability has been afforded added piquancy by the decision of the British Prime Minister to send his own children to a Roman Catholic school. Part of the claim to respectability is lodged in the continued presence of Catholic schools, in areas of urban deprivation where, it may be claimed, they are a presence for good and where they identify their mission as serving the urban poor. At those sites, the argument goes, Catholic schools are making a significant contribution to the alleviation of the worst consequences of poverty and disenfranchisement. They are 'signs of hope' and evidence of the Church's historic commitment to the poor and marginalised; indeed they 'are at the sharp end of the Church's mission to the world' (Department for Catholic Education and Formation of the Catholic Bishop's conference of England and Wales, 1997, p. 50).

Of course the continued presence of Catholic educational institutions in such areas may be seen to be entirely contingent since they are so located due to the existence of significant residual Catholic presences which are themselves a result of demographic trends in the nineteenth and early twentieth centuries(Bossy, 1975, pp. 307-11; Hornsby-Smith, 1987, p. 27). In and of themselves they do not represent a coherent outworking or articulation of either a Catholic philosophy of education or a Catholic educational philosophy. Indeed there are many Catholic schools in Britain where the link with the mission to the poor and marginalised is somewhat attenuated and exists only in so far as there are collections for SCIAF or CAFOD or some other agency, or Christmas boxes. It would be too rhetorically easy and indeed too facile to imply that such efforts are unimportant for the students and teachers in schools serving affluent populations; clearly many individuals in such circumstances believe that these activities are an important outworking of their personal and corporate values system. Nevertheless, of themselves, such activities cannot justify the continued existence of Catholic schools in a modern or, as some would have it, a 'post-modern', democratic polity. In other words, since not all Catholic schools have the same commitment to the poor and marginalised in practical terms it is not possible to justify the continued existence of all Catholic schools in such terms, as if this were a common grounding. Indeed, Arthur (1995, pp. 225-53) documents in some detail the lack of cohesion within the Catholic community as to the continued and future purposes of Catholic schools. Further, he exposes the ongoing discord from the mid-1960s onwards among Catholics as to the purposes of Catholic education. This was manifest in the work of those educationalists and thinkers who claimed unequivocally that the identification of Catholic education with comprehensivisation as a necessary social good since it championed redistributive justice, was fundamentally flawed (Arthur, ibid., pp. 92-105). The fallout from the 1988 Education Reform Act exemplified the lack of consensus among Catholic educators as to both purposes and practices. Many governors and head teachers of Catholic schools chose to ignore the strongly held views of the Catholic Bishops' Conference of England and Wales that opting for grant-maintained status would be damaging to the life chances of many pupils and would potentially dilute the Catholic nature of the school (Pilkington, 1991).

While it might be convenient to regard the justification for the continued existence of the Catholic school in terms of the promotion of social goods or indeed common goods, in itself this is not sufficient grounds for the justification of the continuance of a separate Catholic school system within a polity which no longer has a coherent attachment to a religious worldview. It is logically possible, even if practically difficult, for Catholics simply to transfer their schools in areas of deprivation, together with the relevant insights and expertise they have accumulated over the years, to colleagues in the non-denominational sector.

There are other groups of Catholics who would like to reduce the functioning of Catholic schools to 'lifestyle' enclaves (O'Keefe, 1998); a walled sanatorium inoculating children against the evils of society. They are not, however, and indeed have never been representative of a meaningful or coherent philosophy of Catholic education (Sawicki, 1988). Their position is redolent of a kind of pietistic withdrawal from both the language and the discourse of the reality in which Catholic pupils live; whereas a more authentic tradition continues to be represented by, for example, the insights of Maritain, who points out that

> Christianity is not a sect, not even in the sense of a sect dedicated to the purest perfection... [the] Essenes... lived up to high moral standards... [they] were a closed group, a sect. Christians are not a sect, and this is the very paradox of Christianity; Christianity says, Be perfect as your heavenly father is perfect, and Christianity gives this precept not to a closed group but to all....even to those among us who are most deeply engaged in the affairs and seductions of this world' (Gallagher and Gallagher, 1962, p. 134).

Clearly the lesson to be learned from the Essenes is that sects wither away and that if Catholic education does actually have anything to contribute to the commonweal then it must resist hubristic sectarian tendencies.

Those who wish to identify Catholic schools as 'good' state schools with a conscience and those who wish to preserve the purity of the Catholic heritage are prey to a partial vision of the nature and intentions of Catholic education properly conceived. It is precisely this partial account of the descriptions of and the activities within Catholic schools which allows many within the broader polity to claim that there is no place left in a modern democracy for denominationally based education paid for partially or totally from state funds.

In his speech to the House of Lords in 1998, Lord MacKay (Little, op. cit., p. 24) indicated that Catholic schools were no longer relevant in a modern plural democracy; that the conditions which had led to their establishment in the nineteenth century and their subsequent maintenance no longer obtained and that they were both anachronistic and, at worst, socially divisive. Let it be supposed that those who maintain this, including the General Assembly of the Church of Scotland, which, since 1972, has opposed the continuance of state-funded Catholic schools in Scotland, do not harbour any ill will towards individual Catholics or indeed to Catholicism as a religious institution. Instead they may be construed as simply holding the belief that the polity functions better if all subscribe to a broadly similar set of beliefs as to what is in the best interests of society as a whole (*Times Educational Supplement* [Scotland], 1998). Let it further be admitted that the opponents of the continuance of state-funded Catholic schooling regard a primary function of schools as the communication of the common values and aspirations held by any such society. Finally, let it also be assumed that those who wish to promote the importance of communicating these values, wish to do so in a manner which is anti-indoctrinatory.

Given that opponents of Catholic education in Britain may be reasonably said to hold the above views, then it is not unreasonable to assume that they believe Catholic institutions in general and schools in particular to be indoctrinatory and consequently anti-democratic. Such views rest on a misreading of both the nature of democracy in post-modernity and the purposes of Catholic schools. It might also be suggested that those who mount these particular kinds of challenges to the appropriateness of Catholic education to the contemporary polity are somewhat Quixotic, tilting at illusory or partial representations rather than the more robust accounts offered by some contemporary Catholic educationalists. Unlike, however, the hapless Don Quixote they are without the advantage of a trusty steed since the horse called 'coherent liberal democracy' is itself but a shadow. And it is to this shadow that I now turn.

What is the place of Catholic education in the polity?

It is difficult to know precisely how evidence is to be adduced for claiming that Catholic schools are *ipso facto* indoctrinatory, irrelevant or anti-democratic. Those who make such claims tend to do so by way of assertion rather than by way of argument. This is not to suggest for a moment that there are no particular examples of fundamentalist authoritarianism in Catholic schools but that is not the same thing as asserting that such attitudes are a *sine qua non* of Catholic education. Further, and more importantly, such critics readily assume that liberal education carries within it no doctrinaire or indeed indoctrinatory tendencies. As scholars from Oakshott (1967) to Thiessen (1993) have adequately demonstrated, this very liberal education to which all are asked to subscribe in the interests of civil unity and harmony carries a range of non-rational elements concerned with the initiation into particular views of 'the good'. Liberal education is predicated upon a notion of liberal democracy which, in turn, rests upon a belief that a liberal economy self-evidently produces social goods. It does so in the firm belief that markets are determinative of both what society needs and wants. Claims for such a benign view of markets has little or no rational basis, relying rather on a host of unarticulated feelings that people should 'stand on their own feet'; should 'serve the economy'; should be 'free to choose lifestyles and pathways for themselves' (providing, of course, that such choices prescind from challenging the dominant political and economic order). The term 'feelings' is carefully chosen here since these views tend to be held axiomatically as if they were incontestable.

The interesting question then becomes whether or not these non-rational elements emanating from this 'liberal' conception of the polity are more desirable than the non-rational elements which inhere in that Christian anthropology which informs Catholic education. To assert that particular forms of liberal non-rationality are indeed more desirable than Catholic non-rationality it would be necessary to show that the social goods which they have produced are *de facto* better. Recent political theory would suggest that it is not at all obvious that such a claim is self-evidently justified. In his critique of Fukuyama's somewhat Hegelian assertion that the collapse of socialism presages the advent of 'Western liberal democracy as the final form of human government' (Fukuyama, 1989, pp. 3-18), the political philosopher John Gray argues that it is a serious mistake to believe that only our present form of government has seen human beings flourish. 'Who can doubt', he writes, 'that human beings flourished under the feudal institutions of mediaeval Christendom? or under the monarchical government of Elizabethan England' (Gray, 1993, 1996, p. 246). Whatever the merits of Gray's particular examples it is abundantly clear that the liberal democracy, which opponents of Catholic education suggest makes such education redundant, is itself but a contingent form.

A truly liberal polity recognises itself as provisional, relying not on axiomatic principles but on the best reasoning which may be brought to bear at this or that particular moment in history. The limits on the forms of government and on the public discourse at any time in the life of a liberal polity are adduced from reflection on past experience, best guesses about the future and choices for the present. The limits themselves must reflect the permeability of their boundaries and the provisionality of the systems, structures and discourses that colour and shape the forum of public life. As Berlin puts it, 'to demand or preach mechanical precision, even in principle, in a field incapable of it is to be blind and to mislead others' (1996, p. 53).

The two perspectives from within Catholic education discussed earlier reflect truncated notions of its nature and purpose and consequently have vitiated relationships with the liberal civil polity. The first, advocating integration, knits itself into a seamless robe with the dominant discourse of the polity, becoming virtually indistinguishable from that which constitutes meaning and purpose in non-denominational education. Indeed, those who hold to this view tend to be marked by the ability to respond positively to all that the polity demands with greater enthusiasm than might be expected by their non-denominational counterparts. It is in essence an assimilationist approach. The second, in distancing itself from the polity, inadvertently becomes a side-show to not only the polity but to the universality proclaimed as central to Catholic Christianity; it reconstructs itself as a sect, as having a place only for the elect. The first of these two perspectives offers itself as a hostage to fortune in so far as those opposed to Catholic education may argue that since it is largely indistinguishable from general liberal education it is redundant. If there are a few techniques and practices which offer a charitable dimension to the state school then these may be taken on board and so much the better. In respect of the second view there is in fact no conversation to be had since there is no common language. Opponents of Catholic education may argue that such an education has no claim to public funding because it engages in no public activity, offering nothing to the commonweal from which it cuts itself off.

Ultimately both the justifications for and the challenge to Catholic education which are discussed here are fatally flawed and there is need for a different kind of conversation between Catholic education and the wider polity. This conversation needs to serve both the ends of education properly conceived within the Catholic tradition and the need for the polity to be satisfied that Catholic education makes a distinctive contribution to its well-being.

The stentorian voices of modern educationalists

Before exploring the distinctive contribution which Catholic education has to make to the polity through the *deployment of laughter* properly conceived, it is necessary to make some comments about the recent evolution of educational rhetoric in public political life in Britain (indeed one might argue throughout the English-speaking world). At the time of writing the Secretary of State for Education in England and Wales has just announced the Government's position on homework, suggesting that five-year-olds should complete twenty minutes each evening. This development follows recent proposals on a quasi-national curriculum for pre-fives (Scottish Office Education and Industry Department, 1997).

The obsession with pre-school education represents but the latest move in an ongoing strategy emanating from a neo-liberal view of education wherein children are constituted as '*our* future'; not as their own present; as servants of the wider polity, the parameters of which are constructed by reference to contemporary shibboleths, most especially those of the global economy. The twenty minutes homework scenario places even very young children at the centre of this self-aggrandising economic view, not only of education, but of the social relations which govern our dealings with each other.

It has become deeply unfashionable to suggest that education may serve to support the individual in her or his personal development *qua* human being if this is not, in the same breath, allied to the economy or, possibly worse, some étatist view of 'citizenship' (Qualifications and Curriculum Authority, 1998, p. 7). Further, education is such a 'serious' business that there is little room left for enjoyment, song – and laughter. Of course it is not meant to suggest that individual teachers in particular classes do not laugh with their pupils but that is very different from believing that *laughter* itself is a fundamental and important educational category. It would, indeed, provide a challenge to the most accomplished exegete of educational legislation and governmental 'advice' to find mention of play and laughter, much less a significant treatment of them, in current policy documentation. This poverty of thinking is manifest in *A Curriculum Framework for Children in their Pre-school Year*, alluded to earlier, which, apart from betraying the dubious étatist impulse of having a curriculum for children as young as three, reduces play to a means to other educational ends rather than something which children do in and for itself. Play, we are informed, 'allows them [children] to learn in a broad variety of ways... to consolidate previous learning or to be intensely involved and challenged in new learning' (HM Inspectors of Schools, 1997, p. 13). In contradistinction, the remainder of this essay is concerned with *the rehabilitation of laughter* as a vital category in Catholic educational thinking and a central characteristic in the practice of Catholic education. This rehabilitation is vital if a Catholic philosophy of education is to remain both true to its roots and provide an alternative anthropology to that which currently underpins educational thinking in the polity.

Towards an understanding of laughter

Murray provides a helpful summary of the main elements of a Catholic philosophy of education, indicating that it should be constituted by wholeness, truth, respect, justice and freedom. 'The Catholic tradition of education involves no diminution or distortion of the aims of education [he suggests]. Instead, it gives to the Wholeness, Truth, Respect, Justice and Freedom pursued in education a new depth, a richer possibility, a fuller understanding' (Murray, 1991, p. 22). In this cluster of ideas it might be reasonably assumed that laughter should be regarded as a subordinate feature of wholeness. There is, however, no evidence in Murray's text that this is the case and even if there were it would not satisfy the needs of the Catholic educational community to have laughter as a fundamental category informing ongoing reflection and discussion within and about Catholic education. This present study offers laughter as a supraordinate category in, rather than a subordinate feature of, a Catholic philosophy. If laughter itself had been no more than an element within human wholeness then its place within both the Catholic tradition and the wider polity is unlikely to have been marked with various attempts at suppression and domestication. But it has been, and is, more than that! It is a mode of being in the world rather than a subordinate element within wholeness. If this were not the case then the historic tension between laughter and ponderous solemnity would not have been so marked. Thus we are offered the thought that:

> Comedy does not tell of famous and powerful men, but of base and ridiculous creatures, though not wicked men.... It achieves the effect of the ridiculous by showing the defects and vices of ordinary men. Here Aristotle sees the tendency to laughter as a force for good, which can also have an instructive value: through witty riddles and unexpected metaphors, though it tells us things differently from the way they are, as if it were lying, it actually obliges us to examine them more closely, and it makes us say, Ah this is just how things are, and I didn't know it. (Eco, 1994, p. 472).

So it is that Brother William explains how and why the various deaths and murders which have taken place in the course of Umberto Eco's *The Name of The Rose* are occasioned by the attempt to protect the Christian world from the dangerous ideas lodged in the second part of Aristotle's poetics; the ideas of comedy. Brother Jorge, who is responsible for killing his brother monks, does so to protect them and, as he sees it, Christendom from such inherently dangerous ideas. These ideas about comedy are dangerous, Jorge believes, precisely because they come from 'the' philosopher and not from the carnivalesque and Saturnalian street plays and theatre of the peasantry. This latter could be tolerated because it allowed for a kind of catharsis and it was possible to 'bracket it out' of the divine order. But Aristotle; that was another matter, because he had the ability to transform the comic from the ridiculous into an art form, to enable it to become what Brother Jorge saw as 'the object of philosophy and of perfidious theology' (ibid., p. 474).

Eco's novel is important precisely because it alerts us to both the historic and the present difficulties which the Christian tradition has in holding together its two most important life forces in something approaching creative tension. On the one hand Christianity in general and the Catholic Church in particular takes its mission to educate very seriously. Indeed so seriously that Pius XI claimed that the educative task is 'supremely important in the church' (1929, p. 1). On the other, it is central to the deepest insights of Christian witness to recognise the vanity and provisionality of all human endeavours, especially those such as education in which humanity is particularly prey to its own hubristic tendencies. Education embodies at one and the same time the noblest human aspirations towards service and enlightenment, and the gravest pretensions of human self-sufficiency.

The tensions so perceptively disclosed in Eco's novel are manifest in a wide variety of writings throughout the Judaeo-Christian tradition. Indeed for many of the early Fathers laughter was a site of great confusion. This may be in part due to the variety of forms in which laughter comes as well as being inherent in its connections with play and *eutrapelia*.

In order to focus on the particular forms of laughter which are important for Catholic education it is necessary to adumbrate some distinctions. *Eutrapelia* is that Aristotelian virtue which turns away from both boorishness, where everything is treated as an object of Grobian laughter, and coarse stiffness where there is nothing amusing in word, person or world. Positively construed it is that disposition which treats both serious endeavour and jocular play as jointly constitutive of a 'well-turned' life. In itself *eutrapelia* had been the subject of much controversy and debate in the writings of the Fathers and even of Paul himself when he warned the Ephesians (5:4) to avoid 'smart talk' which is to be equated with the chattering of fools. Indeed there were major differences between the Fathers as to whether or not *eutrapelia* was vice or virtue; a debate which is effectively chronicled by Rahner (1963). Aquinas, drawing on Aristotle, rehabilitates *eutrapelia* (here translated as 'wittiness') as refreshment for both body and soul. He points out that when St John is chastised for playing with the disciples,

> he [St John] is said to have told one of them who carried a bow to shoot an arrow. And when he had done this several times, he asked him whether or not he could do it indefinitely, and the man answered that if he continued doing it, the bow would break. Whence the Blessed John drew the inference that in like manner man's mind would break if its tension were never relaxed (Aquinas, 1921, p. 297).

For a Catholic school truly to reflect the mainstream of a Catholic philosophy of education it is necessary to provide pupils with a site for and sense of balance, a central feature of which is playful laughter. Too often in the contemporary discourse of education has play itself been transmuted into an object of serious study, hence physical education becomes a subject for study, adults organise children's play times and games become 'learning opportunities'. As the stentorian voices of education make the lives of children increasingly serious, the actual, existing Catholic school has a responsibility to ensure an authentic balance; a balance which moves beyond the shibboleths of the global economy and challenges, 'playfully', the increasingly shrill voices of a crude utilitarianism within the political and educational establishment (Munro, 1997). To mount this challenge it is necessary to provide some fundamental distinctions for our understanding of laughter and how it may be deployed in our own time.

As Zwart (1996) points out, the social and educational understandings of the 'official' voices of the polity have their roots in the liberal theories of philosophers like John Rawls and Richard Rorty. Theirs are theories which create an ethics of compartmentalisation which in turn distinguishes between what is to count as public and what is to count as private. Here there is no moral content in the public sphere since there is no metanarrative which can join people together in a common project, rooted in a common set of beliefs; everything is provisional and there are no final categories to be had anywhere. According to Rorty (1989, pp. 73-78), metaphysicians of both the religious and the post-Enlightenment humanist kind are equally misguided, precisely because they subscribe to some essential underpinning belief or beliefs about human nature. Such beliefs, he holds, are unsustainable as absolutes because, through the insights provided by literary critics like Derrida, we have come to recognise the contingency of all speech acts and therefore of all to which they refer. The only route left open to one who recognises this radical contingency is private irony; a kind of philosophic laughter wherein one is able to say to oneself, 'I know my deepest held beliefs and understandings have no ultimate value' and, perhaps more socially corrosively, 'I know that all the claims made for common bonds are no more than temporarily and socially convenient artifice'.

We are assured by Rorty that this position of private irony enables us to discriminate between public questions and private concerns. An example of such a distinction would be between acts of cruelty, which are part of the public domain, and personal fulfilment which is to be seen as a private matter. Why the prevention of suffering as a universal principle of public engagement should be distinguished from any other foundational claims such as Kant's universal principle of treating others as ends in themselves remains a mystery; it is a mystery which, however, needs to be and is explored elsewhere (see Critchley, 1995). Despite this, Rorty's claims are not easily dismissed since there is something deeply appealing about admitting to provisionality, most especially when one takes a long look at the consistent and continuous inadequacies of institutions which make foundational metaphysical claims. However it is important to resist the appeal to private irony or laughter as it appears in post-modern philosophical, political and economic thought since it must lead to a bifurcation or duality in our consciousness and the consequent removal of whole realms of human behaviour from any meaningful public conversation. The laughter which ensues from such a position has nothing to offer common social projects such as education (see also Conroy and Davis, 1999). It is a laughter which prescinds from engagement and offers only sterility to those interpersonal encounters which comprise our social organisation. Ultimately, it must be a laughter which sneers at all encounters since none has any actual significance. Paradoxically, such irony cannot even offer itself as a form of subversive corrective to the foolishness of our more absurd absolutist claims for such things as the axiomatic nature of functioning of the markets in the 'global economy'.

Is there then another, alternative form of laughter which shares some family resemblances with this form of post-modern irony but which does not banish real and substantive ethical and social issues from the agon? If there is such an understanding of laughter, does it effectively move beyond *eutrapelia* or playfulness in order to perform a critical role in our self-aggrandising claims for education? Indeed, there remains, contra-Rorty, a public form of laughter rooted not in irony but in *parody* and which has always offered vitality to the Catholic Christian tradition. This tradition has been explored by Bakhtin, who develops a perception of what may be called the 'responsible carnival' in literature, folklore and behaviour where all parties to the exchange have the possibilities of 'laughing' in all directions (Morson and Emerson, 1990, p. 433ff).

Despite these universal possibilities this form of laughter has a subversive quality which the powerful, with their colonising and acquisitive instincts have always found disconcerting. As public laughter, it may itself be further subdivided into that which appears to challenge institutional interests merely through abuse and sneering and that which is enhancing to the polity precisely because it acts as a kind of humorous mirror to some of our wilder societal excesses. Clarity as to the distinctions to be made between these two kinds of laughter is vital to an understanding of how they affect the conduct of the polity and the place of Catholic education therein. The basic distinction to be made is between laughter which sneers and laughter which challenges.

Sneering laughter is crude, boorish even brutish, distancing itself from the object of its attention. It is a laughter which is devoid of any redemptive quality, either on its own or indeed on its object's behalf. It has a kinship with private irony in as much as it is reserved for the *cognoscenti* and is positioned outside the actual life of the polity. It does not engage with the polity but stands aloof from it, a kind of bird's-eye view of the rest of humanity. One can think of parallels in bullying behaviour where the bully possesses no powers of empathy, only those which demean the victim. There is, however, a distinction to be made with post-modernist irony in that the boorish 'comic' has no capacity for authentic self-criticism within or without the polity, precisely because he or she has no sense of the provisionality of their own language and accompanying behaviours. The cruelty to be inflicted by those who sneer in this way is its own object and has no wider purpose in the public conversation which continues to bind human beings together. It finds itself manifest in a certain kind of television comedy which shouts at and insults both the viewer and the objects/subjects of derision; sometimes they are the same thing.

The second type of laughter which has a vital role to play within Catholic education and which, it will be suggested here, offers one of the most potent justifications for the continued existence of

Catholic schools within the contemporary polity is represented most particularly in the totally engaged laughter of Rabelais and, more especially, Erasmus. Unlike the private irony of Rorty the public laughter of these Renaissance humanists was deeply embedded in its metaphysical foundations. Nevertheless, like Rorty, the humanists recognised the provisionality of the linguistic, social and economic categories deployed by both Church and State. Of course scholars like Rabelais and Erasmus shared the platform of laughter with others such as Luther, who was concerned to use and develop the vernacular as a mode of speech, writing and communication in order to challenge what he perceived to be the pretentiousness and self-aggrandising tendencies of the late Middle Ages. The fundamental difference was to be seen in the positioning of the self as voice in relation to the institutional structures; Luther chose to stand outside whereas Erasmus and Rabelais continued to challenge from within. Erasmus, in particular, adopted an approach which was less bellicose than that of Luther, believing that true laughter was likely to be more effective if used as a rapier rather than a bludgeon (see Todd, 1964). Further, Erasmus' laughter deliberately took the form of interrogation rather than declamation. In his diatribe, *On the Freedom of the Will*, which is a direct challenge to Luther, Erasmus constantly plays down his attack in a mildly self-abasing manner so as not to be distracted by invective (Rupp *et. al.*, 1969). Luther, on the other hand, opens his rebuttal with a full frontal assault, suggesting that Erasmus' arguments are 'cheap and paltry', that he, Erasmus, has defiled himself and his style with 'trash', and expresses himself disgusted at the unworthy manner of Erasmus' expression (Rupp *et. al.*, ibid., p. 102). Luther's decision to take himself outside the Roman Catholic Church provides a licence to adopt a robust, abusive kind of grobian laughter which may be seen to have parallels in some of the more anarchic contemporary comedy genres. Long before his encounters with Luther, Erasmus had made the decision to stay within the Church and argue his case for reform through wit.

Rabelais, on the other hand, probably because he, like Luther, drew on the vernacular, displayed a much more biting comic approach to ecclesiastical institutions (Screech, 1997, p. 223 ff). This was largely because the classical idiom did not possess the range of crude and bawdy vocabulary evident in vernacular French. As a humanist, however, Erasmus would not have contemplated writing in anything but Latin.

In any event Erasmus offers a particular model of laughter which may usefully be deployed in understanding what might count as an appropriate and healthy relationship between the polity and Catholic education. Despite being one of the best loved and most popular figures in Europe, courted by bishops, princes and popes, he remained independent of them all, relying on none to offer him preferences and endowments.[2] His finances were always on the edge but he wished it so in order that he might write and speak in his own voice (Bainton, 1969, p. 139ff). His best known work is undoubtedly *Praise of Folly* which is a parodical account of how so many of his contemporary decision-makers were themselves in thrall to Folly. In this instance Folly is the personified voice of vanity, self-importance and pretentiousness. He parodies, for example, those, such as Seneca, who claim to be wise through having divorced their reason from their emotions (Erasmus, 1971, p. 106). Philosophers and theologians can be like this if they desire and Folly[3] embraces them as missing nothing, never being deceived, able to weigh up all things precisely, self-sufficient, self-satisfied. It is the inability of such high churchmen to understand so little of themselves and their perception that their particular formulation of any given doctrine or indeed answer to any particular theological question is always the last word to be said on the matter. In *Praise of Folly*, Erasmus uses Folly as the parody which challenges those who have divorced themselves from that which they claim to be their origin, the ultimate folly of the Cross. This he does by parodying the truly wise as 'foolish' since they would undermine the fat livings of the clerics. Thus Folly suggests that 'if... your wise man starts blurting out these uncomfortable truths, you can see how he'll soon destroy the world's peace of mind and plunge it into confusion' (ibid., p. 130).

In another work which, though anonymous, is widely attributed to Erasmus, he proposes a witty and clever parody of a conversation between Pope Julius II, St Peter and a Spirit which offers a conflated caricature of the Renaissance Popes. Here Julius is created as the mouthpiece for all those excesses which, while making the Renaissance Church great in material terms, had divorced it from its roots (Bainton, op. cit., pp. 131-36).[4] In his letter to a contemporary theologian, Martin Dorp, Erasmus is at great pains to point out that the purpose of his writings is not to offend the good and just but to challenge the wicked and vainglorious among, but not exclusively among, the most wealthy and powerful. As he puts it himself to Dorp, 'And why is the archbishop of Canterbury not offended? Because he is a man who is an absolute model of all the virtues and concludes that none of them is aimed at himself' (Erasmus, Radice [trans], op. cit., p. 224).

Laughter and Catholic education

So, what then are those of us involved in Christian education to take from the writings and insights of Erasmus, and, in turn, what do these insights offer for our relationship with the polity at a time, certainly in Britain, when Catholic education continues to be viewed with some suspicion? Erasmus' parodies work precisely because they are predicated on the ultimate source of Christian laughter, the Cross. The Cross, he thought, had been forgotten in the maintenance of the Renaissance Church. Indeed it might also be argued, so had the Resurrection. The 'important' questions revolved around, what seem to modern eyes and ears, obscure concerns with whether or not God might be able to turn God's self into a cabbage or questions as to whether the three persons in the Trinity might all occupy one form at one time and so on. For a humanist like Erasmus, who had been schooled in this scholasticism, all of these questions and their varied formulations missed the centrality of the death and resurrection of Jesus. These two absolutes of Christianity reduced all other theological formulations to subordinate roles and for Erasmus provided the source of his laughter.

Erasmus was acutely aware of the provisionality of our modes of expression, our actions and indeed our very existence long before it became fashionable in nineteenth- and twentieth-century philosophy and theology. This is why he laughed at the pomposity of clerics and others who imagined that the particular world they inhabited was described by some final vocabulary which they formulated. Further, he laughed at the idea that human beings might look axiomatically upon the particular forms of their civic and ecclesiastical institutions. Just as Erasmus recognised the flawed nature of the assumptions about how the world actually is and subjected inappropriate claims and activities to the cleansing power of laughter, so too we might apply the same principles to our education system. This recognition of provisionality and the corresponding desire to apply laughter are central to the life of both the individual Catholic school and, more importantly, the entire venture of Catholic education.

It is important to the individual school because those who work within it must be prepared to subject their own formulations and aspirations to critical self-reflection, which finds one of its most potent forms in laughter. Now it might be acknowledged, especially if one is to believe all the surveys conducted on teacher morale, that there is little at which the teacher and student might laugh in the modern globally orientated, competence-driven school. However, such a perspective resides only with those who believe that the educated person is so prepared in order to serve the global economy. The holding of such an article of faith, for that is what it is, expounded upon at length by the current and previous British Prime Ministers (Beresford, 1997; Gray, 1997) requires to

be treated to the force of laughter. It ha
more than one occasion at the hands of
British comedians whose art runs counte.
humour in being understated and paroc.
bound into the plausibility of simulated cc
great and the good of British public life. Takin.   .ile
economic and political facts, they embark upo   .ie-play a
conversation between an interviewer and a prominent
businessman, politician or other public figure. In asking apparently
naive questions, somewhat akin to St Peter in the parody with Pope
Julius II, they expose much of the absurdity which passes for
rational thought about public life, political economy and business
practice in Britain today. Teachers in Catholic schools have a
similar duty to place seemingly naive questions about a range of
matters of import before their students; indeed they have a duty to
equip students to ask these questions for themselves. In so doing it
is not mandatory that they occupy a soapbox but they are required,
by the gospel, not to accept unwittingly or unquestioningly what
counts as educational discourse as if there were no alternatives.

So what then might be the targets of this laughter within the
Catholic school? The high-minded language of accountability as
manifest in individual school targets and individual pupil
attainment presents an obvious first example. School targets, we are
informed, provide a mechanism for improving children's life
chances (Wilson, 1998) though it is not obvious or indeed
demonstrable that the establishment of particular targets for the
school are the means to this (Davis, 1998). Similarly, it is not clear
that the development of traditional Attainment Targets and
Performance Indicators in Curriculum Guidelines (Scotland) or
the National Curriculum (England, Wales and Northern Ireland)
have provided pupils with enhanced job opportunities or more
sophisticated skills which can be deployed in the 'global markets' to
which we all are supposed to pay homage. Interestingly, a report by
the *Royal Society for the Encouragement of Arts, Manufactures and*

(1998) and another by the *Industrial Society* (1998)
suggest that current approaches to teaching and learning in
the education system are largely irrelevant to our projected needs.
Further, it is likely that de-regulation of the financial markets
which took place under neo-liberal economic policies in the 1980s
will need to be reversed as the flight of capital from economy to
economy is seen to have an increasingly damaging effect on the
fabric of whole polities. Of course, in these reports, there is much
made of the need to change from a subject-based curriculum to an
information-led curriculum where skills of utilisation will be more
important than other, more traditional, synthetic abilities.

It is encumbent on the Catholic educator to resist spurious, and
what are inevitably transient, claims to particular forms of
utilitarian education which treat the individual person as a means
in the global economy rather than an end in herself. Within the
realpolitik of schools, with the varied expectations placed upon
teachers from parents, education bureaucrats and politicians, it is
not possible for the individual teacher or indeed a particular school
to refrain from ticking their boxes. Nonetheless, the box-ticking
approach must be relegated to its rightful place; a minor and
sometimes irritating feature in a genuinely educational process.
Tick-boxes of all kinds are generated as forms of social and
educational control, raising themselves from the level of trivia to
the very end of education by inducing fear in teacher and pupil
alike; if success is measured by these kinds of achievement then it
can have no authentic conversation with Catholic education. The
Catholic school should resist the temptation to assimilate itself to a
rhetoric which has so fundamentally confused means and ends (see
Davis in this volume). It should also resist the fragmenting
tendencies of an information-driven curriculum, which reflect a
fragmented anthropology. In so doing it should bring laughter to
bear on the outpourings of those who would fragment the sense of
the individual in and with the community. It can stand out against
these tendencies because it recognises and gives voice to a belief in

the dignity of the individual, the centrality of community and the provisionality of our strivings.

It is possible to see another site of laughter for the Catholic school; recent Government rhetoric and policy in Britain has extolled the virtues of after-school homework clubs. Catholic schools might provide a genuine alternative through after-school play clubs, or alternatively advocate and facilitate the making of local streets safer and more child-friendly so that children might have the opportunity to play with their peers. Children need more than anything else to be exposed to the joy of play and the incisiveness of laughter. The school might examine its financing policies and practices to see how much energy and resources are to be devoted to play time, play space and play equipment, and here the concern is for all education and not only infant education! Allied to this the Catholic school should be a site of laughter; a place which cultivates a facility with language so that pupils can make play with words precisely so that they are not fooled by the politicians, pundits and advertisers – or indeed themselves. Even in the exploration and exegesis of scripture we are provided with myriad opportunities to laugh. One has only to explore some of those ideas communicated in the Infancy narratives to see the possibility of laughter as an exegetical tool; nativity plays so re-worked as to bring together the awesome mystery of the Incarnation and playful incredulity at Joseph's predicament!

And so to the systems of Catholic education; what have they to do with laughter and play as distinct from the role of the individual school? As Jung pointed out, there is always a tendency for the powerful to arrogate to themselves the prerogatives of both wisdom and power; in the Middle Ages it was the Church, in the nineteenth and early twentieth centuries it was the State and, in our own time, it is the transnational corporation (Conroy, 1997 and 1999). Thus transnational corporations can become drunk with their power, creating a particular economic and civic language with which politicians may collude too readily and possibly unwittingly.

This language may in turn shape our reality in particular ways, producing a hegemonic view of both the nature of the polity and of education. Such a hegemonic view may well be built upon sand but it is sustained because it reflects the discourse of power and therefore can have an overpowering effect on popular consciousness, creating a monoglot, monocultural disposition in the polity. This is, in the terms of liberal thinkers like Berlin, disastrous for the polity. While having the appearance of bringing individuals and groups together into common bonds of citizenship it actually reduces freedom to choose, freedom to dissent and even freedom to laugh. It reduces dissent because there are too few competing discourses coming together in the forum which can provide for effective checks and balances. Of course it might be suggested that the advent of mass communication in its presently varied forms provides a bulwark against such hegemonic tendencies in the polity. This argument, however, is only effective to the extent that the media or substantial elements within it have and represent alternative discourses to the dominant, at the moment politico-economic discourse of neo-liberalism; there is no evidence that this is, in any significant way, the case. Even were it so it would not preclude the necessity of having other, alternative, voices within the agon, since education potentially provides one of the few public sites for contesting discourses.

Conclusion

There are those who will suggest that State education already offers the plurality necessary for a healthy polity (Hirst, 1974) and that denominationally-based education runs counter to the aims of a liberal society. This issue is fully addressed elsewhere (Theissen, op. cit.) so that here it is only necessary to focus on one particular aspect of this discussion: the place of laughter. There has been, it might be suggested, an interesting, if somewhat accidental, collusion between liberal philosophers of education and neo-liberal economists in shaping the direction of schooling since the mid-1970s. This 'collusion' has resulted in schools which are not quite so 'liberal' as the rhetoric might have us believe and which are inhabited by those who have lost the perspective to laugh. So, then, how has this come about? The philosophers of secular education such as Hirst and Peters developed an educational rhetoric which assumed that a particular secular view of the world was itself a final form of description as to what might constitute a 'proper', indeed a 'good' education. Similarly the free-market economics of the neo-liberals is regarded by its progenitors as the final form of economic and political activity. Just as Hegel (1955) regarded nineteenth-century rational Christianity as the final and purest form of religious expression, so too the liberal educationalist and the neo-liberal economists see their formulations of the polity as the highest representations of the free society. Because theirs are seen to be final forms they have no mechanism available which enables them to stand back to regard both their educational and economic systems as provisional, as a moment in time. These 'systems' embody absolute truth and their absolute character prohibits the possibility of their being laughed at from within.

Catholic education, on the other hand, has the potential to recognise its own limitations precisely because the Cross and Resurrection are signs of contradiction and therefore signs of the limitations which are to be put on our aspirations. They are important sources of laughter because they laugh at death which is one of the few absolutes shared by all, irrespective of time and space. In and through laughter such education offers a possible corrective to the hegemonic tendencies of the State and the transnational. It is here that the justification for continuing Catholic education within the State sector resides, not in either the assimilationist or the sectarian modes critiqued above. Laughter offers hope!

NOTES

1. While it is certainly the case that Catholic schools in England and Wales, Scotland and Northern Ireland all have different legislative contexts and political relationships, they nonetheless share sufficient demographic and contextual features to enable a general discussion of commonalities to be both relevant and useful. Further, they share many concerns and practicalities with other English- speaking countries such as North America and Australia.

2. Erasmus did enjoy some protection from Leo X though even this did not protect him from serious attack from many who saw his irreverent style as dangerous to Christendom. In any event this protection was offered long after he had produced some of his more swinging attacks on the pompous and foolish of Christendom.

3. It is important to recognise that Folly is to be distinguished from Erasmus and that she has several different voices, the particular application of which depend on the particular context. Here she is happy to draw to her bosom those she thinks are incredibly foolish in ignoring their emotions and indeed the part which the emotional life plays in the processes of reasonable thought and action.

4. In Bainton's volume there is an abbreviated version of this satire which was first published in 1518 and which, it is generally thought, Erasmus either authored or co-authored with Fausto Andrelini of Forli.

3

DISTINCTIVENESS AND THE CATHOLIC SCHOOL: BALANCED JUDGEMENT AND THE TEMPTATIONS OF COMMONALITY

Terence H. McLaughlin

Introduction

It has recently been observed that in the United Kingdom, the United States of America and Australia there has been a new awakening of interest in, and appreciation of, Catholic schools (February, 1998, p.210). In these and other contexts it is widely agreed that there is much to celebrate in the work and achievements of Catholic schools today, and many grounds for optimism about what these schools can achieve in the future.

In England and Wales, Catholic schools have, in general, received favourable reports in inspections recently conducted by The Office for Standards in Education (OFSTED)[1] and the schools enjoy considerable popularity among parents. Catholic schools in England and Wales have not confined their attention to students who are academically able or otherwise privileged. Many Catholic schools have a particular concern for students from poor and disadvantaged backgrounds and are notably successful in relation to them (Bishops' Conference of England and Wales, 1997a). Further, Catholic schools are increasingly responsive to calls that they be open to the educational demands of a liberal democratic society in terms both of the common good in general (Catholic Education Service, 1997) and the needs of members of other religious faiths in particular (Bishops' Conference of England and Wales, 1997b).

A broadly similar picture of Catholic schooling can be discerned in the United States. Andrew Greeley, for example, has argued that research evidence relating to Catholic schools in the US over the last forty years has painted a picture of these schools which is overwhelmingly encouraging in many respects. (Greeley, 1998, esp. pp.181-187; cf. Bryk *et al.*, 1993) In Australia, a similarly positive and encouraging vision of Catholic schools emerges (Canavan, 1998).

In all three contexts, and elsewhere, there has been a recent increase in research effort focused on Catholic schools, evidenced by scholarly publications and by the establishment of research centres, projects and journals.

This climate of interest, appreciation, celebration and optimism in relation to Catholic schools is not uncritical. Quite properly, critical questions are raised about a number of pertinent and important issues. Included here are questions about the precise nature and significance of the 'Catholic effect' in the success of the schools, about priorities in the aims and goals of the schools, about the specific institutional and other challenges and dilemmas which arise for Catholic schools in particular contexts and about practical obstacles and requirements needed for the realisation of the different aspects of the work of the schools. In these and other ways, the 'success story' being told about Catholic schools today is placed in a critical perspective.

Of the critical questions which are posed to Catholic schools today, perhaps the most fundamental, and the most difficult, concern the distinctiveness of Catholic schools. The inescapable requirement that Catholic schools have a distinctive character has been reiterated in the recently published document from the Congregation for Catholic Education, *The Catholic School on the Threshold of the Third Millenium*. The Catholic school, the document reminds us, has 'an ecclesial identity and role' which is '...not a mere adjunct, but is a proper and specific attribute, a distinctive characteristic which penetrates and informs every moment of its educational activity, a fundamental part of its very identity and the focus of its mission' (Congregation for Catholic Education, 1997§11). The fostering of this 'ecclesial dimension' of the Catholic school, the document continues, '...should be the aim of all those who make up the educating community' (ibid.).[2]

It may be argued that Catholic schools exist in order to transmit the Catholic tradition of faith and life and to educate within it. Catholic schools therefore have, or should have, a distinctive educational responsibility and character which is rooted in the distinctiveness of Catholic education itself. Other schools – for example 'common' schools in a liberal democratic society – are based on a somewhat different conception of education and therefore have a somewhat different educational responsibility and character (McLaughlin, 1996). One central difference between these two kinds of school is that Catholic schools, in contrast to 'common' schools, can base their educational influence on a specific and detailed vision of the meaning of human life and of existence as a whole (Congregation for Catholic Education, op. cit., §10).

These claims about the distinctive character of Catholic schools seem to be obviously true. As general statements of the nature of Catholic schools and Catholic education how could they be denied? How could contradictories of the statements be coherently maintained? Could it be intelligibly argued, for example, that Catholic schools exist in order *not* to transmit the Catholic tradition of faith and life and to educate within it? And what sense can be made of a claim that Catholic schools on the one hand, and the 'common' schools of a liberal democratic society on the other, have – and should have – an identical educational responsibility and character?

However, deeper exploration of these statements reveals a number of complexities, arising both in relation to (a) the claim that the Catholic school exists in order to transmit the Catholic tradition of faith and life and to educate within it, and (b) the claim that Catholic schools on the one hand and common schools on the other are, and should be, based on a somewhat different conception of education and have a somewhat different educational responsibility and character.

With regard to (a) ambiguities and questions arise in relation to two matters. First, how is 'the Catholic tradition of faith and life' to be understood? Many disputes about questions of distinctiveness in relation to Catholic schools have their roots in different interpretations of this tradition. These differing interpretations need not necessarily involve fundamental incompatibility and conflict – differences of priority or emphasis may be at stake. Secondly, scope for dispute arises in relation to 'transmit' and 'educate within'. Some disputes here relate to the 'content' of transmission and education and hence, in part, to disputes about the nature of the Catholic tradition of faith and life. Other disputes, however, relate to the notions of 'transmission' and 'education' themselves and to the nature of their practical implications in particular contexts. The concepts of 'transmission' and 'education' are, or can be perceived to be, somewhat in tension with each other, and this tension is apparent, for example, in familiar debates about the appropriate relationship between 'catechesis' and 'religious education' (Astley and Francis, 1994; Gallagher, 1996; Wrenn, 1991). Further, it is clear that the form which 'transmission' and 'education within' should take in given practical circumstances requires institutional and pedagogic interpretation in particular contexts. This interpretation takes place in the complex and partly intuitive practical judgement and wisdom of teachers and educational leaders, and here there is ample room for dispute and differences of view.

With regard to (b) ambiguities and questions arise with regard to the precise account which should be given of the relationship between Catholic schools and 'common' schools. It is important to insist here that Catholic schools on the one hand and 'common schools' on the other are not based on wholly different conceptions of education nor have a wholly different educational responsibility and character. After all, there exists an 'overlapping consensus' (Rawls, 1996, pt lect. 4) between specifically Catholic beliefs and values and the 'public values' of a liberal democratic society, and this consensus extends to many educational beliefs and values also. It is important to emphasise, therefore, that Catholic schools are, and should be, *somewhat* different from their 'common' counterparts with respect to their educational conceptions, responsibility and character (McLaughlin, op. cit., pp.145-148).

Notwithstanding these complexities, ambiguities and questions, however, it is possible to re-state, at least in general terms (a) the claim that the Catholic school exists in order to transmit the Catholic tradition of faith and life and to educate within it and (b) the claim that Catholic schools on the one hand and 'common' schools on the other are, and should be, based on a somewhat different conception of education and have a somewhat different educational responsibility and character. It may be argued, therefore, that whilst the meaning and interpretation of the claims clearly require much analysis and debate, the claims themselves are, at least in general terms, indisputable.

Before proceeding, however, it is worth considering a particular challenge to (a) which arises from a claim that there can be a legitimate plurality of different 'models' of Catholic school. From the perspective of this challenge it is argued that, whilst some Catholic schools have the role of transmitting to Catholic students the Catholic tradition of faith and life and educating them within it, other Catholic schools have a different educational role, for example in relation to the provision of certain forms of service to students who are marginalised or disadvantaged or in relation to the encouragement of dialogue with students of other faiths (Bishops' Conference of England and Wales, 1997b, ch.3).[3] In these other models, it is suggested, the Catholic school has a principled role in relation to students who are not Catholics which does not amount to 'transmission' or 'education within' the Catholic tradition of faith and life. However, whatever the merits of the arguments in support of these alternative models of Catholic school, it seems possible to accommodate these arguments within (a). This is because it seems a necessary part of any coherent attempt to show that these 'alternative models' of Catholic school are indeed Catholic schools that it be claimed that they are in fact engaged in *some sense* in transmission and education with respect to the Catholic tradition of faith and life, though in a particular and more diffuse way (for example, through exemplification and witness).

The present chapter therefore assumes that the general claims made in (a) and (b) are true. The task of analysing their meaning and implications is extensive. This chapter will explore a number of questions relating to the appropriate response of teachers and educational leaders in Catholic schools to the significance of the claims. The chapter has three sections. In the first, I indicate the importance of the claims and offer some thoughts about aspects of their practical significance for teachers and educational leaders in Catholic schools. In the next two sections I consider in turn two general issues relevant to an appropriate response to the claims; the question (related to (a)) of what is involved in the achievement of balanced judgement in relation to the claims in the light of 'the Catholic tradition of faith and life' and the need (related to (b)) to avoid in response to the claims a phenomenon I shall call 'the temptations of commonality'.

Both in the matters selected for discussion, and in the broadly philosophical approach adopted, the present discussion is necessarily partial and incomplete.

The distinctiveness of Catholic schools: importance and practical significance

The importance of questions of distinctiveness for Catholic schools is manifest. This importance extends beyond the familiar point that a shared educational vision on the part of teachers and educational leaders in schools is a generally recognised requirement for educational effectiveness. In the case of Catholic schools, questions concerning distinctiveness are implicated in, even if they do not wholly determine, the criteria of what is to count as effectiveness.

Questions of the distinctiveness of Catholic schools can, and should be, explored in an abstract or theoretical way by theologians, bishops, philosophers, sociologists and others viewing education 'from a distance'. The present discussion, however, seeks to explore some aspects of the practical significance of questions of distinctiveness for teachers and educational leaders in Catholic schools. A number of matters are of relevance here.

At the outset, it is important to recognise that a school is not a seminar concerned with the exploration of abstract or theoretical ideas in a detached and disinterested way. A school is engaged in a practical enterprise of great complexity which calls for many forms of practical knowledge and understanding, judgement and wisdom, skill, disposition and commitment on the part of teachers and educational leaders. In the light of this recognition, a number of questions relating to the practical significance of questions of the distinctiveness of Catholic schools come into focus.

First, it is important to recognise that practical questions and demands relating to the distinctiveness of the Catholic school arise in relation to many issues in the school and in many different ways. The pervasive and polymorphous character of these distinctiveness-related questions and demands can be seen by considering the wide range of contexts in the Catholic school in which these questions and demands arise. At the level of the school as an institution these contexts include the writing and publication of statements of aim and mission, the recruitment, appointment, promotion (and perhaps dismissal) of staff, the admission of students, the 'marketing' of the school (perhaps in a competitive environment) and the prioritisation of resources. At the level of the life of the school as a whole, they include matters relating to the ethos and culture of the school in their various aspects (including liturgy and worship). At the level of the curriculum they include questions relating to pedagogy and 'content' in areas such as catechesis and religious education as well as in areas relating to the curriculum as a whole, including 'cross-curricula' elements such as sex education and specific subjects such as English, Mathematics and Science. At the level of the 'management' or leadership of the school they include processes such as school review, target setting, staff appraisal and the like. Indeed, it can be argued that questions and demands of distinctiveness cannot be excluded from any aspect of the life and work of the Catholic school.

Second, the professional qualities and capacities which are needed on the part of teachers and educational leaders in Catholic schools as a response to the many contexts in which questions and demands of distinctiveness arise are themselves wide ranging. These qualities and capacities include an understanding of issues relating to questions of distinctiveness at the level of general principle (derived, say, from scholarly resources, Church documents and professional guidelines and conferences), an ability to judge what is demanded in practical terms as an expression of the demands of distinctiveness in particular contexts (for example, with respect to decisions relating to staff appointments or to aspects of the ethos and culture of the school), the skill to put such judgements into practice (for example, in leading prayer or engaging in certain kinds of pedagogic practice), the disposition to be concerned about matters of distinctiveness and to act in relation to them, and the commitment to pursue these matters in the face of obstacles and difficulties. The complexity of some of the practical judgements involved in these matters scarcely requires emphasis.

It might be argued that the full range of these professional qualities and capacities cannot be expected of all teachers in Catholic schools. Teachers holding certain posts of responsibility, it might be claimed, can be expected to possess a fuller range of these qualities and capacities than other teachers. Further, it might be argued, certain qualities and capacities can be expected only of Catholic teachers – or, more precisely, Catholic teachers with an appropriate kind of religious commitment and practice who are prepared and able to bring this commitment and practice to bear upon their professional responsibilities. Whilst there is some truth in these claims, caution is needed in relation to them. For example, many teachers will testify that some of their colleagues who are not Catholics make a more significant contribution to the distinctiveness of the school than those who are Catholics. Further, and crucially, it is appropriate to ask all teachers in Catholic schools, whatever their level of responsibility within the school and whatever the nature and degree of their religious commitment and practice, to indicate the ways in which they contribute to the distinctiveness of the school, or might be able to do so. Every teacher, it has been argued, can and should make some sort of contribution to this distinctiveness and this contribution should feature in their formal appraisal.[4] A demand of this kind arises from the aspiration of the Catholic school to exercise a kind of holistic influence (McLaughlin, op. cit., pp.141ff; Congregation for Catholic Education, op. cit., §14, 18, 19) from which no teacher can be exempted.

Third, it is important to consider how these professional qualities and capacities demanded of teachers and educational leaders in Catholic schools by the questions and demands of distinctiveness may be best developed. The varied character of the qualities and capacities that have been identified indicate that no simple answer can be given to this question. The promotion of forms of theoretical study on the part of the professionals involved is only part of the story. The qualities and capacities do not involve a crude 'application' of theory to practice by teachers and educational leaders. It has long been realised that the proper role of 'theory' in relation to educational practice cannot be seen in terms of crude 'application'. A more adequate view sees 'theory' as initially developed in practice as part of the 'professional common sense' of teachers and educational leaders, much of which is unreflective and tacit in character. More explicit and systematic 'theory' (including that developed in relation to the distinctiveness of the Catholic school) has a role in gradually sophisticating this understanding in an appropriate way at various stages and contributing to the development of a body of educational practices informed and justified by defensible 'practical theory' (Hirst, 1990). On this view, abstract or theoretical analyses still have an indispensable value and role. I have suggested elsewhere, for example, that the lack of an articulated contemporary Catholic philosophy of education deprives the Catholic educational community of an important resource for dealing with questions of distinctiveness (McLaughlin, op. cit., pp.138f). Such abstract and theoretical analyses, however, merely have a contributory role in relation to an understanding of and engagement with the practical questions which arise.

Educational practice cannot wait upon the achievement of the sort of clarity required in a philosophical discussion, nor can it proceed in a unduly rationalistic way. Practical experiment, intuition, compromise, 'artistry' and the like are inherent in the very nature of educational practice (McLaughlin, 1994). The sorts of professional qualities and capacities that are being sought are best developed in close relationship with educational practice itself.

It is claimed in some quarters that the sorts of professional qualities and capacities we have been referring to are best conceptualised in terms of the concept of 'the reflective teacher'. Thus, it may be claimed, the questions and demands of distinctiveness will be best addressed if Catholic teachers become 'reflective teachers'. However, despite the insights which are embodied in the concept of the 'reflective teacher', the concept lacks clarity and is apt for use as a vague slogan. An adequate account of the concept requires sustained attention to the meaning and implications of 'reflection' and to its scope and objects. Further, the concept of 'the reflective teacher' seems incomplete. We want and need teachers to have qualities and capacities which extend beyond reflection (McLaughlin, 1999).

The professional qualities and capacities to which we have been referring are better conceptualised in terms of a form of pedagogic practical wisdom or *phronesis* in the Aristotelian sense. Wilfred Carr describes *phronesis* as '...a comprehensive moral capacity which combines practical knowledge of the good with sound judgement about what, in a particular situation, would constitute an appropriate expression of this good' (Carr, 1995, p.71). The full articulation of this notion, and its educational implications, lies beyond the scope of this chapter, and only central suggestive elements of the notion can be indicated here.[5] In *phronesis* practical knowledge of the good is related to intelligent and personally engaged sensitivity to situations, individuals (including oneself) and a tradition of belief and life, in making inherently supple and non-formulable practical judgements about what constitutes an appropriate expression of the good in a given circumstance.

Sustained attention is needed to the exploration of a distinctively Catholic form of pedagogic *phronesis* which could form the basis of distinctively Catholic forms of teacher education and training at pre- and in-service levels and which could constitute the best way in which the professional qualities and capacities which have been identified might be developed. Here an emphasis would be placed on the development of the teacher in a broad way. Dunne comments that the sort of practical knowledge which is at stake in *phronesis* is '...a fruit which can only grow only in the soil of a person's experience and character' (Dunne, 1993, p.358). Dunne continues: 'In exposing oneself to the kind of experience and acquiring the kind of character that will yield the requisite knowledge...[one]...is at the same time a feeling, expressing, and acting person, and one's knowledge is inseparable from one as such' (ibid.). A notion of a Catholic form of pedagogic *phronesis* involves the wide-ranging formation of the teacher in the Catholic tradition of faith and life in general, and the Catholic educational tradition in particular. Such a wide-ranging formation, in which spiritual development has a central place, has some affinities with kinds of formation offered to members of religious orders.

Several of the demands of distinctiveness seem apt for satisfaction by *phronesis*. These include the need for teachers and educational leaders to exercise complex contextualised judgement and to exert influence of relevant kinds through their personhood and example.

The suggestion that a Catholic form of pedagogic *phronesis* might be explored may encounter a number of objections and difficulties. Joseph Dunne draws our attention to '...the complicity of *phronesis* with an established way of life' (ibid., p.373). In the case of the kind of *phronesis* under discussion, this is the Catholic tradition of faith and life. The difficulty here is whether this tradition, in the circumstances of present-day life, is sufficiently 'established' in the required sense. Further, the notion of 'pedagogic *phronesis*' seems to demand flourishing and relatively stable 'communities of practice' (Pendlebury, 1990). It might be argued that we do not, at least in Britain, enjoy a sufficiently robust Catholic form of life and a sufficiently flourishing 'community of practice' among Catholic educators for the notion of a Catholic 'pedagogic *phronesis*' to get off the ground. A further difficulty, it might be claimed, is that we lack a sufficient number of Catholic teachers with the relevant commitments. We ought, however, to move towards the implementation of this notion, albeit in a gradual way.

However, in the absence of the specification and enactment of a wide-ranging formation for teachers and educational leaders in Catholic schools of the sort associated with the notion of a Catholic 'pedagogic *phronesis*', it is nevertheless possible for a number of valuable steps to be taken in relation to the development of the professional qualities and capacities which have been discussed, and many of these steps have been taken in England and Wales and elsewhere.

Some of these steps include encouraging teachers and educational leaders to go beyond 'edu-babble' (imprecise and platitudinous rhetoric) in their handling of the questions and demands of distinctiveness (McLaughlin, 1996). Further, the understanding by the professionals of the issues at stake can be enhanced by a number of initiatives and practical strategies and requirements. These include publications and statements (Catholic Education Service, 1996b; Catholic Education Service and *Briefing*, 1997), courses of various kinds, professional exercises and policy requirements. Prominent among potential misunderstandings concerning the questions and demands of distinctiveness is the mis-perception that they arise only in relation to a part of the life and work of the Catholic school and in relation to certain members of staff only.

Needless to say it is important to emphasise that the questions and demands of distinctiveness cannot be dealt with teachers and educational leaders in Catholic schools in isolation from other important agents and influences, such as Church authorities and the educational policies of the state. These broader influences require consideration in a fuller account.

The development and exercise of the professional qualities and capacities needed by teachers and educational leaders in Catholic schools relevant to the questions and demands of distinctiveness give rise to many issues. I focus attention in turn below on two of these: the need for teachers and educational leaders to achieve balanced judgement in relation to the Catholic tradition of faith and life and the need for them to avoid what I shall refer to as 'the temptations of commonality'.

Balanced judgement and the Catholic tradition of faith and life

In his book *Travels in Sacred Places*, Geoffrey Robinson, Auxiliary Bishop of the Archdiocese of Sydney and Chairman of the Catholic School Board in that city, recalls a vision of God which is widely seen as having been dominant in the minds of earlier generations of Catholics. This is a vision of an 'angry' God, who frowned on enjoyment and 'this-life', inspired fear and demanded unquestioning obedience to detailed rules. As the Bishop reminds us 'the Catholic Church is famous for its angry God' (1997, p.6). Whilst acknowledging the need to take a balanced and carefully judged view of the conception of God which was in fact presented to, and experienced by, Catholics in earlier times, the Bishop nevertheless considers that, for many people, the image of an 'angry' God was dominant and overwhelming (ibid., ch.2).

Such a vision of an 'angry' God is, the Bishop insists, deeply flawed in many respects. It is clearly damaging to the health and growth of individuals psychologically and spiritually and can be mis-used as a device for manipulating people. A vision of an 'angry' God involves a distortion of the Christian message. For good reasons, he notes, contemporary Catholics have reacted against the conception of God as 'angry', and seek to avoid the transmission of such a conception of God to their own children.

In the face of this the Bishop poses an interesting question in relation to this reaction. Has it, he asks, gone to an opposite extreme, and generated a conception of God which is inadequate in other ways? He describes this reactive conception in the following terms: 'This new God is full of love, tenderness, compassion, kindness and warm feelings. This God permanently consoles, never challenges, doesn't forgive because there is no such thing as sin and thus nothing to forgive, and often doesn't even encourage, for encouragement could imply challenge' (ibid., p.9). Such a vision of God, observes the Bishop, ascribes 'unintelligent love' to God and limits God's response to all human situations to something akin to the giving of a 'big hug'. It is a vision of God which is, in his view, not only unintelligent and limited but also undemanding and unsatisfying. Further, the Bishop implies, this reactive vision of God is false and harmful.

In place of this kind of exaggerated reactive vision of God, the Bishop urges the acceptance of a deeper and more adequate vision, which preserves in a delicate balance the notion both of a God of love and a God of challenge.[6]

Bishop Robinson's discussion serves as an illustration of the indispensability of balanced discernment and judgement in matters of faith, and the need to be alert to the dangers of distorted perception and reaction. In the Catholic tradition of faith and life, as elsewhere, balanced discernment and judgement are essential.

Any attempt to illuminate the notion of 'balanced discernment and judgement' in the Catholic tradition of faith and life involves issues of great complexity. To sketch matters roughly, a first move in any such illumination requires an outline of the clarification of the general features of the tradition in which 'balanced discernment and judgement' is to be exercised.

There have been many attempts to elucidate the central features of the Catholic tradition of faith and life. Richard McBrien offers the following general answers to the question: 'What is Catholicism?'

> Catholicism is a rich and diverse reality. It is a Christian tradition, a way of life, and a community... it is comprised of faith, theologies, and doctrines and is characterised by specific liturgical, ethical and spiritual orientations and behaviours; at the same time, it is a people, or cluster of peoples, with a particular history. (McBrien, 1994, p.3)

> '...the Catholic Church is a community of persons (the human dimension) who believe in God and shape their lives according to that belief (the religious dimension); who believe in God as triune and in Jesus Christ as the Son of God and the redeemer of human kind, and who shape their lives according to that belief (the Christian dimension); who ritually express and celebrate that belief especially in the Eucharist, and who... recognise the Bishop of Rome to be 'the perpetual and visible source and foundation of the unity of the bishops and of the multitude of the faithful' (the ecclesial dimension). To be Catholic, therefore, is to be a kind of human being, a kind of religious person, and a kind of Christian disciple belonging to a specific eucharistic community of disciples within the worldwide, or ecumenical, Body of Christ. (ibid., p.1187)

McBrien holds that the distinctiveness of Catholicism consists in a particular and unique configuration of characteristics including the principles (or themes) of sacramentality, mediation and communion, and of tradition, reason, analogy and universality. The task of articulating these characteristics, and Catholicism itself, in detail is clearly an extensive one, in which reference to such resources as the Catechism of the Catholic Church (1994) is important.

The notion of balanced judgement is involved in relation to the Catholic faith and life in a number of ways. First, the notion of balance is inherent in the very nature of Catholicism itself. McBrien emphasises the centrality of the notion of balance to Catholicism by referring to its embracing of 'both/and' rather than 'either/or' approach:

> It is not nature or grace, but graced nature; not reason or faith, but reason illumined by faith; not law or Gospel, but law inspired by the Gospel; not Scripture or tradition, but normative tradition within Scripture; not faith or works, but faith issuing in works and works as expressions of faith; not authority or freedom, but authority in the service of freedom; not unity or diversity, but unity in diversity. (ibid., p.16)

An emphasis upon the notion of balance in the structure of Catholic faith and life is a central feature of Kevin Nichols' recent book *Refracting the Light: Learning the Languages of Faith* (1997). Nichols focuses his attention upon four interrelated 'languages of faith': narrative expression or story, doctrine, liturgy and Christian morality. The need for balanced judgement is inherent within each of these 'languages of faith' and between them. With regard to balanced judgement within each 'language', Nichols illustrates how, for example, such judgement is required in relation to the 'language of story' in the discernment of the 'truth' of stories (ibid., pp.32-41), and is aided by the role of metaphor in unifying diverse elements of faith (ibid., p.41). Such judgement is required in relation to the 'language of doctrine' in achieving an appropriate understanding of the nature and importance of doctrines, and in ensuring (for example) that they are not on the one hand mistaken for the objects of faith nor on the other hand seen as insignificant for faith or as merely relative or provisional: whilst doctrine develops and is not exhaustive, Nichols maintains, it is nevertheless true (ibid., pp. 56-64). Further, such judgement is required in discerning the 'hierarchy of truths' of the faith. Such judgement is required in relation to the 'language of liturgy' in discerning its distinctive character as a mode of expression of faith (ibid., ch.3). Balanced judgement is also required in relation to the 'language of morality', in such matters as the achievement of an understanding of the proper relationship between the moral demands of, on the one hand, law, authority, general principle and the avoidance of sin, and on the other of love, conscience, the making of contextually sensitive concrete decisions and the development of virtue.[7] With regard to balanced judgement between the various 'languages' of faith, Nichols illustrates the mutual interaction, nourishment and correction that exists between them (ibid., p.22).

As well as the notions of balance and balanced judgement being inherent in the very nature of Catholicism itself, these notions are clearly required in the process by which individuals appropriate the tradition of faith and life. One reason for this is that the tradition cannot be conceived as wholly fixed, static and transparent. Nichols points out how a balanced grasp of the different languages of faith in relation to each other is necessary to guard against distortions and narrowness of perception and vision. And since the languages of faith do not have a precise grammar and syntax, being a Catholic is best seen, in Nichols' view, in terms of being the occupant of a house. He writes:

> It is a way of knowing which is oblique and partial. It is not
> knowledge which we are meant to do up in neat packages and

present cockily to others as a set of ultimate facts. We are meant, rather, in humility, to draw others into this way of understanding... It is a house in which we have space to live and breathe, to relate to others, now intimately, now stormily. It is a house in which we are never bored though sometimes afflicted; often also surprised by joy. (ibid., p.152)

The achievement of 'balanced judgement' in relation to the Catholic tradition of faith and life is clearly important for teachers and educational leaders in Catholic schools in their handling of the questions and demands of distinctiveness. This is for a number of reasons. One reason concerns the need to avoid distortion and bias in the interpretation of the Catholic tradition. This general concern about distortion and bias can be illustrated by reference to the case of catechesis. The General Directory of Catechesis (1997, pt. 2, chs I and II) insists that catechesis involves a normative content to be transmitted in a way which is comprehensive, systematic, structured and approved on behalf of the universal Church, since catechesis is an ecclesial activity. Therefore, catechists must be able to '... "integrate",... [and be]...capable of overcoming "unilateral divergent tendencies"...and ...[be]...able to provide a full and complete catechesis. They must know how to link...orthodoxy and orthopraxis, ecclesial and social meaning...lest tensions arise between them' (ibid., §238-245).[8] A somewhat similar set of concerns underlies recent attempts to specify in more detail the aims and content of religious teaching in Catholic schools (Bishops' Conference of England and Wales, 1996a). This concern to do justice to the Catholic tradition of faith and life has application beyond the specific areas of catechesis and religious education to all the aspects of the work of the teacher and educational leader in the Catholic school.

Apart from concerns about distortion and bias, however, a balanced grasp of the Catholic tradition of faith and life is needed by teachers and educational leaders in Catholic schools if their work in relation to distinctiveness is not to be merely superficial. The achievement of 'balanced judgement' in relation to the Catholic tradition of faith and life is not, however, straightforward. It involves the kind of *phronesis* which was outlined earlier, and the sorts of difficulties and obstacles noted in relation to the acquisition of 'pedagogic *phronesis*' apply here also. A further difficulty emerges by confronting the question: What is to count as a balanced judgement in relation to the Catholic tradition of faith and life? The notion of 'balance' is, in itself, a purely formal one and is uninformative about what precisely a balance is to consist in with regard to any specific judgement. A significant issue relevant to this matter is dispute and disagreement within the Catholic tradition of faith and life about a number of issues and the phenomenon of lack of unity and cohesion within the Church.[9] The existence of disputes and disagreements of these kinds was indicated earlier as explanatory of many disputes and disagreements with respect to the questions and demands of distinctiveness. On the part of teachers and educational leaders in Catholic schools these disputes and disagreements may require the adoption of approaches and attitudes such as those distinctive of the 'Catholic common ground' project in the United States.[10]

A balanced grasp of the Catholic tradition of faith and life is also important if Catholic teachers and educational leaders are to avoid what I shall call 'the temptations of commonality'.

The temptations of commonality

The 'temptations of commonality' can be seen as arising in the form of a reaction to an earlier distorted vision of Catholic education. Just as Catholicism used to be famous for its 'angry God,' so too, it might be argued, it used to be famous for a form of education which emphasised authority, guilt creation, doctrine, orthodoxy, rigid rules, sanctions and rituals, and the development of a Catholic identity somewhat defensive with respect to the wider world. Such a view of Catholic education, it is claimed, failed to awake a real understanding of and commitment to the faith on the part of young people, and frequently amounted to a form of mere 'sacramentalising of the unevangelised'. Further, it is urged, this form of education was seriously deficient with respect to the attitudes to the wider world which it conveyed. As with the conception of God as 'angry', this view of Catholic education needs to be seen in a clear and fair perspective; caricatures need to be avoided and the true nature and value of earlier emphases appreciated (O'Donoghue, 1997). However, again as with the 'angry God' this model of Catholic education is sufficiently recognisable for its dominance in the experience of earlier generations of Catholics to be acknowledged.

A typical reaction to this model of Catholic education is discernible in a recent piece of research which explored the distinctiveness of a system of Catholic secondary schools run by a religious order. Here the particular details of the research are not at issue, but rather the general picture of Catholic schools which it presents. The research showed that there was much evidence of forms of distinctiveness in the culture and life of the schools which was authentically derived from the charisma of the founder of the order. However, these forms of distinctiveness were mainly concerned with extensions of, or specific emphases relating to, values commonly recognised in society as a whole such as caring, social justice, self-esteem and 'the spiritual quest' broadly conceived. The researcher found that, despite the centrality to the thought of the founder of specifically religious aims and concepts (in particular the importance of catechesis), in the schools there was a lack of clarity about their religious and ecclesial purposes, that these matters lacked clear and consistent expression, that there was considerable ambivalence concerning the spiritual purposes of the schools, that the staff did not see their efforts as aiming at 'traditional Catholic practice' on the part of the students, that the more specifically religious goals of the schools were not strongly subscribed to by the students, that both the students and the staff were 'largely disconnected' from the 'institutional Church' and that parents were sending their children to the schools less and less for specifically religious reasons. What is interesting about this research is that the phenomena identified were seen by staff in the schools not merely as *de facto* states of affairs dictated by practical, and perhaps regrettable, realities, but in some cases as expressions of what Catholic schools today should properly be aiming to achieve.

The concept of the angry God led to the over-reaction of the concept of an unrestrictedly nice God which was equally (though differently) inadequate. Has the concept of the dogmatic Catholic school led to the over-reaction of a Catholic school unduly dominated by variants of common values?

Indeed, the researcher in question raises the issue of whether the schools in his study had, in their emphasis upon variants of 'common' values linked to the charisma of the founder in a sometimes platitudinous way, brought about a diversion of attention away from Jesus and the Gospel.

The attractions of 'commonality' are easy to understand. It is clear, for example, that the Christian message has implications for the world and for engagement with its issues and problems. Further, the Catholic tradition of social teaching can be shown to have telling application in relation to the notion of 'the common good'. It is also true that attention to matters of 'commonality' is needed for purposes of student motivation and engagement. Michael Paul Gallagher, for example, argues that inhibitions or blockages to religious faith experienced by many young people today requires educators to engage in a kind of analysis and critique of contemporary culture, '...helping students to identify the dehumanising factors present in life-styles and assumptions...' (1997, p.25).

The attractions of commonality become temptations when they prevent due attention being given to the specifically religious concepts and perspectives which a properly balanced perspective on the Catholic tradition of faith and life requires. This is not to suggest that Catholic schools are as a matter of fact succumbing to temptations of these kinds, merely that vigilance is needed with respect to them.

Conclusion

In this chapter I have attempted to illuminate the importance and practical significance of the questions and demands which arise for teachers and educational leaders in Catholic schools relating to the distinctiveness of these schools, and have indicated two issues requiring particular attention. A number of steps can and have been taken in relation to the development of the range of professional qualities and capacities needed by teachers and educational leaders in Catholic schools if they are to deal adequately with these questions and demands. However, it has been suggested that the nature both of the questions and demands and the professional qualities and capacities needed in response to them indicate the need to explore the notion of a distinctively Catholic version of pedagogic phronesis as the most favourable context in which relevant forms of professional formation and development can take place.

NOTES

1. On the performance of Catholic schools in England and Wales in recent OFSTED inspection reports see, for example, Catholic Education Service, 1995, 1996a. For analyses of the reasons for the academic success of Catholic schools in England and Wales see, for example, Morris, 1998a, 1998b, 1998c. Compare Bryk *et al.,* 1993.
2. Congregation for Catholic Education 1997 §11. For a sensitive and comprehensive discussion of matters of distinctiveness in relation to Catholic schools see Sullivan, 1998.
3. See also Bishops' Conference of England and Wales, 1997b, ch.3. Compare Arthur, 1995, ch.7.

4. I owe this point to John Sullivan. See Sullivan, 1998, Appendix One.
5. For such articulations see, for example, Carr, 1995, ch.4, Dunne, 1993, esp pt.2. For an articulation of the notion of practical judgement in the context of moral judgement see, for example, Smith, 1997.
6. See esp. chs. 6,8-11, 28, 30, 33-42, 46-48.
7. Ibid., pp.110-111; 126-129; ch. 5.
8. See also §67, 78f, 282, 284f, 219, 236f, 238-248, 249.
9. On this matter in relation to catechesis see, for example, Congregation for the Clergy, 1997, esp §28.
10. 'On the Catholic Common Ground Project' see *The Tablet*, 17 August 1996, p.1085; 7 September 1996, pp.1156-1159. Compare Robinson 1997, ch. 48.

4

THE CATHOLIC SCHOOL IS AS GOOD AS ITS ETHOS

John Brick

Introduction

This chapter argues that Catholic schools are founded upon a rich ethical tradition which brings together respect for the person and a dynamic theology of community. This occurs in their special environment, education, which has as its fundamental task the care and nurture of the young. Individual schools revitalise themselves and heighten their effectiveness when they regularly revisit their underlying ethos. In doing so, they have the substantial resources of the Conciliar and post-Conciliar documents of the Second Vatican Council.

Humanity – the measure of all things?

Schools do not exist in some ethical vacuum. Every moment of a school's existence is characterised by the encounters between the individuals who make up the school's community. At every moment each person who is participating in the life of the school is answering the question, 'how ought I treat the other?' The morality which emerges from these personal encounters will give a clear indication as to what constitutes the ethos of the school, and, in large, its version of life's meaning.

One version of life which has persisted through history is that creation is dark and that life is not only meaningless but is pitiless and inexorably mean. Perhaps it is Job lamenting thus: 'Has not man a hard service upon earth, and are not his days like the days of a hireling? ... My days are swifter than a weaver's shuttle, and come to their end without hope' (7:1-7).

Or, again, Macbeth describing his experience of the aridity of life:

> Out, out, brief candle!
> Life's but a walking shadow, a poor player
> That struts and frets his hour upon the stage
> And then is heard no more. It is a tale
> Told by an idiot, full of sound and fury,
> Signifying nothing.
>
> (5:v:35-40)

Closer to our own time, in the social and political turmoil of the 1930s, Malcolm Muggeridge concluded that,

> when there is no God, nothing in the wide universe more than Man, no wisdom greater than his, no being more lasting than his being or patience exceeding his patience, then the Word is Flesh indeed, and desperate becomes the need for imperfection to signify perfection, finitude to signify infinitude. Blessed are the poor in heart, for they shall see God; cursed are the impure in heart, for they shall see man. (1967, p. 251)

Several millennia after Job, Charles Handy reflects on American Vice-President Al Gore's insight that 'we have constructed in our civilization a false world of plastic flowers and Astro-Turf, air-conditioning and fluorescent lights, windows that don't open and background music that never stops, days when we don't know whether it has rained, nights when the sky never stops glowing' (1994, pp. 12f). At this point Handy goes on to suggest that Gore could have made it sound a lot worse, had he described the wastelands of many inner cities. In these wastelands there are mindless murders of tiny children, rapes of old ladies, burglaries and thefts every thirty seconds in some places, a total disregard for human life and property, senseless anonymous violence.

In developing this topography of contemporary society, in the post-Second World War period, the eminent Lutheran theologian Paul Tillich offered the following diagnosis:

> We may nevertheless elaborate two main characteristics of man in industrial society. The first of these is the concentration of man's activities upon the methodical investigation and technical transformation of his world, including himself, and the consequent loss of the dimension of depth in his encounter with reality. Reality has lost its inner transcendence or, in another metaphor, its transparency for the eternal. Since the beginning of the 18th century God has been removed from the power field of man's activities. He has been put alongside the world without permission to interfere with it because every interference would disturb man's technical and business calculations. The result is that God has become superfluous and the universe left to man as its master (1959, pp. 43f).

The result of the Western subscription to eighteenth-century rationalism has, for Tillich, led to a world where '...the structures of destruction in personal and communal life, are ignored or denied. Educational processes are able to adjust the large majority of men to the demands of the system of production and consumption. Man's actual state is hence mistakenly regarded as his essential state, and he is pictured in a position of progressive fulfilment of his potentialities (ibid.)'. Further it has resulted in a situation where the education system itself may be seen to be uneven at best and leaves many young people deprived of the opportunity to achieve even fairly rudimentary levels of literacy and numeracy (Wickens, 1995).

Tillich's rich analysis holds as well today as it did when he first wrote it four decades ago. Gore's description in some ways enfleshes

Tillich's more overarching view. It might be claimed that Tillich's interpretation was optimistic, particularly where he regards education as successfully 'adjusting' most people to an economic system, a major feature of which seems to be to condemn a significant number of school leavers to be victims of chronic unemployment. The suicide rates of the young, combined with statistics reporting accidental death from drug or alcohol abuse, leave even less comfort for the contemporary observer than was the case when Tillich was writing. The gravity of the situation is not lost on the Catholic Church.

Catholicism's response

Of course the Catholic Church is not blind to the very real and sometimes dramatic way in which the lives of the young are worked out. The concern of the Church for people in such circumstances is articulated in Conciliar and post-Conciliar documents where there is a strong sense of the Church addressing itself to what it sees as a huge challenge (Congregation for Catholic Education,1988, §13). The daunting nature of the challenge is apparent when it is realised that the Church must respond almost in spite of itself, since, as institution, it is often identified with the problem rather than the solution. Yet the Catholic school has the potential to present students with a coherent and convincing account of life which is not sunk in pessimism or despair. The Catholic school exists precisely to demonstrate in a living, human way that there is an alternative vision of life which denies the darkness of a Job or Macbeth and which sees people transcending those philosophies which seek to reduce them to figures on a balance sheet.

What the Catholic school can bring to the lives of the people who make up its community – students, parents and staff – is a breadth of vision founded upon St John's text that 'in Him was life, and the life was the light of men. The light shines in the darkness, and the darkness has not overcome it' (Jn1:4f). It might be argued that it is the breadth of vision held by each Catholic school which will describe the goodness of that school. One pathway into understanding the notion of breadth of vision can be found in the work of Anthony Padavano, who suggests that 'seen from outside, man is but an episode in the vast process of nature. Seen from within, each man is a universe in himself with a dignity that touches us poignantly' (1996, p. 6). The very flow of Padavano's language is an immediate antidote to the reductionist machine language of industrialism, and its adoption confers upon the school a power to combat robotisation of the person. In this respect, language is the potent tool for building ethos, and schools must consciously encourage a language which actually does recognise the uniqueness and dignity of each of its people.

In their attack on the limitations imposed by technocratic language forms on describing reality, Conroy and Davis (1996) propose that the language of poetry can be a source of empowerment for teachers and students by providing modes of expression which are clearly more human and meaningful, and hence carry more dignity, than the language of technocracy which pervades commercial society. They are correct in suggesting that 'poetry returns to the hearer a vocabulary which enables her to begin the process of self-reflection, in a language which captures the imagination through exposing the pupil to passion, anguish, anger, hatred, fear and betrayal as well as love, joy, relief and hope'. But the poetry itself is framed within a wider context. The foundation for that of the Catholic school is to be found, initially, in the teachings of the Second Vatican Council.

Vatican II: The nature of the person – dignity and freedom

When seeking the foundations of the ethos upon which Catholic education is built it is necessary to explore sources of the fundamental teachings of the Church. These are to be found in the Documents of the Second Vatican Council and those subsequent statements and reflections which derive their inspiration from the Council. In many ways it is refreshing to review the Documents for, in a world which often seems characterised by self-inflicted disaster and tormenting meaninglessness, these Documents breathe hope through the many ways they reflect faith in the goodness of God and the way in which it confers dignity upon humans. Upholding and nurturing this dignity is one of the most important motifs running through the language of the Documents of the Council and, as such, is an abiding concern for the Church. It is worth considering these Documents at length because they do provide the foundation for the vision of the person which makes Catholic education unique and valuable. They put forward a persuasive alternative to the dark self-centredness seen in a Job or a Macbeth.

When read in the school setting they offer the basis for school ethos and, by implication, criteria for constructing educational objectives, curriculum content, and the selection of teaching methods. More generally, they describe what ought to be a disposition towards a spiritual unity of those who are the school community and which, by extension, would encourage adoption of acceptable modes of interacting between members of that community. The importance the Church attaches to this dignity of each person may be seen throughout the Documents and most especially in *Lumen gentium: The Dogmatic Constitution of the Church* §32, which begins by iterating the metaphor of the Mystical Body of Christ wherein each individual is different but integral to the whole. The Constitution goes on to describe this wholeness thus,

> Therefore, the chosen People of God is one: 'one Lord, one faith, one baptism' (Ep 4:5). As members they share a common dignity from their rebirth in Christ. They have the same filial grace and the same vocation to perfection. They possess in common one salvation, one hope and one undivided charity. Hence, there is in Christ and in the Church no inequality on

the basis of race or nationality, social condition or sex, because 'there is neither Jew nor Greek; there is neither slave nor freeman; there is neither male nor female. For you are all "one" in Christ Jesus.' (Ga 3:28, Greek text; cf. Col 3:11).13 (Abbott,1966, p. 59).

Consequently, Christian educators are invited to be people who see through and beyond the physical and sociological characteristics of their students. While teachers may know more than their students, at least as far as the curriculum is concerned, they are nevertheless joined with them in the need for healing and the longing to be one with God. In this respect no one in the school is superior to another. If this is the case certain ways of speaking to students and interacting with them will be consistent with this common humanity while other ways will be inappropriate. It is sometimes too easy to dismiss such sentiment as sentimentality and place 'reality' as central; the reality of sometimes loud and aggressive students; the reality of an over-burdened curriculum and so on. These 'realities' are, in fact, no more pressing than that which issues from the central beliefs of the Christian Church as articulated in these Conciliar documents. The way schools approach this understanding is the way in which they create their ethos.

As it is a central contention of this essay that the ethos of the Catholic school should be located in a coherent understanding of the documents it is necessary to interrogate some of them further at this stage. The Council describes the theological basis upon which Christians generally, and the Catholic school in particular, build their ways of perceiving others. *Gaudium et spes: Pastoral Constitution on the Church in the Modern World* §14 concisely and powerfully describes the nature of the person.

Now, man is not wrong when he regards himself as superior to bodily concerns, and as more than a speck of nature or a nameless constituent of the city of man. For by his interior qualities he outstrips the whole sum of mere things. He finds re-enforcement in this profound insight whenever he enters into his own heart. God, who probes the heart, awaits him there. (ibid., p. 212)

This view of the person strips away the egocentricity seen in the notion that I am my own creation. Rather, it suggests that the I is embedded in a creation greater than the external material world. At once, this person recognises the humility of contingency and the glory of being part of an eternal benevolence. To this extent, 'Man judges rightly that by his intellect he surpasses the material universe, for he shares in the light of the divine mind' (ibid., p. 212)

The Church's understanding of the nature of the person is then developed in a discussion on the meaning of conscience. This discussion amplifies the meaning of the dignity of the individual and the nature of personal responsibility. The dignity is bound up in the recognition of personal responsibility as articulated in what is perhaps the most famous statement of the Council, that 'conscience is the most secret core and sanctuary' of the person (ibid., p. 215).

Finally, the Church tackles the difficult question as to what represents the authentic person and the life lived authentically. It answers this question within a framework which focuses on the interrelationship between the nature of freedom and how it is reflected in the nature of the person. In this same Constitution, under the heading 'The Excellence of Liberty', it argues that 'Only in freedom can man direct himself toward goodness. ... authentic freedom is an exceptional sign of the divine image within man. For God has willed that man be left "in the hand of his own counsel" so that he can seek his Creator spontaneously, and come freely to utter and blissful perfection through loyalty to Him. Hence man's dignity demands that he act according to a knowing and free choice. Such a choice is personally motivated and prompted from within. It does not result from blind internal impulse nor from mere external pressure.' (ibid., p. 214).

Finally, Vatican II describes the Church's multiple but integrated tasks of preserving and interpreting Holy Scripture, positing a view of creation as benevolent and eternal, seeing itself as on a never-ending journey which seeks an ever clearer understanding of God, and within all of this, affirming the individual as dignified and worthwhile, and destined for unity with God. This reaches to the heart of the complex relationship which the Church has both to the world at large and, more particularly, to those who are in communion with it. It does this by guarding the heritage of God's word and drawing religious and moral principles from corporate reflection, 'without always having at hand the solution to particular problems' (ibid., p. 639). This acceptance of the provisionality of the answers has always been a central feature of the reflection of the Catholic Church. 'She desires thereby to add the light of revealed truth to mankind's store of experience, so that the path which humanity has taken in recent times will not be a dark one' (ibid., p. 640).

What may schools draw from this? From one perspective these statements propose a very positive and very optimistic view of the person. God is goodness itself and goodness is intrinsic to the make-up of every person. In this respect there is an orientation for adults in the school to develop a disposition towards students and to each other of seeking the good in the other. It is part of the adults' task in the school to give effect to just that description – they are adults and they have a special responsibility to those who are at pre-adult stages. For teachers in particular, it is their pedagogically-special task to study and think about what 'pre-adult' means, and to create a suitable pre-adult environment which allows the goodness to flow. In the special relationship of care which ought characterise any Christian community, the Catholic school, in particular, must have as one of its perennial tasks the regular assessment as to how well its adults are creating an environment which permits the maturing learners to explore ideas of faith and to exercise judgement of conscience. To the extent that it does this the school will create moments when each person has time to be at peace with their in-dwelling God. The practical decisions which issue from these reflections on central questions about the very nature of Christian communion will point to the particular ethos of each particular school.

The text suggests that there are prior and ultimate ends in life, and in the school setting, there is a continuing demand to ensure that the 'feverish activity' say, often associated with final year examination classes, is not allowed, intentionally or unintentionally, to generate an educational ethos wherein the means justifies the ends. To offer such resistance in an environment which increasingly exerts pressure on the school and its students to perform in precisely these ways would indeed be the mark of a school community characterised by the reflections of the Council. Indeed, it is here that teachers reach deep into their resources as pedagogues in order to demonstrate in an ethical way to the adolescents who are enduring yet another of society's rites of passage – the school exit examination – that their dignity and self-worth as persons are not to be measured by academic results.

The Declaration on Christian Education

The centrality of education in and to the thought of the Council is marked by the decision to devote a document to its consideration. In doing so it intimated that, for the Christian, it meant much more than a means of self-aggrandisement. Alternatively, at its heart, it offers an ethic of the Christian person as communal-oriented and caring for the other, and through an appropriate education, becoming better able to bring Christian values to bear on social questions. To this end, *Gravissimum educationis* observed that as people grow more conscious of their dignity and calling, they prefer to take an increasingly active part in the life of society, especially in economic and political matters. 'Since every man of whatever race, condition, and age is endowed with the dignity of a person, he has an unalienable right to an education corresponding to his proper destiny and suited to his native talents, his sex, his cultural background, and his ancestral heritage. At the same time, this education should pave the way to brotherly association with other peoples, so that genuine unity and peace on earth may be promoted'. (Abbott, ibid., p. 639)

The Declaration regards teaching as an evolving discipline, a claim which ought to prevent teachers from being too prescriptive or categorical and that 'children and young people have a right to be encouraged to weigh moral values with an upright conscience, and to embrace them by personal choice, and to know and love God more adequately' (ibid.). Analysed, these statements provide an outline for the development of a school philosophy and curriculum. The Declaration speaks of education as a means to self-fulfilment through engaging in bringing Christian understandings to bear on economics and politics. It speaks of personal development, spiritually, intellectually, physically and sexually. It reiterates the basic value of respect for the dignity of the person. And, if these reflections are supplemented with the insights which come from *Dignitatis humanae: The Declaration on Religious Freedom*, the profundity of the anthropology which underpins Catholic attitudes to the place of the individual person within the educational system becomes increasingly transparent. Thus, 'the truth cannot impose itself except by virtue of its own truth, as it makes its entrance into the mind at once quietly and with power. Religious freedom, in turn, which men demand as necessary to fulfil their duty to worship God, has to do with immunity from coercion in civil society' (ibid., p. 677).

The Catholic school takes on the responsibility to acquaint its students with the teachings of the Church as manifest in the Conciliar and post-Conciliar documents and in a manner which ensures that the language used and the manners adopted are themselves rooted in this holistic view of the human freedom in community. Exercising freedom of choice comes after knowing what choices there are. Schools or systems of education which do not analyse or discuss religious understandings of meaning and destiny have in effect a truncated vision of both education and the person.

The Catholic ethos of education is one which engages with the secular society, taking on aspects of its curriculum, abiding by the socio-legal framework within which it must operate, but providing for its entire community the opportunity to investigate and experience ways of seeing and living over and above the secular. The ethos within which this vision of education is able to live clearly rejects certain past principles and practices which were evident in some Catholic schools that would be hard-pressed to demonstrate a commitment to a belief in the dignity and innate goodness of their students. These include linguistic and social practices which, irrespective of the intentions of the perpetrators, had (or continue to have) the effect of undermining and denigrating the person and treating natural and other resources as of no consequence. This vision is multi-faceted. When looked at from the perspective of the special tasks carried out by the school, a number of questions can be put to the school in order to attempt to see how any one school incorporates this vision into its life. The special nature of the school centres around an idea of community. This is not a generalised, inchoate notion but one founded upon a deeply held belief that true humanity is discovered through communion with others. This is partly what is meant by living an authentic life.

Authenticity and conformism

As Cardinal Karol Wojtyla, and prior to becoming Pope, John Paul II's exploration of authenticity in *The Acting Person* provides an interesting and incisive analysis of the sterility of conformism.

> The term 'conformism' derives from 'to conform' and denotes a tendency to comply with the accepted custom and to resemble others, a tendency that in itself is neutral, in many respects positive and constructive or even creative. This constructive and creative assimilation in the community is a confirmation and also a manifestation of human solidarity. But when it begins to sway towards servility, it becomes highly negative. It is this negative tendency that we call 'conformism'. It evidences not only an intrinsic lack of solidarity but simultaneously an attitude of evading opposition; in short, a noninvolvement. ... Instead of being the actor or agent responsible for building his own attitudes and his own commitment in the community man then fails to accept his share in constructing the community and allows himself to be carried along by the anonymous majority. Even when the servile attitude of conformism does not become an outright denial or limitation it always indicates a weakness of personal transcendence of self-determination and choice. (1969, p. 289)

The Pope's close analysis of the nature of the authentic life is a reflection of the Christian understanding of the person as one whose destiny is not confined to temporal concerns. It also raises the hugely important question of the school's attitudes to conformity both within its own walls and within the wider society. The ever-present temptation offered by education systems which never engage in that exploration which takes them beyond the mechanical is that they encourage an ethos wherein individuals may lose their essential identities to their socially-determined functions. Numerous references are made to authenticity throughout the Conciliar documents and this again returns us to *Gravissimum educationis,* which has as the focus for education the Christian's willingness to participate with others in the betterment of social life. The proposed curriculum is meant to empower Christians to be able to work effectively to that end. For the school, a pathway into a religious understanding of life can be by way of positively using the notion of authenticity. It can be seen in the ways in which the school educates all of its participants to develop the knowledge and skills which enable them to engage in the never-ending task of bringing Christian perspectives to inform whatever it is they may be engaged in. In this respect knowledge and skills are not ends in themselves but means towards achieving the vision of persons – dignified, worthwhile, deserving respect, having God as their centre and destiny – as described by the Church. Hence, the study of economics, for example, becomes the means whereby we might discover ways to have individuals realise their innate dignity which is made difficult if not impossible if they are forced to live with hunger and disease. Economics then rediscovers its origins in political economy which, in its turn, is clearly embedded in a discussion of how individuals ought to treat each other.

The school then does not teach subjects in some sort of disciplinary isolation, but sees them as part of a greater whole whose object is nothing less than the study and understanding of the eternal destiny of the person. As the Chief Justice of Australia, Sir Gerard Brennan, opined at the 1996 Australian National Catholic Education Commission Conference,

> There can be no contradiction between the purpose of Christian formation and the purpose of instruction in secular subjects. Nor can some false priority be accorded to one aspect or another of human development. To those who believe, human personality is completed, not diminished by human faith. If the system is to be true to itself, there must be a

confident proclamation of gospel truths. Freedom to think, to question, even to reject, is of paramount importance. Without that freedom, virtue is impossible. A will constrained by ignorance or sanction cannot respond freely to the love of God or humanity. But a mind which is free to accept or reject the loving message of faith is enriched by a positive response and finds peace in its warm relationship with God and other people. (1996, p. 15)

A difficulty experienced by some teachers is the confusion of goals of discipleship and independence. Sometimes they forget that education's primary task is not to construct disciples but to create adults who are independent and who decide in their own right to become disciples, not of others, but of Jesus. It is too often forgotten that it is not the institution or the individual who is to be followed but God. As a constant reminder of this the story is recounted by Klinger (1964, p. 80) of how Cardinal Tardini, the first Secretary of State for Pope John XXIII , would complain when asked to confer with John that 'The one up there is calling me again', i.e., to the papal apartments on the third floor of the Vatican. After one particular consultation John took Tardini aside and said to him, 'Caro Tardini, I should like to straighten you out on one point. The one up there is the Lord of all of us, the eternal Father in heaven … I am merely the one on the third floor.'

Didion quotes Lionel Trilling as sounding a warning of an inherent danger, which seems to be intrinsic in the nature of the work associated with the helping professions, in reminding us that 'we must be aware of the dangers which lie in our most generous wishes. Some paradox of our nature leads us, when once we have made our fellow men the objects of our enlightened interest, to go on to make them the objects of our pity, then of our wisdom, ultimately of our coercion' (Didion, 1969, pp. 161f). From the point of view of the Catholic school an important question concerns the nature of faith and the power of the Spirit. In this respect, coercive methods may be seen as contradicting the spirit of faith which permeates the Council's understanding of person.

In practical terms it may be difficult (and probably neither desirable nor feasible) to have this image of the holistic curriculum at the forefront of each individual lesson. Nevertheless, each school conducts its business within an ethos, and if regular opportunities are not taken to revisit the philosophical and theological foundations of the school, narrow day-to-day preliminary concerns may become, by default, the definers of the school's vision. It may be the case that a school allows others to decide its focus. For example, while the particular task of the school is about learning and academic progress, has it allowed its vision to narrow down so that it has become little more than an examination factory where position on some 'league table' provides its *raison d'être?* As human institutions, schools are always at risk of allowing the vision to escape. As the Sacred Congregation on Education notes, ' ... the Catholic school is particularly sensitive to the call ... for a more just society. It does not stop at the courageous teaching of the demands of justice even in the face of local opposition, but tries to put these demands into practice in its own community '(1977, §58). But as human institution it has not always been apparent that the bearing of the name has been contiguous with this mission (ibid. §65). This is not a closed criticism but an invitation to place schools as institutions in a creative context. The Congregation goes on to argue that ' ... loyalty to the aims of the Catholic school demands constant self-criticism and return to basic principles, to the motives which inspire the Church's involvement in education'. (ibid. §67) This, in turn, reflects an underlying thrust of the discussion about education in *Gravissimum educationis* which saw education as not standing still either in content or in the pedagogy which is to be brought to bear in the whole educational enterprise. It is consistent with the vision described in *Gaudium et spes: The Church in the Modern World* of Christians as living inside a community of faith which is ever seeking deeper expressions of truth. The idea that existed in certain historical versions of the Church Triumphant that it, the Church, owned truth in a form immutable and incontestable which must be applied in all situations and for all times has given way to the understanding of Church as pilgrim, as journeying, or, as Pope Paul VI expressed it when opening the Second Session of Vatican II.

> The Church is a mystery. It is imbued with the hidden presence of God. It lies, therefore, within the very nature of the Church to be always open to new and even greater explorations (Pope Paul VI, quoted Dulles, 1978, p. 22).

The special work of educators

It is in the context of the reflections of the Conciliar and post-Conciliar Church, as well as the murkiness of actual life explored in the first part of this essay that educators have their special work to do. They have a crucial part to play, not only as deliverers of a particular curriculum, but also as professionals who are engaged in refining the theory and practice of expressing the Christian vision of person in a way which is comprehensible to their students. It is here that their expertise is to be deployed as pedagogues who have studied and continue to study how best their students learn and how content must be transmitted in a way appropriate to these growing and changing children and adolescents.

In the first instance, learning takes place within particular relationships. Robert Starratt describes this as schooling based on an ethic of care which '… places the human persons-in-relationship as occupying a position for each other of absolute value; neither one can be used as a means to an end; each enjoys an intrinsic dignity and worth, and, given the chance, will reveal genuinely lovable qualities' (1996, p. 163).

Working within this ethic, teachers' understanding of the stages of growth that their pupils are experiencing, their expertise in developing structures in the classroom which encourage and expedite effective learning, their contemplation of what is actually worthwhile learning and what is not, and their understanding of the love, fear, and anxiety parents have about their children, and how to harness these for the good, place the whole task of schooling on a profound and, not to be shy about it, noble level. The poet Thomas Gray (Smith, 1926, p. 369), on observing Eton College, remarked that 'where ignorance is bliss,'Tis folly to be wise', and reminds teachers that they might have a part to play in attempting to help individuals avoid a desiccated life:

> Perhaps in this neglected spot is laid
> Some heart once pregnant with celestial fire;
> Hands, that the rod of empire might have sway'd,
> Or wak'd to extasy the living lyre.
> But Knowledge to their eyes her ample page
> Rich with the spoils of time did ne'er unroll:
> Chill Penury repress'd their noble rage,
> And froze the genial current of the soul.
> Full many a gem of purest ray serene,
> The dark unfathom'd caves of ocean bear:
> Full many a flower is born to blush unseen,
> And waste its sweetness on the desert air.

> (ibid., p. 375)

Schools have a very real part to play in nurturing students' special gifts. However, this may present an equally real difficulty where curricula are weighted away from gifts evidenced by some students or their (the school's) inability to provide the resources necessary to provide for individual giftedness. It may be the ethical thing here to advise the family that this school will only hold back the development of the student. In some cases schools may not be able to serve students as they deserve to be served. However, in other cases it may be that, tragically, some children bring to school with them family situations which are anything but noble. Too many school communities are familiar with Thomas Hardy's description of one such collection of children:

> All these young souls were passengers in the Durbeyfield ship – entirely dependent on the judgement of the two Durbeyfield adults for their pleasures, their necessities, their health, even their existence. If the heads of the Durbeyfield household chose to sail into difficulty, disaster, starvation, disease, degradation, death, thither were these half-dozen little captives under hatches compelled to sail with them – six helpless creatures, who had never been asked if they wished for life on any terms, much less if they wished for it on such hard conditions as were involved in being of the shiftless house of Durbeyfield. (1981, pp. 61f)

While schools may be relatively powerless in the face of what is really child abuse thinly or not so thinly disguised, they are able to show the children and adolescents in their Christian community that everybody is deserving of love and respect. Sometimes sacrificing the demands of the curriculum which may be adding yet one more source of stress in an already overloaded young life may, temporarily, make that life just that more liveable. The Christian call for love may mean that the school becomes a haven, not another burden for some children. This requires great institutional courage in the face of a political culture which attaches little value to the individual being, preferring to map them as a 'part' in/of the economy.

It is not always possible to estimate the effect that the ethos of the school today will have on the student who becomes the adult of the future. If the ethos of the school and the practices deriving from it are founded on the belief that God is to be found in the heart of every person, there will always remain the Christian virtue of hope to shed light even in the darkest circumstances.

A critically important part of what creates ethos and what contributes to the overall effectiveness of the development of faith and learning concerns just who the teacher is. While many things may seem remote from the influence of the individual teacher, this is one thing which can be identified. In *The Religious Dimension of Education in a Catholic School* the teacher of religion is characterised as the key to the 'organic presentation of the faith'; as one who brings 'many gifts', is 'capable of genuine dialogue' and brings that most fundamental of qualities, already discussed above, 'authenticity'. In addition to teaching the faith they must also teach what it is to be human; they must bring 'balanced judgement, patience... and prudence in the way they respond to the task of teaching'. They must have a clear vision of the Gospel and invite and assist young women and men to enjoy such a vision for themselves' (Sacred Congregation for Catholic Education, op. cit., §96). But there is no reason to suppose that these qualities should not extend to all staff in the school. Teaching is a special vocation and the theologian Paul Bernier (1992, p.237), when speaking of ministry, develops this idea further, claiming that 'Christians must develop "inner freedom" (1 Co 2:11-16) in order to live with integrity and in strength'. Further, he goes on to suggest that because this is so for a teacher then 'destructive passions must be let go ... and we must have the courage to live the vocation to which each of us is called [witnessing] to spirituality' (ibid). This is to be seen not just in the word but in example. Thus, 'the love and service that builds the community is the most powerful message we can give a world starved for meaning. ... the force that will change the world is the example of a truly Christian life. This is the fundamental Christian vocation'.

Schools and ethical leadership

Schools do have the special task of educating to carry out, but they do this in particular contexts. It is significant to note that coming through management literature today there is a growing concern about what ethical management practices mean. For example, Patrick Duignan and Mac Macpherson (1992, p. 183) argue that an integral component of educative leadership is the consideration by leaders of, simply, what is right. Schools benefit from engaging in this conversation, on the one hand because valuable insights are being offered by these writers and, on the other, because much of Catholic understanding of the person can be heard echoing through this literature. A cognate example is to be seen in the work of the Robert Greenleaf Foundation. Robert Greenleaf's notion of servant-leadership has an immediate resonance with Christian thought. The Greenleaf leader is not one who seeks self-aggrandisement through the exploitation of others, but rather, acts in a manner consistent with Matthew's Gospel which tells us that Jesus led his followers away from a dispute about precedence and favouritism when he told them that

> You know that the rulers of the Gentiles lord it over them (their followers), and their great men exercise authority over them. It shall not be so among you; but whoever would be great among you must be your servant, and whoever would be first among you must be your slave; even as the Son of Man came not to be served but to serve, and to give his life as ransom for the many. (Mt 20:25-29)

The application of these ideas of leadership to the education of children and adolescents who are in the midst of growth stages, the experience of which will be critical in creating the people they will become, can be seen in Greenleaf's description that 'the best test [of the servant-leader], and difficult to administer, is: Do those served grow as persons? Do they, while being served, become healthier, wiser, freer, more autonomous, more likely themselves to become servants?' (1977, pp. 13f). The Greenleaf Foundation (Spears, 1995, pp. 5ff) has taken this work forward and, in a recent anthology on leadership, suggests that servant-leadership displays the following characteristics:

Ten characteristics of the servant-leader
 1. Listening
 2. Empathy
 3. Healing
 4. Awareness
 5. Persuasion
 6. Conceptualisation
 7. Foresight
 8. Stewardship
 9. Commitment to the growth of people
10. Building community

While there is not space to examine each one of these in detail, they do provide a basis for thinking about how ethos might be conceived of in the school setting in the way each or any of these is expressed in school policies and practices.

Peter Drucker, who has been working in the field of management theory and practice for more than fifty years' summarises his conclusions about the characteristics of effective leadership and, again, the ethos which picks up issues of personal integrity has application to school leadership at whatever level. Thus he can say about effective leaders, that

> They did not start out with the question, 'What do I want?' They started out asking, 'What needs to be done? Then they asked, 'What can and should I do to make a difference?' ... They constantly asked, 'What are the organization's mission and goals? What constitutes performance and results in this organization?'

They were extremely tolerant of diversity in people and did

not look for carbon copies of themselves ... But they were totally – fiendishly – intolerant when it came to a person's performance, standards, and values. They were not afraid of strength in their associates. (1966, p. xiii)

One way or another, they submitted themselves to the 'mirror test' – that is, they made sure that the person they saw in the mirror in the morning was the kind of person they wanted to be, respect, and believe in. This way they fortified themselves against the leader's greatest temptations – to do things that are popular rather than right and to do petty, mean, sleazy things.

Fortunately, education has always had those who would resist pressures for conformism and exploitation. For example, Scotland is one place in particular that can be proud of the way that it nurtures organisations such as the Scottish Consultative Council on the Curriculum (SCCC). Not every country is able to claim ownership of a public body which can place into the perennial debate on the nature of education documents such as *The Heart of the Matter*. This document speaks very sensibly of schools having, as part of their task, the development of dispositions on the part of students (1995). Such qualities as respect for self and others are familiar to teachers who are concerned with faith and learning. Caring for others is at the heart of Christianity. The very existence of Catholic schools is predicated on the belief that education is a religious enterprise. As such it is concerned with much more than academic performance although this is not unimportant. Barbara Lepani's (1996, p. 15) model for a hierarchy of learning can serve as a checklist for schools as to where the emphasis of the overall educational programme is placed.

The hierarchy of learning

Wisdom
Insight

Foresight
Knowledge
Information
Data

Programmes devoted to exploring faith and learning and discussions about school ethos lay at the base of the Catholic educational venture. Without them Catholic education has little reason for continuing. In an understanding of education which has at its centre the person as a being directed towards the Christian God, the regular discussion of faith and ethos are signs that school communities are remaining true to their vision. It is in offering schools nurtured on the richness of the Catholic tradition that we may provide an alternative to the nihilism explored at the opening of this chapter.

TURBULENT TIMES – A CHALLENGE TO CATHOLIC EDUCATION IN BRITAIN TODAY

Albert Price

Introduction – the context

There is a sense in which a case for change in education need not be put. Education must always be changing – finding new responses to new circumstances – bringing a necessary vitality to individual lives and society. Whenever there is change the motives are always numerous and complex, the experience is usually turbulent. The change taking place in our education system is fundamental and, without doubt, turbulent. This is more than a question of wishing to raise educational standards. It represents an ongoing attempt to change radically and irrevocably the system put in place by the 1944 Education Act. This new system is intended to deal with the major problem of the increasing cost of education; the perceived 'fact' of surplus places, the accusation of wasteful use of resources, a conviction that education had lost its way under decentralised Local Education Authority (LEA) control and teacher autonomy – and of course the issues surrounding achievement, attainment and accountability. It is inevitable that such widespread, root-and-branch change is contested by many, resented by some and welcome to others. However, the divisions go even deeper still. The issue is said to be one of standards but the questions being raised are about the nature of standards, the nature of human beings and the nature of society, the purpose of education, the relative value of heritage, tradition and progress. It is always so when education is reformed.

There have been more than thirty major reforms in education since 1989 and these have affected every aspect of school life; some apply more particularly to England and Wales but they all, in one way or another, impinge on education throughout Britain (Great Britain, 1994; 1996a; 1996b).[1]

structurally:	the reduction of the power of the Local Education Authority in England and Wales and, indeed, in Scotland
administratively:	increased independence
financially:	devolved budgets
philosophically:	market forces and competition
curriculum:	the national curriculum
organisationally:	pupil groupings and forms of teaching, the evolution of centrally 'approved' pedagogies
accountability:	SATs, exams, inspection, league tables, appraisal, individual school targets
relationships:	pupil contracts, parental contracts

As these changes have been put in place it becomes increasingly clear that we are seeing the creation of a whole new system – a widespread reform (Paten, 1993). The challenge we face is not simply how to respond to any single reform – crucial though each one is – but how we envisage the root-and-branch totality of what is happening and respond to an entirely new approach in education.

It is to be expected that the Catholic Church which has worked in close partnership with the State in the provision of a major sector of education should continue to press its concerns on how such changes will affect that partnership and how its own interests and the interests of true education will be protected. To these ends it is also our responsibility, and pertinent to our role as educators, to ask what values and principles, what views of human nature, of society and of schools and colleges inform and underpin the motives which have generated change on such a scale. It is our desire and our mission to help to improve education and we do have concerns to protect and a contribution to make.

Many have given voice to similar concerns to those raised here about the person, society and the purpose of education (Buber, 1947) and their voice is afforded new poignancy by the living out of changes which appear to militate against more traditional personalist understandings of Catholic education. The questions raised in the present climate have become commonplace. In view of the rapidity of change it may be helpful to muse for a moment on the following range of definitions of education.

> He is to be educated not because he makes shoes, nails and pins but because he is a man. (Tyron Edwards)

> The important function of education at any level is to develop the personality of the individual and the significance of his life to himself and others. This is the basic architecture of life, the rest is ornamentation and decoration of the structure. (Grayson Kirk)

> The real object of education is to give children resources that will endure as long as life endures, habits which time will ameliorate but not destroy, occupations which will render sickness tolerable, solitude pleasant, age venerable, life more dignified and useful and death less terrible. (Sidney Smith)

> The primary concern for education is to cultivate in the largest number of our future citizens an appreciation both of the responsibilities and benefits which come to them because they are citizens and free. (James Bryant Conan)

> Education is both an inward and an outward journey with no beginning and no end. Inward to the very soul of the being where answers are not memorised, knowledge not learned by

heart, and stored for examination recall, but part of the self and therefore very much alive. And at the same time outward with the courage to find freedom and justice to bind us together as a community, to judge certain values such as faith, hope, love, truth as of ultimate concern – to take the jump and stake all on these values. (Unknown)

All of these images of education hold the person and her/his growth as central to all our endeavours and, for the Christian, education is a process of sowing and harvesting. This, the biblical image of vision and practice offered in the parables of Jesus and explaining to us the coming of the Kingdom, is also an image which contains the presence of teaching and learning (the sower and the seed) as a sign of hope in a new life. Without such hope, linked to the coming of a new life, our work in schools is just another chore.

Education is a moral transaction between one generation and the next (Eliot, 1948). It is not a political transaction nor an economic transaction. In our own time a moral transaction can only endure which has at its heart the idea of a common good as well as the equal value of each person. We are all part of one body. It is a mutual activity stimulated by all that is involved in love and living together. In being mutual it offers solidarity around shared values and ideals such as love, hope, truth and justice as evidence of the importance of a vision of education in our lives. It is this solidarity which helps to unify faith and life in the community and to hold our lives together.

Out of these reflections images crowd the mind about the person and the purposes of education; important concepts in education and society, both for the individual and for the community.

The functional being, the citizen, the wholeness of human beings, body, mind and spirit – all these find a focus in a range of practical issues such as:

effectiveness	and	efficiency
self-fulfilment	and	self-satisfaction
individuality	and	equality
cooperation	and	competition
liberty	and	restraint
diversity	and	uniformity
the person	and	the community

choice, justice, hope, opportunity and many more besides.

The earlier quotations exemplify the range of views in a society such as ours when the foundational questions are raised about being a person and the nature of education. They also show that all of those who are active in education operate on the basis of some view of the nature and destiny of humankind. In the attempt to find answers to these questions many recognise that values always lie at the heart of any radical agenda in education since education is always about the values which underpin individual development and social interaction.

The main issue, therefore, is not the detail in the changes taking place in education but the particular in all of them – not the value of each part but the motive behind them all. What is the essence of the whole – the beliefs, ideals and values which give the whole its cohesion? It is the string which holds together the corporate value of the pearls and it is this string which must be held up for scrutiny.

The philosophical basis of Government policy is not easily discerned and that gives rise to some uneasiness. This unease lies not in some gap between Government and Catholic philosophy and practice, but in what seems to be a gap between what is stated to be Government philosophy and its own practice. Many of the promises offered by Government (Dept of Education and Science, 1985) warm the heart: the importance of equal educational opportunity; breadth and balance in the curriculum; the centrality of religious education; stress on spiritual and moral development and the attention given to special needs. At the same time the undertone of the words used to describe learning, such as children will be 'stretched', 'driven', 'required' and 'informed', chill the circulation. The espoused intentions in the policy carry one message – the language and the tone of debate another. Is it possible that Government philosophy is a random collection of attractive themes and slogans? There is much to substantiate this observation. Is it likely that reform is a disjointed accumulation of instant recipes which do not come together as a total programme? There is much to substantiate this also.

If the diagnosis is correct, all that can be done in the search for standards is what the Government now seems to be doing: interfere more and more, bring in more changes, question reading schemes in the infant school and literature in Key Stage 3, castigate grouping policies and non-specialist teaching in junior schools, compel governors to ballot on the GM option, force through a raft of tests, set targets for individual schools. The main thrust is to keep up the activity, keep looking for a missing ingredient, blame others: LEAs, teachers, parents, educationalists. The desperate search for the key to success goes on and on and on. As part of this search an attempt is to be made to hold the reform of the public education service together through the power of competitiveness between schools. Within the warp and the weft of the more than thirty changes which have occurred, six fundamental market principles have emerged:

1) *Autonomy* – this is absolute independence. A school must be free of concern for, and obligation to, all other schools and the LEA.

2) *Diversity* – a host of different types of schools should exist so that the choice between schools can increase.

3) *Flexibility* – a school may decide its own admission criteria, leaving the way open to an increase in pupil selection.

4) *Accountability* – published results, league tables, inspection, school brochures, individual school targets, etc.

5) *Specialisation* – schools should be able to develop a speciality – Music, Art, Modern Languages – and select a number of 'gifted' pupils.

6) *Targeted funding* – All funding is to be targeted, beginning with devolved LEA funds, and then gradually through grant-maintained status, City Technology Colleges and curriculum initiatives. In time, it is likely that all schools will have to meet criteria for all forms of funding and all protective funding for schools in disadvantaged areas will gradually disappear.

Together, these are the principles of privilege and not opportunity, irrespective of the Government's ideological hue. They are meant to establish the pre-eminence of market priorities in all planning and operational detail. Every achievement of value can be measured and compared. All that is valued can be targeted and produced more cost-effectively. The best way to increase the number of successful schools is to build on the advantage which the best schools can carve out for themselves in a competitive market. Those who advocate these changes support their argument with a vision of what schools and children should achieve.

The changes will produce results. Undoubtedly the academic performance of those schools which are already successful will increase and their number will increase; the peaks will rise but the failure of schools which cannot compete will be more severe, more frequent and more public. The troughs will deepen. In urban areas, where schools are close to each other, there is likely to be a greater increase in failure than success. Many urban schools, secondary, junior and infant, will be able to cope with the scramble for advantage which surrounds them. The changing character of family life, the changing character of school intakes and staffing establishments and the changing character of school funding is likely to destabilise many schools. As this happens some schools are becoming dysfunctional.

Whatever the quality of leadership, management or teaching, some schools will lack the essential security derived from consistency in pupil numbers, stable staffing and reliable finance to maintain competitiveness and standards. Decline is rapid and so damaging that when the time comes to improve such schools many will need to be healed before they can be cured. Teachers will continue to leave or, at best, wish to leave the profession early and in increasing numbers. The numbers entering will decline and appointments will become more difficult. Headship is increasingly seen as being unattractive, whatever the pay, and recruitment will become a more serious problem than it already is.

It is profoundly important that all who are involved in the planning and delivery of an education service should recognise that the question of beliefs about the nature of people and the purpose in educating them cannot be evaded. There is no such thing as value-free education. If certain vital questions are not answered prior to planning then they will be answered in diverse and conflicting ways in practice. At this stage the vision of what can be achieved is not likely to be true or achievable. Put simply, an education service cannot be built solely upon what, it is claimed, is affordable, nor upon how it is funded. Nor can it be built upon what you hope to produce. If a school or a school system has little else to guide it but an ever-increasing range of conflicting expectations, ideas and plans (whatever their merit) urged on only by a competition for resources, then it will be almost impossible to retain or improve its reliability or standards. Such a dismal outcome is at least a strong possibility and it will be a disappointing reward for the sacrifice, commitment and effort being asked for in a much needed reform of education.

A credo for education

It seems, in education, that we pursue a false notion but one which has endured for a long long time. There is too much anxiety about the implementation of knowledge and the acquisition of skills so that a proper relationship with values, personal and religious, has been lost. In doing so something profoundly false about the meaning of human dignity and human life is iterated. The reality is that questions of achievement and implementation in education are of no consequence until the vision around human nature and the purpose of education can be imagined. The weakness in the government and in the schools is not in a power to implement or measure but in a power to believe and imagine.

In education, all that has to be implemented, all that has to be achieved and measured can only be held together by what is believed about the pupils and what is imagined about what they can become. These two realities underpin standards and are discovered through faith and ideals and not through budgets, ballots and league tables. Our schools are paralysed by detail and starved of vision. If the practice must be two realities in harmony, then to be so both must rest upon the truth about the nature and destiny of all people. Whether or not the times are turbulent we are required to be constant in who we are and certain of the purpose of education.

The value and quality of our contribution as Christians to education and to a public service is our commitment to two equally important and inseparable realities. These two realities, vision and practice, must always co-exist in life and in education.

1) We are an Easter people formed in the image of God. Our vision of the world proclaims God as Creator, Christ as Saviour and the Holy Spirit as Inspirer. We are redeemed and made whole by the incarnation, life, death and resurrection of Jesus Christ.

2) Education does not make us whole but must meet the needs of the wholeness we already possess. Our practice in education is our opportunity to fulfil all human attributes and to build a salvation on the way all God's people live together. Every genuine creative process has to be held together by vision and mission. Education is the most creative process in our lives (Flannery, 1975).

It is so easy to underestimate the importance of a unity of vision and practice to the integrity and the standards of a genuine education service. When vision and practice in education come apart then what is offered is always inadequate for all and the way it is offered will always be unjust to many. I believe this is the most likely reason why so many schools are already in trouble and why so many teachers are weary and disillusioned. A market cannot hold vision and practice together, it cannot dispense hope or justice. This is not its function. A market is not capable of producing a good school for every child and it will always neglect the most needy. In its more candid moments even this is acknowledged by official agencies such as *Ofsted* (1993) who maintain that, 'most schools in... disadvantaged areas do not have within them the capacity for sustainable renewal'. The contrast between what is happening now and what is actually needed is stark and presents Christian educators with many new challenges. This mission of our Church in education is a great responsibility. We are not Christians for ourselves alone. Nor is our first responsibility the survival of Catholic schools. We are not part of a public education service simply to go with the flow whatever the cost. Our first concern has to be the nature, purpose and practice of education itself. Where there is no true education there is no safe haven for Catholic schools.

We are Christians for what we can offer to others in defining a vision and relating it to a mission which others can follow. We have a responsibility to sustain hope and to promote justice, to plan a whole curriculum and to raise all standards. It is the belief of this author that in our faith and through our people we should be in the vanguard of education, raising a beacon for others to follow.

What follows is our educational creed. It consists of two inseparable realities in one enterprise. We offer this to others. This is our vision – what we believe, and this is our mission – how we try to put it into practice.

We believe that all human beings have a divine origin and an eternal destiny. All are created in the image of God.

We should always teach children who they are. We should say to each of them: Do you know who you are? God created you. You are a marvel, you are unique. In all the world there is no other child like you. In the years that have passed, or in those to come, there has never been and will never be another like you. You have the capacity for anything and when you grow up you can harm another who is like you, a marvel. You must cherish one another, you must work, we must all work, to make this world worthy of its children.

We believe that each individual is both unique and equal to others regardless of sex, nationality, colour, creed, class, intellectual ability or emotional, social or physical handicap.

We seek to build a view of education which establishes all that we do as a moral and spiritual transaction between ourselves and all people. We have no time for alienation, discrimination and separation. Ours is a mission of truth, hope, justice and love – a total process which believes in the unlimited future of all humanity. Our creativity must always be awake, our sensitivity must always be alert, our commitment and conviction must always be alive so that we continue always to stimulate an enterprising and creative spirit in people and communities.

We believe that the whole person includes the dimensions of body, mind and spirit and that the dimensions of human personality are fully realised in community and not in isolation.

The individual is not an independent being. All our learning takes place in the context of an intricate network of human contacts, love and relationships. The family is not an isolated unit. Parents' responsibilities for helping children to grow is shared in a partnership of care and trust with other groups in society, the Church, the school, the media, the locality, friends, relatives – the State. The involvement of parents in an active partnership with others is central to the process of education for it provides vital support to each participant and contributor. The school is not an autonomous institution. Any risk that it could become so is a threat to its true function and to its partners. Rather, a school should be encouraged to see its life and purpose as a partnership with others and with the concerns of many people. Education is a mutual activity.

We believe that all people are formed, sustained and armed through a process of love and relationship with others. If we are to be individuals there is no escape from our interdependence.

Love, not intellect, is at the centre of learning. People become fully human through their understandings, particularly of 'relationships' with others. Affective learning provides the stimulus for cognitive learning (Gardner, 1996). At its centre is affirming love. People must relate to one another as a primary category of their being. We are each unique individuals with a strong conviction of our own individuality. We each know there is no one else quite like us and yet we are each totally dependent on others to show us who we are; to define, validate and affirm our individual identity. We need other people to confirm our individuality. And others need us for the same purpose. We cannot achieve individuality without accepting each other as equals. Individuality and equality are the two inseparable parts of what it means to be truly a person. They cannot exist separately.

We believe that education is a moral transaction between one generation and the next. It takes place in communities, the home, the school, the parish and the locality.

Knowledge is not to be considered as a means of material prosperity and success but as a call to serve and to be responsible to others now and in the future. Self-satisfaction and self-fulfilment are two different experiences. There is a variety of gifts but always the same creation, there are many kinds of service to be offered but always the same creation. The quality and skills of our individuality are the very essence of our responsibility and service to the society in which we live; every right carries a responsibility, every opportunity carries an obligation, every possession carries a duty. We must always see life steadily and see it whole.

All of this helps us to see and understand the interdependence between the educational needs of the individual and those of society. Such a philosophy will avoid both an education which is self-indulgent and an education which is a mere instrument for the satisfaction of a society's material functions. These 'abuses' are not mutually exclusive. They often exist together in an illusory balance. For the Christian a genuine education service must always seek to harmonise individual and collective aims. The main difference between the Christian and the secular approaches to the development of the individual and of society is the importance we attach to the centrality of faith in our educational process. Our belief in the nature of the person and the purpose in educating them gives us a clear aim: that of integrating the development of the person around a love of Jesus Christ and of their neighbour.

This is to be done by immersing students' enriching experiences in a full curriculum which seeks to hold together a vital unity of purpose in life and faith (Treston, 1998). Our schools and colleges are established to raise communities of people united by common beliefs which provide an inspirational philosophy to guide both their planning and action in education towards individual fulfilment and universal salvation. Catholic schools and colleges are asked to form a 'distinctive service', offering an induction into a way of life in which belief is put into practice. The aim of a Catholic school is to help pupils/students to achieve complete dignity as persons in a relationship with Jesus Christ and with each other.

Christian educators need to be confident that our faith and the philosophy it provides empowers us to hold together all our careful and careless decisions – in the curriculum, in the grouping of pupils, in managing resources, in the involvement of parents, in celebrating achievement, in handling disappointment – indeed in every aspect of school life. Ours is a faith tying all our decisions and actions into a purpose based on love, truth, justice – where our God is no longer in the margins and in the gaps but in the middle of life in the middle of the school, where God is in all things. We do not just hope this will make a difference – we 'know' it makes the difference.

Towards some practical expressions of distinctiveness

Thus, we educators in the Catholic tradition find ourselves holding in our hands the stewardship of the conduct of one of the most vital enterprises in the formation and salvation of the human person. How crucial it is that as a task force, for that is what we are, we share the fundamental values of a common mission, and because we are the practitioners we must possess some common interpretation for the implementation of some practicalities in that mission; a mission for schools with its roots in our Christian vision and its wings in all that we do in living our Christian faith together; schools which think, pray, reflect and try to act theologically in everything they do.

The life of a distinctive school begins in the distinctive lives of the adults who lead it. A school where teaching and learning is offered in such a way as to indicate that the pupils are loved for what they are and what they can become. A curriculum with breadth and balance so that the gifts of all might be released as God intends in a service to others. A school which welcomes everyone, celebrates difference, encourages and praises the outcomes of all genuine effort, rejoices in and gives support to a range of aspirations and achievement so that hope is offered to all. A school which can sustain its unity of vision and practice into a communion with other schools. It can share its work with others and also rely upon others to offer help in return.

A distinctive school is always vulnerable, indeed ours is a faith which makes us vulnerable and not unassailable. A vulnerable school has to be ready and willing to resist the separation of vision and practice whenever that unity is threatened. Leaders[2] in such schools should always be gracious and determined challengers since many will come to help who will not be aware of the cost to vision and practice which even a favour can present. At times the cost of refusal can be high – and sometimes the cost of acceptance is greater. But this is what it can mean to be distinctive. Such leaders want others to understand that theirs is a school with an active mission and that the belief in the vision truly exists to unify the things you try to do. No one lights a lamp to put it under a tub!

Vision and practice are to be seen together in all concerns and bound together in all solutions; seen together in all objectives and bound together in all achievements; seen together in all values and bound together in all principles. If others are to see God in the work of Catholic schools then they have to be able to learn from the particular Catholic response to the problems all educators also have to handle. People who can do this to help others are distinctive and the schools they work in become distinctive. Thus Matthew offers the key obligation on Catholic educators that,

> [Their] light must shine in people's sight, so that seeing your good work they may give praise to your father in heaven (Mt 5: 13-16).

All our hope and all our effort in this quest for distinctiveness is derived from and sustained by a cradle of religious education and catechetical programmes in the curriculum of our schools. These programmes must be clearly distinctive both in what is taught, through a rich liturgical provision, and in good interpersonal relationships, a concern for justice, a fostering of the talents and achievements of the whole community and a deep sense of cooperation and service between the school/college and its locality.

In such a way a creative governing spirit is set up and sustained in the school and in the community within it and around it. It is the practical expression of this spirit, the vital task of organising the school, which can bring other dimensions of Catholic distinctiveness to the fore in day-to-day activities which are visible and accountable. We have to plan the openings for the work of the spirit of our faith in the warp and weft of the fabric of school life. We must be able to celebrate distinctive practices which are tangible to the teachers and the pupils if what we teach in religious education and proclaim in worship is to belong to them.

I wish to bring to the fore some further expressions of distinctiveness which give substance to questions raised in a public address by Cardinal Hume, who gave voice to what we know instinctively but frequently ignore: that 'pupils quickly sense what a school really considers to be of importance and they respond accordingly, so do parents and visitors' (1992, p. 11). To begin, it is necessary to accept that distinctiveness is neither an isolated nor exclusive quality. Some of the good things we claim for ourselves are shared with others and sometimes done better by them.

Distinctiveness emerges from a particular approach in faith to the tasks which all schools have to take on. Distinctiveness begins with the small things. Different is separate – distinctiveness is particular and enriching but belonging. Some distinctive Christian approaches will be found in other schools, hopefully most of them or better still all of them will be found in a Catholic school.

Leadership is crucial and the quality of it must always be improving. I am speaking of leadership, not leaders. The absence of leadership in a school is not a vacancy in the staffing establishment but a void in the centre of the enterprise. The most important task of leadership is custodianship of the vision of the importance of the person and the purpose of the task. This requirement on leadership applies to the governors, the head teachers, the teachers. It is a shared task, a ministry in the Church. In this task the mission statement is vital (Bishops' Conference of England & Wales, 1990). It is the keystone in management development and activity, the source of authority and the touchstone for decisions. These general principles translate into clear objectives.

1) The management of beliefs and values of love, hope and justice must precede the management of finance and resources with expectations that the former will inform the latter and not vice-versa. We must plan the management of these values with more care than we give to other aspects of our work.

2) A Catholic school will prepare a presentation on a vision statement as a prelude to a mission statement. This must be a proclamation as to what we believe about the children we teach and why we are educating them. We will advertise our vision statement in our booklets and on our notice boards.

3) The staff, governors and parents, all who share in the welfare of the school, will share one heart, a *cor unum*, a recognition of the preciousness of children and the fulfilment of sharing in

their education. School-based in-service days will be organised to reflect on these things and to renew and reflect on the vision and mission of the school.

4) The school will know that teaching and learning come alive in the hands of teachers. The teachers will know that if there is a positive exchange of feeling, and aspirations between the teachers and the taught, satisfying to both, then there is a describable curricular reality. But if there is no such exchange, if there is a total absence of mutual satisfaction, the curriculum simply remains as an idea, a structure, in the mind of someone somewhere.

Much of the in-service work will be about teaching; much of the talk will be about children and how they learn – not about test results; students' assessment will be diagnostic and formative, used to evaluate teaching as well as what pupils have achieved. This kind of work will be seen in practice and will be part of school planning and development.

5) In considering the curriculum we shall be primarily concerned with human beings whose feelings, emotions and aspirations are far more real and immediately important to them than their cognitive development.

This raises important questions in respect of what is to count as relevant in education, as between the claims of the pupil on the one hand and the claims of the parents, the government, the industrialists on the other. Teaching and learning comes alive in the hands, relationships and satisfactions of teachers and pupils together. If it doesn't come alive there, then it doesn't come alive at all. We should not forget that it is difficult for the sincere teacher to be enthusiastic about something they do not believe in. Teachers should devote more time to talking to pupils than to writing about them. Pastoral structures should be designed to create relationships and not to complete administration or to deal with problems. Teachers should give time to individual pupils and groups of pupils. This should be planned. All teachers should have a pastoral role clearly detailed and agreed which is seen as distinct from registers and form periods. Teachers should be aware of the need to be seen to be loving and just.

6) The school will challenge the predilection for labelling children. Average, below average, dull, backward, ESN, E2L, SEN, SLD, MLD, TVEI, Newsome, Rosla, all convey the image of deficit models. The only label which is a compliment is bright. It is of course difficult to shed popular language but if this is the baggage taken to teacher decisions it can be no surprise that much of what is achieved in most schools with many children is self-fulfilling (Bishop's Conference of England & Wales, 1997, p. 37f). The school will fill its children with hope rather than label them with self-fulfilling titles.

7) This change in mood will be seen in the staffroom which is full of affectionate laughter at the things children do and say – mixed at times with the expressions of frustration and irritation at the problems they cause. But never trivialising them as people, whatever their limitations or differences.

8) A distinctive school has a carefully worked out grouping policy; it is one which knows that there is no such thing as a homogeneous group of human beings. The school rejects the theory that a child is a compartmentalised accumulation of undeveloped specialisms which can all be developed to the different potentials possessed by setting. A distinctive school is one which does not have a blanket response to grouping for it knows that the causalities would be too heavy, even if it has over 70% with five A to C grades.

A distinctive school dislikes both élitism and uniformity as both are abrasive to human individuality. Community distinctiveness lies in finding the love, patience and understanding to hold the tension between these two so that pupils can be properly cared for.

9) A distinctive school knows that to select individuals by prescribed criteria and then put them in a group produces the stereotype and is the antithesis of individuality. Setting, streaming, mixed ability are grouping policies which represent some tools of the trade and teachers should decide their use. The keener the criteria used to define what are said to be good people, then the fewer good people there are, and the fewer scientists, the fewer mathematicians. A distinctive school knows that there is little purpose in telling pupils that they are all valued equally when all the signals the children receive from the organisation of the school tells them that this isn't true.

10) A distinctive school gives a just consideration to the deployment and development of teachers. The way in which the timetable in the school is constructed is a reflection of the task of the school. Policies on appraisal, in-service, staff groupings and salaries are all integral to this process.

11) There should be very little awareness of rank or status amongst teachers but clear evidence of stature. Tasks are attached to salaried posts in a changeable way so that people and subject hierarchies are only briefly established and never entrenched. There should be little risk that they will become counter-productive and harmful. Only one area should be rooted in entrenched attitudes: that is, the concern and care for the individual child or adult which lasts for the duration of that child's or adult's stay in the community. The school should be able to exemplify this care in particular strategies for both pupils and teachers. It has to be something more than a

warm feeling or a line in the school handbook. The care given to the grouping of pupils and deployment and development of teachers are necessary safeguards against a hierarchy of subjects – and therefore of knowledge.

12) A distinctive school has a Parent/Pupil/Teacher Association, not a Parent/Teacher Association. This brings families together in shared activities and on shared occasions. Further, it is an educational enterprise, not a fund-raising body.

13) A distinctive school does not train governors on the detail of the curriculum but on the origins of it, so that they know the moral basis for what is done in their name.

14) The distinctive school knows the moral justification for breadth and balance in the curriculum. It gives support to an expansive and rich view of what human maturity might be and what it surely ought to be. To do justice to all its members a school or college is obliged to provide a breadth and balance of opportunities which corresponds to the aspirations of a complex range of individuals and the integral and personal development of each of them. If breadth and balance are to be important planning principles then they must be more substantial than an agreed list of common subject titles in the timetables of pupils and students. If all the resources, time, finance, space, teachers, etc. which govern the quality of what is provided are distributed in such a way as to retain unacceptable equalities between schools, colleges, subjects, classes and individuals, then breadth and balance is not a reality of the curriculum. There will be an abundance of evidence in the planning of a distinctive school which indicates the care given to implementing breadth and balance as comprehensive principles in planning and framing curricular opportunities.

15) Much thought and practice should be devoted to the importance of and implementation of whole school attitudes to courtesy, care, bullying, discrimination, intolerance – and the love and justice to carry them through. The school avoids instant recipes and single-issue management, tempting though this frequently is.

16) A wealth of display – plants, pictures, artefacts – in primary and secondary schools should provide a rich environmental backdrop within the buildings and the surroundings. It should always be up to date and continually renewed.

17) Academic success should be evidenced in depth – it should be celebrated and proclaimed (without boasting) for children to whom success is familiar, to those who shine steadily without dazzling, and to those who grit their teeth and with encouragement struggle on. The corollary is that there be few suspensions or expulsions (ibid., 1997, p. 39).

18) The arrangement of furniture in the classrooms should tell of a range of teaching styles practised by confident teachers who are able to concentrate on the task with little worries about control and much more.

Catholic schools, the principles on which they are based and the ethos and working climate they seek to create, have to be worth the effort. They must not regard the reference point as being solely our own community but recognise that, at their best, they can do much to provide alternatives to the frailties and falsehoods in purely secular objectives. There is a Christian response to every aspect of school life.

It does no harm to remind the State that it is not the primary agent in education. It receives its rights and its finance from its citizens. It is bound to all its citizens by principles of ethical justice in deciding its policies and principles of distributive justice in the allocation of resources – and ballots do not absolve politicians from these responsibilities.

All parents must be free to choose schools and colleges for their children in accordance with their convictions and conscience (United Nations, 1948; Great Britain, 1989, 1995). It follows that the citizens in the State, and the members of faith communities, rely upon their political leaders to exercise great care in planning an education system and in providing a comparability of opportunities across a range of choices. This is particularly important in a society of plural values.

The best way to remind the State of the value and importance of our approach and their responsibilities is by distinctive example. This is central to our vision and mission. The many contributions to that Catholic effort, including those of our friends and partners of other faiths and beliefs, are all important because individually they represent what is true and best about the human person and collaboratively what is just, hopeful and caring about life lived in a community.

These truths, upon which a wholesome enterprise is based, can be fostered in the leadership and management of schools and colleges, whatever the situations and whatever the challenges which have to be faced. Put simply, what we have to impart, by what we do and by who we are, is a vision and a way of living a full life, and the majority have always wanted to share that with everyone.

It is vital that we continue to adopt and promulgate the message of hope in these turbulent times.

NOTES

1. Although some differences of emphasis exist in Scotland, the broad thrust of policy remains similar throughout Britain.
2. Leader here is not synonymous with senior manager or head teacher etc. but refers to those who are 'guardians' of the mission.

6

TOWARDS THE MILLENNIUM – CATHOLIC EDUCATION: IDENTITY, CONTEXT, PEDAGOGY

Vincent J. Duminuco SJ

Introduction

On the threshold of the third millennium Catholic education faces a number of challenges, three of which may be described as follows:

1) In many developing countries and in the former Soviet Union there is a strongly expressed need for more Catholic schools, colleges and universities. The problem here is the lack of trained personnel and financial resources to meet the needs.

2) In parts of Western Europe Catholic education is being eroded under the influence of secularism, expensive demands of some trade unions and attempts by some governments to limit registration in Catholic schools so as to preserve jobs in Government-run schools at a time when the birth rate is dropping dramatically.

3) In many Developing World countries under the influence of increased professionalisation and the stress upon schooling for the professions, some wonder whether the formational aspects of Catholic education can survive.

In what may be construed as a confusing worldwide situation the identity and mission of Catholic education must be clear if it is to serve wisely the formation of future generations of men and women for others. In this paper I will attempt to shed a little light on three pivotal issues: the essential identity of Catholic education, the challenges posed to Catholic schools, colleges and universities by the context we live in, and then point to an emerging pedagogy that offers concrete hope in our mission.

Identity

The demand for a more explicit definition of the identity and distinctiveness of Catholic education is one of the most pressing concerns today among Catholic educators and parents as well as among many members of the Church hierarchy. There are many reasons for this concern. With the declining number of religious in the schools, it is no longer possible to take for granted a common set of assumptions held by all or the majority of the faculty. Lay persons, formerly just a sprinkling within the almost solid ranks of religious, especially in the United States, have become the overwhelming majority in virtually every Catholic school. Their presence brings true richness. But they emerge from a Church context which is diverse and confusing rather than from the ecclesial environment of a generation ago which was clear, distinct and sure of every answer and practice! They come to the schools with a variety of backgrounds, motivations and perspectives. It would, however, be a serious error to suggest that the need for clarity concerning identity is focused only because of the increase of lay faculty members. The rapidly changing context within the Church and religious congregations has left members of religious groups almost equally in need of systematic programmes to clarify, develop and encourage their religious involvement in schools.

At the same time as the number of teachers from religious orders has declined and the diversity of faculty backgrounds has multiplied, there has also emerged, from other sources, an increasing urgency to show how the Catholic school is distinctively religious. This demand originates both internally – from teaching faculties who are continually searching for redefinition of their function and purpose in a shifting Church, and externally – from parents and the Catholic community in general who are both less sure of the purposes of Catholic education and are simultaneously expected to increase their support of increasingly expensive school operations. ⁰ 🗶

In the attempt to address some of these issues, this essay will outline a response to the key question of identity: 'What makes a Catholic school, college or university "Catholic"?'

Firstly, Scripture and tradition assist our understanding of the nature and mission of Catholic education. For example, Genesis tells us that God looks upon creation and sees that it is very good. In the New Testament Jesus speaks of God's continuing creation, his loving intervention, not only in the Incarnation, but in every breath we breathe. 'Are not fine sparrows sold for two pennies? And not one of them is forgotten before God. Why even the hairs of your head are all numbered' (Lk 12: 6f). These are but two examples of God's continual interest in the human situation and experience which stem from the engagement with Scripture. Here there are important implications for the philosophy of Catholic education which rejects many of the principles of Platonists and Neoplatonists, who regarded material reality as a source of evil limitation. Christians, on the other hand, look upon material creation in a very real sense as a source of good. And, as a matter of fact, education, the very process of helping young people to come to know and explore the material creation and its developments in culture and language, in science and social studies, is really a way of helping them to find God in all things; to find God in and through God's creation. Thus education itself may be considered as a way of assisting young people to understand revelation, God's revelation of God's goodness and love in the world around us and in our own human experience.

Secondly, freedom is God's consummate gift to humanity. God risks in the giving of this gift, because we can reject God. And so, within Catholic education, there is an inherent challenge to indoctrination. Education is to be construed as a freeing process, wherein understanding is critical: understanding of basic facts, understanding of overriding principles, understanding of values. All of these are vitally important precisely because young people, as they grow and mature and become capable of making judgements, may be truly free, rather than the victims of indoctrination, whether that comes from the State, or cults, or the media. Thus it becomes critically important that Catholic education be, in reality, a process in the first instance of education, of exploring reality and its possible uses, of serious consideration of alternatives and their consequences. In this way education becomes a freeing experience, beyond freedom to attachments or reputation, 'What will people think?', 'Everybody's doing it'. Education is meant to be precisely a freeing experience interiorly so that the individual may be helped to move beyond the entrapment of those assumptions and networks of values that form so much of contemporary culture and are simply taken for granted.

Many young people (Grimmitt, 1987) going through adolescence are highly vulnerable in terms of their identity and self-worth; they crave acceptance. From an educational perspective, Catholic education must take into account the threat of tyranny over children's minds by materialism and its salespersons, who have billions of dollars to lure all, even within their own living-rooms. Insidiously, consumerism would have adolescents believe that their self-worth is inextricably tied to their possessions – the right brand of jeans, the newest colour video recorder, or the latest model car. Christian educators and the young people they serve are being asked to sell their birthright for a 'mess of pottage'. Or consider the gospel of immediate gratification: 'Fly now, pay later!'; 'Take this aspirin rather than that one because it will give you relief ten seconds faster.' Or think for a moment about the very format of those weekly dramas on TV. Within sixty minutes, minus fifteen minutes for advertisements, some of the most complex problems of human being and relations are presented. They begin, rise to a climax and are resolved. This very format creates an impression that problems and challenges can be dispensed with quickly. You don't have to put up with problems. Be good to yourself. How far from reality is the gospel of immediate gratification.

Given the pace of change and alleged sophistication, if Booth Tarkington (1981) wrote *Seventeen* today, he'd have to call it *Twelve*. Educators are working with a group of young people who, at progressively earlier ages, are very politely sceptical, and who feel they've been bamboozled once too often – by parents, presidents and professors. As a result, from puberty onward, a teenager's greatest fear is being 'uncool', 'sad' (or whatever the latest slang may be), taken in, hoaxed (Barker *et al.*, 1992). And we have problems getting cynics to make an act of faith.

Superficially appealing, these are truly entrapping networks. It is incumbent upon Catholic educators to ensure that young people do not lose their freedom. To do so requires a challenging and exploratory environment, thus 'By their fruits you shall know them' (Mt 7:16).

Thirdly, in all Scripture, human experience is seen as dramatic. The forces of light and darkness are real and active in every human life. Human beings experience contradictory tensions. Any significant human choice in this day and age is never clear cut. With all the competing values that bombard humanity daily, making choices is never easy. Today, it is rarely found that all of the reasons for a decision are on one side and all the reasons against on the other. There is always a pull and tug; it is a matter of balance and discernment. Thus it becomes extremely important that the young are helped to consider more explicitly the criteria they use in making choices; the concrete way in which they express their God-given gift of human freedom.

Fourthly, it is worth recalling Christ's striking assertion: 'I would rather have you cold or hot; the lukewarm I vomit out of my mouth!' (Rv 3:16). Mediocrity has no place in a Christian calling.

What the Christian educator seeks to do is help young people to live and work for the building of the Kingdom, the greater glory of God. Catholic education therefore is interested in the formation of leaders, who will be young men and women of competence. And so, academic excellence is important because our students must know what they are talking about. But we aim to form Christian leaders, people of competence and conscience, where there is a value system, a sense of priorities, and a sense of right or wrong. Without that, the assumption that 'knowledge is virtue' is not true. George Steiner provides a timely reminder that a person who is intellectually advanced can at the same time be morally bankrupt. We now know that such a person can listen to Bach and Schubert at sundown; he can read Goethe in the evening, and the next day go to his daily work at the concentration camp to gas his fellow men and women. 'What grows up inside literate civilisation,' Steiner asks, 'that seems to prepare it for the release of barbarism?'(1974). Steiner's comment not only highlights the dilemma but also dramatises the disillusionment that has taken root in the midst of contemporary being and culture.

There is a growing understanding that education does not inevitably humanise or Christianise. There is a loss of faith in the 'childish' notion that all education, regardless of its quality or thrust or purpose, will lead to virtue. Increasingly, then, it becomes clear that if Catholic education is to exercise a moral force in society, it must insist that the process of education takes place in a moral context. This is not to suggest a programme of indoctrination that suffocates the spirit, neither does it mean theoretical courses that become only speculative and remote.

What is needed is a framework of inquiry in which the process of wrestling with big issues and complex values is made fully legitimate.

At a practical level, the key problems that face men and women on the brink of the twenty-first century are not simple. What single academic discipline can legitimately pretend to offer comprehensive solutions to real questions like those concerning genetic research, corporate takeovers, definitions concerning human life – its start and its end, homelessness and city planning, poverty, illiteracy, developments in medical and military technology, human rights, the environment and artificial intelligence? These require empirical data and technological know-how. But they also cry out for consideration in terms of their impact on men and women from a holistic point of view. So they demand, in addition, sociological, psychological, ethical, philosophical and theological perspectives if the solutions proposed are not to remain sterile.

These questions are not solved in an undisciplined manner since they embrace human and not simply technical values. Every day of the week, there are debates about the beginning of life and the preparation of instruments to end it: Are students prepared so as to know, to really believe because they know, that simply because some technological advance is possible that its development and use is justified? Are the leaders of tomorrow challenged to reflect critically on the assumptions and consequences of 'progress'? Are they challenged to ponder both the wonderful possibilities and the limits of science? Are they assisted in recognising that significant civil financial decisions are frequently not just political manifestos but also moral statements?

Fifthly, the entire effort and vision of Catholic education is centred on the person of Christ, the Word of God that is spoken to us incarnated. The reality of the Incarnation affects Catholic education at its core. For the ultimate purpose, the very reason for the existence of Catholic schools is to form men and women for others in imitation of Christ Jesus, the Son of God, the Man for Others *par excellence*.

The Incarnation is world-affirming, comprehensive, places emphasis on freedom, faces up to sin, personal and social, yet at the same time points to God's love as more powerful than human weakness and evil. It is altruistic, stresses the essential need for discernment, and gives ample scope to intellect and affectivity in forming leaders. Are not these matters essential to the values of a Catholic school, college or university? In confronting the human condition from such a point of view Catholic education challenges much that contemporary society presents as values.

Thus Catholic education, faithful to the incarnational principle, is truly humanistic. As Arrupe writes in *Men for Others:*

> What is it to humanise the world if not to put it at the service of mankind? But the egoist not only does not dehumanise the material creation, he dehumanizes people themselves. He changes people into things. by dominating them, exploiting them, and taking to himself the fruits of their labour. The tragedy of it all is that by doing this the egoist dehumanizes himself. He surrenders himself to the possessions he covets; he becomes their slave – no longer a person, self-possessed but an un-person, a thing driven by his blind desires and their objects (Arrupe, 1979, p.12).

In the quest for meaning in and the renewal of schools in the fuller understanding of Catholic education, it is necessary that formal learning becomes a truly humanising, incarnational experience.

Finally, the test in Catholic education is not propositions, hypotheses, philosophies, or even examination results. The test is realism. It is not everyone who says 'Lord, Lord!' who will be saved; it is the person who hears the Word and does it. And so Catholic education succeeds not merely by presenting the young with a diploma or trophy. The test of the success of Catholic education is deeds, not words. What students do with their education is of central importance. Such educational systems and those who serve within them are not indifferent as to how alumni use that empowerment which is their Catholic education.

The pursuit of each student's intellectual development to the full measure of God-given talents rightly remains a prominent goal of Catholic education. Its aim has never been simply to amass a store of information or prepare for a job, though these are important in themselves and useful to emerging Christian leaders. The ultimate aim of Catholic education is, rather, that full growth of the person which leads to action – especially action which is suffused with the spirit and presence of Jesus Christ, the Man for Others. This goal of action, based on sound understanding and enlivened by contemplation, urges students to self-discipline and initiative, to integrity and accuracy. At the same time, it judges slipshod or superficial ways of thinking unworthy of the individual and, more importantly, dangerous to the world that he or she is called to serve.

Context – a major challenge

Idealistic goals and good intentions are not enough. This may be illustrated anecdotally.

Before arriving in Rome some thirteen years ago, I lived in Washington, DC. The community house was about three blocks from the Argentine Embassy. In November of one year a new ambassador arrived from Argentina. He was a man of some aesthetic sensitivity. He noticed something that the neighbours had noticed for a long time, namely, that the place had been let go on the outside. He decided to do something to beautify the front of the embassy. So just around Thanksgiving time, shortly after his arrival, he went out and bought two Norfolk Island Pine trees. He planted one on each side of the entrance. They were about six feet tall and quite beautiful. But on Christmas Day of that year, they were brown and completely dead. Why? Because the ambassador did not understand the context in which he was living and working. He did not realise that the Norfolk Island Pine is a tropical tree; it is not a true pine. It requires a tropical climate. Secondly, he did not know that in Washington, DC that

December, as happens from time to time, the temperature could go to nine degrees below zero.

Now what is the point of this narrative? What did the man do? Firstly, he had good intentions; secondly, he did not stop with velleity, he actually went out and did something. But, thirdly, all of his efforts were completely frustrated because he did not understand the context within which he was working. I suggest that if we are serious about achieving the mission of Catholic education we need to look at the context of our ministry of teaching.

'And the Word was made flesh and dwelt among us' (Jn 1:14). From its very start, Christian ministry has been contextualised. This is the meaning of 'incarnation'. The 'context of ministry', then, is the placement of the following of Jesus in its historical, concrete situation. To serve effectively as ministers, we must know this context. This need to know the context of ministry is affirmed strongly in *Gaudium et spes: The Church in the Modern World*, where Catholic Christians (and others) are urged to discern the signs of the times, the context of ministry. Without sound social analysis of the real context of our ministry, apostolic choices run the risk of being either visionary and romantic or simply misguided and irrelevant. Let us consider just a few signs of the times to focus our analysis.

Typically, under the best of circumstances, adolescence is a trying and confusing time for a growing person (and indeed, for his or her family). The teenager's conflicting needs to conform and to be an individual, the struggles with emerging sexuality, the thirst for order and simultaneous rebellion against rules, the pervasive lethargy punctuated by brief moments of athletic super-performance, the need for friendship and concomitant fear of vulnerability to others, the quest for meaning are readily recognised. Much of this confusing collage would also have been true for the immediately preceding generations. But then there were supportive structures that provided a context for more constructive growth – things like stable nuclear families and the extended family living nearby, a common set of values and assumptions flowing from a more consistent religious and/or civic milieu, clearer boundaries for acceptable behaviour, an attitude of trust in significant institutions.

But today, as revealed in the European survey of values of youth (Barker, *et al.*, op. cit.), individualism, a stress upon the supreme value of the individual as key decision-maker, and concern for self-development as the primary value becomes all but an absolute. Relationships between persons are increasingly reduced to an instrumental level: 'What can I get out of this relationship?' This seems to be reflected even in young people's attitudes towards marriage: their reluctance to enter into its commitments and responsibilities, 'We're living together!', and an increasing willingness to abandon a spouse if all is not well. The very concept of a binding lifelong commitment seems incomprehensible to many young people, whether that commitment be in marriage or in religious life.

But there is a price to be paid for the me-first priority. The strong sense of self-interest is matched by an underlying loss of coherence. In wishing to develop and further the sense of self and the authenticity which goes with it, the links of common life based on a shared narrative or explanation of what life is really all about are loosened. This, together with the drive of each sector of human living for its own authority and competence, leaves the individual in a place not only of considerable excitement, but also of anxiety and fear of isolation. At the heart of this conflict of values lies a deep desire to be in touch with the underlying coherence and meaning of life, the existence of which most people seem certain of instinctively. The pathway to deeper growth, in other words, is the exploration of a mystery, not the answering or explaining of a problem.

Two important implications for Catholic educators flow from these observations. In the first place it is important to be constantly aware of the moments in life when young people are open to this 'mystery'. There are times when the questions which for so long remain unformulated begin to reach the surface of conscious reflection with greater insistence. Some such times are obvious because of the drama involved and the way in which they touch the very 'fact' of life. For some time now studies have explored the significance of the experiences of birth, sickness and death as key moments in the human person's search for coherence and compassion (O'Malley, 1992). But other moments are also important, and often form the starting point and the dynamic of that search for deeper coherent growth: among them is the confusing and turbulent experience of adolescence. Life is full of such experiences which challenge the personal synthesis by which we may have lived to that date, or, alternatively, reveal the absence of any such synthesis. These are the moments when the door for deeper human formation is wide open. We have to be alert to these moments of *kairos*.

The second key aspect of pastoral awareness which must always accompany the 'moment' is the realisation that people today are open to such approaches only from those whom they know and in whom they have some initial trust. Both research (Flynn, 1975; 1979; 1983; 1993) and experience suggest that this means someone from within their own family or friendship network, or teachers who show personal interest in students, persons sufficiently close to have an initial 'entrée'. In other words, there is little part to be played in this personal exploration of the mystery of life by either the travelling evangelist, whether on the train or the TV, or the 'professionally religious' – bishop, priest, monk or nun – unless that person has already established a considerable foundation of personal knowledge and trust. And for many, it would seem, that that no longer comes automatically with the office. It has to be won!

It must be clear that the challenge to Catholic education being developed here is not one of offering an *apologia* for Christian values. One of the features of individualism, and the personal autonomy it espouses, is that exclusive appeals to 'objective truth' tend to fall on deaf ears. What must be sought, therefore, is not bringing people to agree with what they perceive as our 'personal convictions', but rather the exploration with us of the central, life-giving mystery of God, and God's creation in its many aspects, to be discovered in a study of the gamut of subjects taught in our schools, colleges and universities. The entry points into such exploration are much less those of rational argument than of the appeal of goodness and love, the raising of the senses, and the attractiveness of beauty, the example of fairness, the witness of sacrifice.

This, of course, is not new. It is the emphasis given by Pope Paul VI in his encyclical *Evangelii nuntiandi* in which he reminded the Church that the quality and coherence of the witness is what will attract attention, especially of the young. In that encyclical the Pope reminded us that, 'Today young people do not listen seriously to teachers, but to witnesses; and if they do listen to teachers it is because they are witnesses' (1976, p.464; 1974).

But how, more specifically, do these pervasive contextual challenges confront Catholic educators today?

1. A limited view of education

The purpose of education is often presented as cultural transmission, i.e. passing on to new generations the accumulated wisdom of the ages. This is certainly an important function to assure coherence in human endeavours within any society and in the human family at large. Failure to inform and train youth in what previous generations have learned would result in the need for each new generation to reinvent the wheel. In fact, in many places cultural transmission is the dominant, if not the sole purpose of public education.

But the purpose of education in today's world, marked by rapid changes at every level of human endeavour and competing value systems and ideologies, cannot remain so limited if it is to effectively prepare men and women of competence and conscience, capable of making significant contributions to the future of the human family. From a purely pragmatic point of view, education which is limited to cultural transmission results in training for obsolescence. This is clear when we consider programmes such as training for technology. Less apparent, however, may be the results of failure to probe human implications of developments that inevitably affect human life such as genetic engineering, the image culture, new forms of energy, the role of emerging economic blocks of nations, and a host of other innovations that promise progress. Many of these offer hope for improved human living, but at what cost? Such matters cannot simply be left to political leaders or the captains of industry; it is the right and responsibility of every citizen to judge and act in appropriate ways for the emerging human community. People need to be educated for responsible citizenship.

In addition, therefore, to cultural transmission, preparation for significant participation in cultural growth is essential. Men and women of the third millennium will require new technological skills, no doubt; but more important, they will require skills to understand lovingly and critique all aspects of life in order to make decisions (personal, social, moral, professional, religious) that will impact on all of our lives for the better.

2. Christian values

A value-oriented educational goal such as that represented in and through Christianity – forming men and women for others – will not be realised unless, infused within our educational programmes at every level, our students are challenged to reflect upon the value implications of their studies. Mere appropriation of knowledge does not inevitably humanise either the individual or the community. One would hope that it is generally recognised that there is no value-free education. All teaching imparts values, and these values can be such as to promote Christian values, or work, whether partially or entirely, at cross purposes to the gospel of Jesus Christ.

A value literally means something which has a price; something dear, precious or worthwhile and hence something that one is ready to suffer or sacrifice for, which gives one a reason to live and, if need be, a reason to die. Values, then, bring to life the dimension of meaning. Values provide motives. They identify a person, give one a face, a name and a character. Without values, one floats, like the driftwood in the swirling waters of the ocean. Values are central to one's own life, and to every life, and they define the quality of that life, marking its breadth and depth.

Each academic discipline within the realm of the humanities and social sciences, when honest with itself, is well aware that the values transmitted depend on assumptions about the ideal human person, which are used as a starting point. Catholic educational institutions make their essential contribution to society by embodying in the educational process a rigorous, probing study of crucial human problems and concerns. It is for this reason that Catholic schools, colleges and universities must strive for high academic quality. This is indeed something far removed from the facile and superficial world of slogans, ideology or purely emotional and self-centred responses, and of instant, simplistic solutions. Teaching and research and all that contribute to the educational process are of the highest importance in our institutions because they reject and refute any partial or deformed vision of the human person. This is in sharp contrast to those educational institutions which often unwittingly sidestep the central concern for the human person because of fragmented approaches to specialisations.

3. Complexity – habits of reflection

The values embedded in many areas of life today are presented subtly. This gives rise to the need to discover ways that will enable students to form habits of reflection, to assess values and their consequences for human beings in the positive and human sciences they study, the technology being developed, and the whole spectrum of social and political programmes suggested by both prophets and politicians. Habits are not formed by chance occasional happenings. Habits develop only by consistent, planned practice. And so the goal of forming habits of reflection needs to be worked upon by all teachers in Catholic schools, colleges and universities in all subjects, in ways appropriate to the maturity of students at different levels. But the challenge consists in how to do this. For example, what are the perspectives used to engage our students as they study history, literature, science and culture? Are they inclusive of the poor? Do they raise significant questions about how the marvellous gifts of God's creation should be used and shared with those less fortunate? This fundamental concern of Catholic education is rooted in the biblical understanding of gift. Theologians observe that in Scripture all gifts – talents, wealth – move in a circle. First there is the openness to perceive that the gift is from God; then it is received and appropriated; next, one grows through the gift by sharing it with others; and finally the gift is returned to God through praise and thanksgiving. But at the moment when sharing should take place, there can come the great temptation to hold on to the gift and turn it into a means of accruing personal power. And so the terrible temptation to seek more and more power through wealth becomes insatiable. Thus the seeds of injustice are sown. Reflection like this can help our students to avoid facile and false solutions to real problems they face as they grow.

4. Feelings of insecurity

One of the major reasons contributing to the widespread quest for easy answers is the insecurity many people experience due to the breakdown of essential human institutions that normally provide the context for human growth. Tragically, the family, the most fundamental human society, is disintegrating in countries around the world. In many Developed World countries, one out of two marriages ends in divorce, with devastating effects for the spouses and for the children. Another source of insecurity and confusion is found in the experience of historic mass migration of peoples across the face of the earth. Millions of men, women and children are being uprooted from their cultures due to oppression, civil conflicts, or lack of food or means to support themselves. The older émigrés may cling to elements of their cultural and religious heritage, but the young are often subject to culture conflict, and feel compelled to adopt the dominant cultural values of their new homelands in order to be accepted. Yet, at heart, they are uncertain about these new values.

Insecurity often expresses itself in defensiveness, selfishness, a me-first attitude, which blocks consideration of the needs of others. Emphasis on reflection to achieve meaning can assist students to understand the reasons underlying the insecurities they experience, and to seek more constructive ways to deal with them.

5. Prevalence of pragmatism

Another major source of insecurity reported by students and teachers today revolves around the possibilities of employment when young people complete their education. This concern is certainly justifiable. In a desire to meet goals of economic advancement, which may be quite legitimate, many governments are stressing the pragmatic elements of education exclusively. The result is that education is reduced to job training. This thrust is often encouraged by business interests, although they pay lip service to broader cultural goals of education. In recent years, across the world, many academic institutions have acceded to this narrow perspective of what constitutes education. And it is startling to see the enormous shift in student selection of majors in universities away from the humanities, the social and psychological sciences, philosophy and theology, towards an exclusive focus on business, computer science, economics, engineering, or the physical and biological sciences.

Catholic educators cannot simply bemoan these facts of life. They must be considered and dealt with. This means that Catholic education must insist upon the integral formation of its students through such means as required core curricula that include humanities, philosophy, theological perspectives, social questions and the like, as part of all educational programmes. In addition, infusion methods might well be employed within specialisations to highlight the deeper human, ethical and social implications of what is being studied.

6. Global frame of reference

The dawn of the third millennium also raises a challenge concerning the breadth of our preparation of the younger generation. We live in an era where global thinking and action is the immediate future. International business conglomerates multiply rapidly, adapting to the world community, airlines are fast becoming 'world carriers', the media are beaming programmes around the globe by satellite. We who are missioned to build the kingdom of God cannot remain limited to parochial or individual enthusiasms. Will a distinctively Christian education really help to form men and women for others in the world community of the twenty-first century if Christian educators do not adapt to the changing international culture? And this is a corporate responsibility, with all of us participating in some way according to resources and interests, and with a genuine desire to help others.

A number of Catholic educational institutions have made strides in international collaboration. These are signs of the typically 'catholic' impulse to incorporate a global dimension into our educational programmes, not as occasional special events, but as part of the fibre of what it means to be Catholic educational institutions. But the challenge lies in the purpose of international programmes. Are they thinly veiled tourist outings or are they designed to help young people to realise that difference is not inferiority? Such international consciousness can only help to equip our students for life in the global village through increased understanding and respect for other cultures and the richness they bring to the human family.

7. Collaboration

The enormity of the mission calls all Catholic educators as both individuals and within educational communities to work together in the face of an enormous paradigm shift of values throughout the world. Pope John Paul II in his Post-Synodal Apostolic Exhortation, *Christifideles laici* (1989), reiterated that the role of the laity in this effort is a sharing in the mission of Christ. The roots of lay collaboration in ministry set out by the Second Vatican Council are theological. Vatican II reminds all Catholics that they are called to share in the triple charism of Christ by virtue of their baptism, that is, called to share in the sanctification of God's creation (priest), to proclaim the Word of God in deed as well as word (prophet), and to share in Christ's kingship of service – the Son of Man came not to be served, but to serve, and to give his life as a ransom for many. Recall that the only time Christ wore a crown was on the cross, and it was a crown of thorns. Events of the last quarter of a century have accelerated the need for implementation of this colleagueship.

But attitudinal challenges remain. Are religious, and more importantly, the hierarchy, willing to share responsibility with lay people or do they insist on an employer-employee relationship? Are lay professors and administrators willing to accept apostolic co-responsibility for the integral formation of their students, or do they wish to remain solely academic professionals? And is the Catholic population at large willing to understand and prize such collaboration in ministry as truly Catholic?

What relationships are needed in order to achieve effective collaboration? How can a Christlike spirituality be shared in ways that will assure a living Gospel tradition in these institutions in the third millennium? What forms (personal, communal, legal) are important to assure that we avoid the extremes of total control by Church authorities on the one hand, or abdication of their indispensable role as guarantors of the religious charism of the institution on the other? How can respectful mutual accountability as colleagues in this mission be achieved? The very questions are still in the making. The answers, in anything like their fullness, still lie ahead, to be discovered only in the genuine effort of collaboration.

But collaboration is not an end in itself. It exists precisely so that we can offer more effective service to those who need us. Today society provides special challenges for all who engage in the Church's mission. If our educational institutions are not finally instruments for hope, for the Good News, then their identity is in crisis as Catholic apostolates. Teachers, administrators, staff, trustees of Catholic educational institutions, beyond being qualified professionals in education, are called to be men and women of the Spirit. And because the task is so great, the extent of collaboration that is sought cannot be limited to the campus itself. Former students are potential colleagues for the transformation of the world. Thus there is a need to invite and to challenge Catholic graduates to go beyond awareness and beyond rhetoric, to engage in action for justice, for the poor. Through personal experience of the problems of poverty and injustice, and by reflection, graduates can individually and together, become a positive force for effective service for their less fortunate brothers and sisters. Our challenge is to fashion effective ways to enable our former students to continue to grow in these dimensions of Christian maturity.

8. Burnout

Catholic schools throughout the world are blessed with many excellent teachers and administrators who are totally committed to the ministry of teaching. Yet too many workaholics in too few years burn out and are lost to this important ministry. Even if burnout does not result in a physical or psychological breakdown, it often manifests itself in an inability to reflect and to grow. At base I suspect that this is motivated by a false sense of Messianism, whereby we assume that if we don't do everything, the kingdom of God will be lost. Isn't this, looked at in the cold light of a day, a form of pride? What we are about is the work of the Lord. Certainly we cooperate with God in service to his people. But ultimately all is in God's hands.

The challenge for each of us is to establish a rhythm of life that will allow us to grow individually and as school communities as contemplative in action. This means that we have to make hard decisions concerning priorities, and then live by them.

How to do?

Pedagogy is the way in which teachers accompany learners in their growth and development. Pedagogy, the art and science of teaching, cannot simply be reduced to methodology. It must include a worldview and a vision of the ideal human person to be educated. These provide the goal, the end towards which all aspects of an educational tradition are directed. They also provide criteria for choices of means to be used in the process of education. A Catholic pedagogy, therefore, must assume the worldview of Christ and suggest more explicit ways in which gospel values can be incarnated in the teaching-learning process.

From a Christian standpoint, the model for human life – and therefore the ideal of a humanely educated individual – is the person of Jesus. Jesus teaches us by word and example that the realisation of our fullest human potential is achieved ultimately in our union with God, a union that is sought and reached through a loving, just and compassionate relationship with our brothers and sisters. Love of God, then, finds true expression in our daily love of neighbour, in our compassionate care for the poor and suffering, in our deeply human concern for others as God's people. It is a love that gives witness to faith and speaks out through action on behalf of a new world community of justice, love and peace.

The pedagogy needed is that which endeavours to form men and women for others in a post-modern world where so many forces are at work which are antithetical to that aim. We need a model of how to proceed that promotes the goal of Catholic education, a paradigm that speaks to the teaching-learning process and has practical meaning and application for the classroom.

I mention here briefly only three crucial characteristics of such a pedagogy:

1) It must address human questions through a process of infusion, not by accretion to an already overloaded curricula.

2) For centuries, education was assumed to consist primarily of accumulated knowledge gained from lectures and demonstrations. Teaching followed a primitive magisterial model. And memory was the critical human faculty developed.

Such a teaching model is seriously deficient in Catholic education for two reasons:

a) In Catholic schools the learning experience is expected to move beyond rote knowledge to the development of the more complex learning skills of understanding, application, analysis, synthesis and evaluation.

b) If learning were limited to memory and skill mastery, it would lack the component of reflection wherein students are impelled to consider the meaning and significance of what they study, and to integrate that meaning as responsible learners who grow as persons of competence, conscience and compassionate commitment. Thus an appropriate pedagogical model must rest upon Experience, Reflection and Action.

In addition, a comprehensive Catholic pedagogical paradigm must consider the context of learning as well as the more explicitly pedagogical process. And it should point to ways to encourage openness to growth through evaluation – even after the student has completed any individual learning cycle. Thus five steps are involved. At the crucial step in this process, reflection, the memory, the understanding, the imagination and the feelings are used to capture the meaning and essential value of what is being studied, to discover its relationship to other aspects of knowledge and human activity, and to appreciate its implications in the ongoing search for truth and free action.

Thus, reflection is the process by which meaning surfaces in human experience:

- by understanding the truth being studied more clearly;
- by understanding the sources of the sensations or reactions I experience in this consideration;
- by achieving personal insights into events, ideas, truth or the distortion of truth;
- by deepening my understanding of the implications of what I have grasped for myself and for others;
- by coming to some understanding of who I am… and who I might be in relation to others.

3) Time is necessary for the preparation of teachers for this pedagogy. Repeated research studies over the last twenty years

have demonstrated conclusively that teachers, being intelligent persons, will agree with something that makes sense. But, they will do that with which they are comfortable (Society of Jesus, 1993). Thus, to be effective, any introduction of a meaningful pedagogy will require time to allow teachers to practise methodologies that contribute to the aims intended in relatively non-threatening circumstances, and to master them so they are comfortable with them one by one. In this way there is greater likelihood that they will be used.

Such a pedagogical programme has recently been developed by the Society of Jesus and is now being introduced in Jesuit schools, colleges and universities on five continents.

During their adolescent years and into early adulthood young men and women are still relatively free to listen and to explore. The world has not yet closed in on them. They are concerned about the deeper questions of the 'why' and 'wherefore' of life. They can dream impossible dreams and be stirred by the vision of what might be. The Church has committed so much of its personnel and resources to the education of young people precisely because they are questing for the sources of life 'beyond academic excellence'. Surely, every teacher worthy of the name must believe in young people and want to encourage their reaching for the stars. This means that your own unifying vision of life as teachers, as parents, as pastors must be tantalisingly attractive to your students, inviting them to dialogue on the things that count. It must encourage them to internalise attitudes of deep and universal compassion for their suffering fellow men and women and to transform themselves into men and women of peace and justice, committed to be agents of change in a world which recognises how widespread is injustice, how pervasive the forces of oppression, selfishness and consumerism.

Admittedly, this is not an easy task. Like all of us in our pre-reflective years, our students, our children have unconsciously accepted values which are incompatible with what truly leads to human happiness. More than young people of previous generations, your students have more 'reasons' for walking away in sadness when they see the implications of a Christian vision of life and a basic change of worldview which leads to rejection of softness and the distortedly glamorous image of life purveyed in slick magazines and cheap films. They are exposed, as no generation in history, to the lure of drugs and the flight from painful reality which they promise.

Catholic teachers and professors in a Catholic school, college or university, beyond being qualified professionals in education, are called to be men and women of the Spirit. Who teachers are, speaks louder than what we say. Words about total dedication, service of the poor, a just social order, a non-racist society, openness to the Spirit and so on may lead students to reflection. A living example will lead them beyond reflection to aspire to live what the words mean.

Conclusion

To feel uneasy about facing up to the challenges and responsibilities of being a Catholic teacher is to recognise one's own limits, but it is also to know that these limits are shared! Know, also, that for every doubt there is an affirmation that can be made. For the ironies of Charles Dickens' time are with us even now. 'It was the best of times, the worst of times… the spring of hope, the winter of despair' (1938, p.13). And there is still great encouragement to be gleaned from a growing desire on the part of many in countries around the globe to pursue more vigorously the ends of Catholic education which, if properly understood, will lead our students to unity, not to fragmentation; to faith, not cynicism; to respect for life, not to the raping of our planet; to responsible action based on moral judgment, not to timorous retreat or reckless attack.

In conclusion I recall that when Christ left his disciples, he said: 'Go and teach! I shall be with you…'

PART ONE
Catholic Education – Inside-Out/Outside-In

SECTION TWO
Meditations on the Content of Catholic Education

CATHOLIC FAITH AND RELIGIOUS TRUTH

David Carr

Introduction

What is it to be Catholic? Clearly, such features as baptism, regular
attendance at Mass and recognition of papal authority are crucial
constituents of being counted a member of the flock. But there is
surely more to it than this – and, indeed, there are surely
circumstances which would incline us to deny that someone who
fulfilled all these criteria was genuinely Catholic. In this sense,
Catholic membership turns less upon contingencies of baptism,
upbringing or cultural inheritance, more upon assent to that
particular system of belief or doctrine which marks off Catholic
Christianity from other religious (Christian and non-Christian)
confessions. It is in this sense that – despite the enormous
sacramental importance of baptism and its significant role in
determining whether or not someone counts as a Catholic – many
formerly baptised as Catholics might now be considered to be so in
little more than name.

Truth and value

To be a Catholic in any substantial sense, then, is a matter of
subscribing to that particular set of beliefs which define Catholic
faith. To believe something, however, is to hold that it is *true*.
Actually, in the case of faith-constitutive beliefs it is to do rather
more than assent to truth; it is also to commit oneself to what the
beliefs enjoin in the way of practical conduct. From this point of
view, it is common for the kinds of beliefs that define moral

perspectives, religious faiths and political ideologies to be referred to as values. But this, of course, is precisely where we begin to encounter certain difficulties about any idea of Catholic (or any other religious) truth, for, according to a very powerful philosophical tradition hailing from the rational enlightenment, there is no clear connection between values and truth. On the contrary, in the empiricist tradition of Hume (1969) and his philosophical heirs (Ayer, 1967), values are precisely dissociated from truth in virtue of a logical distinction between facts and values; only facts can have the kind of evidential support which warrants talk of truth, and values are therefore consigned to the realm of subjective preference.

I shall not here engage in lengthy refutation of such attempts to divorce fact from value. It seems to me that the modern – now apparently widely popular – belief that values are merely subjective preferences is perverse to the point of culpable stupidity. To be sure, it would be but further folly to accuse a philosopher of Hume's undeniable greatness of stupidity; but like many great philosophers Hume seems to have allowed arguments of some philosophical dubiety to paint him into the corner of a position which common experience gives us no good reason to hold. If to value something is *inter alia* to regard it as good, then I can clearly value effective dentistry in the absence of any (at least occurrent) preference for visiting the dentist, and for reasons which are clearly grounded in evidential connections between healthy teeth and human flourishing. Moreover, there is no reason to doubt this general point about value – even if one is here more Kantianly inclined to distinguish moral from prudential values (Kant, 1948): there is clearly just as much of an evidentially based connection between culturally universal abhorrence of murder and equally plain facts of human welfare; getting murdered can ruin your entire day.

Indeed, similar arguments to those directed against Hume and his emotivist descendants can be levelled at the non-cognitivist heirs of Kant (Hare, 1952); we do not call actions good because we are disposed to commend or prescribe them, but commend or prescribe them insofar as we consider them good – and, in the moral realm as any other, we generally have grounds for regarding this or that conduct as good or bad which have fairly direct reference to plain facts of human flourishing. We disagree morally but that is no reason to embrace the rationally defeatist position, in the moral sphere more than in any other, that entitlement to one's own opinion morally justifies whatever a person might believe; racists, child pornographers, drug barons and slave merchants may be entitled (in a sense) to their own opinion, but they are just as clearly immoral.

From this point of view, I am inclined to think that the very idea that values are subjective is more oxymoron than falsehood – a plain contradiction in terms; if a state of heart or mind is to count as a value it must be based on reasons or considerations which go beyond the realm of subjective preference. A value is a *principled* preference (Carr, 1991) which precisely entails reasons or grounds; as I have no reason for preferring strawberries to raspberries, it would be odd to number such a preference among my values as distinct from, say, my tastes. In fact, I believe that the prime source of error here is confusion of the subjective with the rather different notion of the personal. However, I can clearly have reasons for valuing things which are at once both personal *and* objective. I may, for example, prize a particular item of property – a photograph or an ancestral home – for reasons of personal association which are not (perhaps even could not be) shared by others; it would be appropriate to speak of my valuing such objects and to number treasuring them among my values – as it would not be in the case of my taste for asparagus.

Still, one might say, while the distinction between the subjective and the personal goes some way towards defusing notions of subjective value, any admission that there can be personal values gives considerable hostage to the fortunes of that other bogy of modern moral and social theory – ethical relativism. Might it not be that whilst values are objective, at least to the extent of resting on evidentially based reasons or justifications, they are nevertheless grounded in considerations which are entirely local and particular to the interests of those who hold them? Of course, relativists do not normally relativise values to the circumstances of particular individuals, regarding them rather as the shared product of social consensus or cultural inheritance. In other words, they are to be regarded as socially constructed for the purpose of harmonious and cooperative human co-existence. But there are undoubtedly values which are relative in this way; the present question is that of whether moral and religious beliefs are values of this kind.

On views of this sort, moral values are endorsed much in the manner of rules of club membership. Just as in joining the Masons, the Brownies, or the Labour Party, one agrees to abide by a certain creed or code of conduct which one accepts as conditional upon continued membership, so one accepts certain rules of conduct as conditional upon one's continued membership of the civil or social order in which – by birth, circumstance or choice – one happens to find oneself. But just as membership of the Brownies is quite consistent with the recognition that rules of Brownie honour are not at all binding upon non-Brownies, endorsing the code of moral values of a given society is quite consistent with recognising that they might not be appropriate or relevant in other social and economic circumstances. Ethical relativism upholds a 'live and let live' attitude to cross-cultural differences of belief and conduct. From our point of view, we deplore the cannibalism, slavery, polygamy, child prostitution and female circumcision which is practised over there – but then, who are we to judge? There can also be no doubt that in the presently prevailing 'post-modern' climate of hostility to liberal enlightenment ethics, such relativism has gained considerable ground – sometimes aided and abetted by religiously driven moral and social theorists of a so-called 'communitarian' bent.

The philosophical trouble here, as so often, lies with the idea that because some values are socially constructed, all must be. We have already seen, however, that this is not so; although there are corporate values which I am well warranted in requiring other members of my social group or club to observe, there are also personal values which I have no right to require of anyone else; I might be justified in forbidding Phoebe to wear that hat at a jaunty angle if she wants to be a true Brownie, but I've no business requiring anyone else to share my enthusiasm for cockroach racing or trainspotting. All the same, why shouldn't there be values that I am justified in requiring everyone to observe, irrespective of their local interests? One might say that even if there are, it may be doubted whether moral values are among them; but it is precisely in the realm of moral values that some of the greatest of philosophers have located them. For example, Wittgenstein (1965), in his famous lecture on ethics, argued that although we could accept as a reason from someone we observed to be playing tennis badly, that he did not wish to play better, we could not accept the excuse of not wishing to behave any better from someone who had maliciously injured or humiliated someone else. Wittgenstein's point here is that the latter ought to want to behave better – and here he gives precisely the same universal force to 'ought' that Kant also gave to his moral or *categorical imperative* (Kant, 1948).

Without endorsing Kantian or Wittgensteinian rational strategies for justifying the universal force of moral imperatives, one may still accept their general point that it is usual for people to think of their moral values as having not just local but universal application. There is something rather fishy about the idea of someone holding, as a moral value, that it is wrong to eat people, to have more than one wife, to own others as slaves, to commit abortion and so on, whilst simultaneously maintaining that it is quite acceptable for Muslims, Mormons or Xavantes to do such things. Thus, contrary to the teachings of many prophets of postmodernism, it is not at all natural for us to take an 'ironic' stance

(Rorty, 1989)[1] with respect to our deeply held moral beliefs, and it is hard to make sense of holding a moral belief that one would not at the same time wish to be held by every other sane and sensible human being. To be sure, there are important moral disagreements between people about abortion, divorce, capital punishment, euthanasia and the like – though it is also worth noting that none of these disagreements are about whether these are bad things – but it seems that these are invariably disagreements, not between moral agnostics, but between people who take what they believe to be true or right. It is also worth pointing out to ethical relativists, moreover, that moral judgment is not always or necessarily culturally colonial or ethnocentric; we can and do compare the moral practices of our own society or social group *unfavourably* with those of other cultures.

Generally speaking, then, it seems likely that moral subjectivism and relativism follow from a tangle of fairly elementary – and readily discernible – conceptual confusions. First, there is the confusion of the subjective with the personal. There is then equivocation, on the part of those non-cognitive theories which hold that morality is a matter of individual self-legislation, over senses in which moral values are a matter of personal choice or decision; for it clearly does not follow from the fact that people are free to choose what they shall believe or do morally, that it is up to them to determine what shall count as a moral value. A similar equivocation is discernible in the moral relativist claim that morality is a matter of *social agreement*; for it would not follow from the truth (if it is a truth) that moral rules are arrived at through some kind of social agreement, that they are automatically justified by such agreement. Indeed, to the extent that social groups can collude, for all sorts of hegemonic and economic purposes, in perpetuating the most beastly cruelties and injustice – this is surely quite false.

A general confusion which seems to underlie all these views is the idea that moral rightness or wrongness is but a human artifact, that there is, in the words of the Prince of Denmark, 'nothing either good or bad, but thinking makes it so' (*Hamlet*, 2. ii. 255). From this point of view, it is deeply disconcerting that a recent item of influential documentation from official educational sources should take the key values of education question to be that of, 'whose values?' (Ofsted, 1994). It is a question which though apparently innocent is in fact profoundly corrupt. It is fatuous enough to raise the question 'who says this is bad?' when I am suffering toothache from dental neglect; it is downright obscene to ask it when a maladjusted individual guns down innocent infant children in a primary school classroom. Thus, while it is only right to observe that there are local social customs and cultural affiliations which we may have an interest in preserving or upholding as members of particular cultural constituencies, it is culpable folly to deny any common human condition underlying such cultural differences by which we might determine what counts as general human wellbeing or harm.

TRUTH AND CATHOLICISM

At all events, it seems *prima facie* reasonable to state that there are different reasons for holding, or different levels at which we can hold, values of one sort or another. We may subscribe individually or personally to a value which we would not require anyone else to share, we may subscribe as a member of a group to values which we are entitled to expect other members of that group to share or we may endorse a value which we would want to be shared by every other human individual, irrespective of local affiliations. It should also be apparent, moreover, that personal, corporate and universal reasons for holding a given value are by no means mutually exclusive; in fact, we can now return directly to present concerns by observing that the Catholic faith would appear to be something to which one might subscribe for personal, communal or universal reasons – or *all* of these.

First, it is clearly possible for someone to embrace Catholicism for purely personal reasons; he or she approves of Catholic ethical thinking, gains considerable aesthetic satisfaction from attending Mass, derives much spiritual solace from confession, and so on. Nevertheless, the benefits derived are regarded as entirely personal and there is no expectation that anyone else, even those who also call themselves Catholics, should value the faith for the same reasons that the private Catholic does; it may even be held by such personal Catholics, perhaps under the influence of phenomenological or existentialist theologians, that no-one could share anyone else's precise experience of Catholic faith. One might well consider it strange, given the pronounced communitarian emphasis of Catholic life, that anyone should take this view, but it is not impossible that they might do so.

It is certainly possible for people to hold to Catholicism on largely communitarian grounds and to accept the rules of Catholic engagement as one might largely accept the rules of club membership. Certainly the ritual practices of some traditional religions would appear to be followed by their adherents in some such way; it is likely, for example, that at least some contemporary Jews observe the rituals of Judaism more in the spirit of cultural affiliation and loyalty than belief in the God of the Old Testament. But this is probably also true of many Catholics living in the largely secular circumstances of such non-traditional and immigrant societies as the United States. Since a sense of identity is for many people associated with cultural affiliation, the only recourse in societies lacking such common cultural roots may to seek the communal ties afforded through loyalty to ancestral religious traditions – even if one is no longer persuaded of the literal truth of the associated religious doctrines. At this level, of course, it is open for such socio-cultural Catholics to criticise other club members for holding Catholically heterodox views, but no real question necessarily arises as yet of criticising non-Catholics for not attending Mass or Confession.

In fact, precisely what does not arise at either of the levels of Catholic involvement which we have considered so far are any questions of the objective truth of Catholic belief or doctrine. For anyone stuck at the personal level, belonging to the Catholic faith is little more than engagement in rituals and practices which entrain certain experiences I happen to find more satisfying than those I might get from spending my Sunday mornings attending stock car races. But the personal Catholic is not in the least committed to thinking that what is a potent source of satisfaction for her need be so for others – still less to the idea that such experiences need be more than 'true for her'. But again, although the involvement of the social Catholic is very much a matter of association with others – an association which enjoins a degree of moral censure of those who do not abide by the rules of club membership – there is still no requirement for Catholics at this level to believe in the absolute, objective or literal truth of the beliefs and doctrines which have traditionally been held to define Catholicism. Indeed, it would appear that Catholic affiliation at this level is an almost exclusively moral matter, in that rather narrow contractual or conventional sense of morality which has dominated much post-enlightenment ethical thought. Consequently, one suspects that certain kinds of misconduct – divorce, abortion or adultery – would here generally be regarded as more serious breaches of Catholic decorum than denial of the Resurrection, the virgin birth or the real presence.

There cannot also be much room for doubt that reflection upon the question of what it is to be a Catholic has been caught up in certain currents of contemporary thought about the nature of religious faith and commitment in general, which strongly incline religious believers to fixation at the personal and social levels. There is little doubt, for example, of the influence of existentialist and phenomenological modern theology, from Kierkegaard onwards, on those current curriculum initiatives (SOED, 1992) which speak of religious education largely as a matter of 'personal search'; a position which I have critiqued elsewhere (Carr, 1992). Again, it seems likely that the currently prevailing 'post-modern' climate of social and moral theory has greatly served to reinforce the idea that all knowledge – not just this or that claim to religious revelation – is socially constructed for all too human purposes. On such views, there can be no ultimate divine truth of the kind St Paul characterised in 1 Corinthians 13:12 as only presently dimly perceived; there are only rival myths of narratives adopted by human beings as useful for their own local and partisan ends. It is also worth noting that some of the influential moral and social philosophers most closely identified with the communitarian end of such recent strongly perspectival and narratival thinking about the nature of human belief systems are actually Roman Catholics (MacIntyre, 1981, 1987, 1992; Taylor, 1989). Such theorists are largely inclined to resist the possibility of universal conceptions of virtue and justice which cut across local differences, and are often implacably hostile to any culturally colonial designs which majority cultures might have with respect to minority ones.

Where, however, does this leave any possibility of holding that Catholicism is just actually *true;* of maintaining that it is not just proper to regard the faith as individually applicable or as applicable to a given individual insofar as she is a member of the social group which calls itself Catholic, but as potentially applicable to every human agent irrespective of her particular social circumstances or current cultural affiliations? Moreover, since the beliefs of many other faiths are clearly inconsistent with those of Christianity, what of the possibility of regarding other ideologies or religious creeds as mistaken? Of course, insofar as all human beings are, according to the central tenets of Catholicism, potential brothers and sisters in Christ, this would be an occasion for treating them with just the same love and concern that Jesus extended to Gentiles. Further, it would also be a matter of seeing that love as in a large part expressed in a concern (though only, to be sure, by means consistent with the love of Christ) for their conversion to the true faith. Isn't such a point of view utterly and hopelessly illiberal and condescending, particularly in the circumstances of most advanced late-twentieth-century liberal democratic polities? How could anyone possibly have the arrogance to claim that Roman Catholicism is the one true faith in a multi-cultural, global village in which the followers of other ideologies and religions already outnumber Catholics, and in which large numbers of people who would actually call themselves Christians are evidently seriously sceptical of some of the traditional truth claims of Christianity (McLaughlin *et. al.*, 1996).[2]

But it is no less than this which seems to be the general position of Pope John Paul II in *Crossing the Threshold of Hope*. Indeed, in relation to present concerns this work could hardly be more resolute on three main points: (i) that the traditional beliefs and doctrines of Roman Catholicism are *true* in an *absolute* or *universal*, not merely local, sense; (ii) that insofar as other faiths and creeds are inconsistent with those of Catholic Christianity, they can only be regarded – however respectfully or sympathetically we might otherwise treat them – as significantly *mistaken*; (iii) that to the extent this is so all faithful members of Christ's flock have a crucial *evangelical* responsibility to spread the truth of faith:

> Against the spirit of the world, the Church takes up each day a struggle that is none other than *the struggle for the world's soul*. If in fact, on the one hand, the Gospel and evangelization are present in this world, on the other, there is also present *a powerful anti-evangelization* which is well organised and has the means to vigorously oppose the Gospel and evangelization. The struggle for the soul of the contemporary world is at its height where the spirit of the world seems strongest (*Crossing the Threshold of Hope*, p. 112).

Whilst, to be sure, such claims as these must widely appear extraordinary in the general intellectual, moral and socio-political climate of late modernity, they leave us in little doubt that the apostolate of John Paul II is every bit as firm as that of the first rock of Christ. But, of course, such claims must also raise doubts about the status as Catholic of any educator who is less committed – granted some room for interpretative manoeuvre – to the actual *truth* of the defining beliefs and doctrines of the Church. In that case, however, it cannot but be a cause for concern that contemporary confidence in the truth of Catholic Christianity seems to have been shaken by modern accounts of the nature of knowledge which seem to undermine the very possibility of speaking of *any* human belief as true. But, in this respect, it seems to me that no serious defence of Catholic belief and doctrine can be mounted in the absence of something continuous with a traditional realist conception of knowledge and truth in general, and religious truth in particular and, of course, the most conspicuous characteristic of so-called 'post-modern' epistemology is an anti-realism or anti-objectivism about knowledge (Rorty, 1981).[3] In the space which remains to me, then, I shall attempt to contribute something towards clearing the rubble in the path of such a redeemed realist notion of religious (and by implication Catholic) truth which must carry with it some substantial implications for Catholic education.

A realist account of truth and Catholic education[4]

First, we should probably recognise that there are very many kinds of religious fact or truth which are interrelated in different religious perspectives in many conceptually complex ways. This should not come as much of a surprise, since the same applies essentially to such other familiar areas of human enquiry as natural science. In general, any given mode of natural scientific discourse requires to be understood as a complex construct of general laws, hypotheses, observational data, mathematical calculations and so on, each aspect of which is, at least in principle, liable to confirmation or correction, or susceptible to normative appraisal as true or false, right or wrong. It is also important to note, however, that most scientific accounts of nature contain significant ingredients of metaphor and analogy which can also be evaluated as more or less right or appropriate – a point which is also of some significance for proper thinking about the nature of religious truth.

First, then, many of the major world religions such as Christianity, Judaism and Islam clearly make significant historical claims to the effect that the word or the will of God was revealed in particular historical episodes or events. In the Nicene creed, for example, Christianity claims that 'Jesus Christ became incarnate from the Virgin Mary and was made man', that 'He was crucified under Pontius Pilate' and that 'on the third day He rose again'. There can be no doubt that such claims have come to be regarded with increasing contemporary scepticism. This is rooted in a perception that they seem to fly in the face of what secular scientific rationality is prepared to concede as reasonable belief about human nature. All the same, Christians are required to regard such claims, on the authority of the Scriptures and the witness of those on whose testimony the Christian faith is largely founded, as historically factual; hence, those modern theologians who have sought to offer figurative or allegorical accounts of what the Gospels claim to have been actual historical events – accounts which effectively deny their historicity – are at best engaged in something like serious heresy, at worst not speaking on behalf of anything recognisable as Christianity at all. There is much of philosophical interest to be said on the topic of modern theological scepticism about the historical claims of Christianity. For now, we shall merely note that much of such scepticism seems blatantly question-begging in its covert acceptance of a kind of implausible scientific reductionism which excludes the possibility of other than physicalistic explanations of the natural order, explanations which may themselves be impotent to account for certain quite familiar phenomena of the life sciences (Smart and Haldane, 1996).[5]

But if the reductive or deconstructivist scepticism of some modern theologians is at odds with orthodoxy with respect to the truth of such a historically rooted religion as Christianity, the uncompromising literalism of fundamentalists is in its own way also quite misplaced. Thus, we need no more construe biblical stories of Eden and Noah as descriptions of actual historical events and locations, than take the parables of Jesus to be reports of true adventures of actual prodigal sons of forgiving fathers. There is, beyond doubt, a significant and ineliminable allegorical, figurative or poetical dimension to religious discourse in general which is given to the expression of spiritual truths about the relationship of human to divine more in terms of metaphor and analogy, than in the straightforward literal language of direct observation and description. Hence, one is liable to miss the religious point of the story of Noah quite seriously if one takes it to be about weather prediction, boat-building, navigation and animal husbandry, rather than the relationship of sin to judgment or virtue to redemption.

There are perhaps two main reasons for the large element of metaphor, simile and analogy in the expression and communication of religious truths. First, the human search for truth is not generally well modelled on the idea of exclusively cognitive organisation, via general epistemic principles and categories, of the world of sense perception. Since truth is of significance to humans primarily from the perspective of how well it serves to explain or make sense of their peculiar existential predicament, explanations connect with human understanding in ways which go beyond so-called 'cognitive' capacities – to engage also with the motivational and the affective. Moreover, it may be that what especially serves to bring together cognitive and affective aspects of human understanding is what is commonly referred to as the *imagination*. Indeed, one obvious way in which the hermeneutical aspects of human intellectual endeavour go beyond the information actually given is through the imaginative construction of various models, metaphors and analogies. It should be stressed here that this process is as ineradicable from scientific explanation and understanding as it is from religious knowledge and enquiry – and metaphors and similes abound in natural science; thus, the image in classical physics of the universe operating like clockwork, the modern idea of the brain (or even the mind) as a kind of computer or that of light behaving like a wave or a particle, are all at heart metaphors.

However, a second crucial reason for the extensive deployment of figurative or poetic rather than literal language in religious discourse reflects the central concern of religious explanation and understanding with not directly observable spiritual aspects of human existence. It is for this reason that much religious language cannot but be indirect or oblique, for in attempting access to an existential realm which is by definition beyond the bounds of human experience, at least as available to the senses, it has little option but to do so by way of parables and analogies drawn from more familiar realms of everyday human experience. Hence, in the Gospels, as elsewhere in Christian literature, we encounter extensive deployment of metaphors: God as father, Christ as good shepherd; the kingdom of heaven as a mustard seed; which precisely aspire to disclose what may not otherwise be communicated through literal description.

But this raises the awkward problem that it is not now clear how there may be a route to determining the appropriateness or otherwise of religious metaphors of a sort more obviously available in the case of scientific metaphors. For if, say, I am inclined to reject certain scientific theories or hypotheses about the operations of human reason on the grounds that they are based on some misleading analogy between brains and computers, presumably my arguments will rest on observations to the effect that the mind just does not appear to function in this way. The analogy just does not fit the facts. But if it is given as the reason why we have to convey religious truths metaphorically that what is revealed or explained in such terms cannot be, even in principle, a matter of direct perception, what remains of an independent basis upon which to judge the appropriateness or otherwise of religious metaphors? In short, in order to make sense of the aptness or otherwise of metaphors and analogies, must we not also be able to identify literal truths, that is, truths of experience, against which such metaphors can be measured?

Much here clearly turns on what is meant by truths of experience – and philosophers are too readily inclined, under the enduring spell of empiricism, to suppose that there may be no truths of experience which are not deliverances of direct empirical perception. But even the sciences recognise different kinds and levels of truth which relate to observation and experience in a variety of complex ways. Thus, as well as observations of natural science there are also social scientific observations, for example, that human perception structures experience according to Gestalt principles, or that societies beyond a certain level of economic complexity are liable to class divisions. Although all these are truths about facets of human experience, they are not all truths of direct perception; moreover, there is no compelling reason to suppose that laws and truths of biological development are reducible to physical principles concerning the organisation of inanimate matter, or that laws of social organisation reduce to those of individual psychology.

But might we not suppose that as well as these truths of natural and social science, there are also religious or spiritual truths; the deliverences, in their own distinctive way, of human observation and reflection? As examples, we might cite: 'man does not live by bread alone', 'no man can serve two masters' and 'what doth it profit a man to gain the whole world and lose his soul?'. None of these is obviously reducible to the other kinds of truth already mentioned. 'Man does not live by bread alone' is evidently not a lesson about nutrition, and 'no man can serve two masters' is not concerned with the limits of human psychological possibility as to what people can or cannot do as a matter of natural mental capability, but with ultimate human goals and values and the actual implications for spiritual flourishing of how or in what way we have chosen to invest our ultimate loyalties.

Indeed, although the religious and spiritual are, especially in much educational literature and policy documentation, often closely linked with moral development, we may also distinguish such spiritual truths from moral prescriptions. Thus, 'no man can serve two masters' and 'man cannot live by bread alone' unlike 'do not do unto others what you would not have them do to you' are not generalisable prescriptions or even primarily prescriptions at all. It is not as if we should always try to will it that attempting not to live solely by bread or only serving one master should become universal laws. For though I can certainly not do unto others as I would have them do unto me without thereby falsifying my conduct (though in so doing I may well be unfair) the point of asking rhetorically 'what doth it profit a man to gain the world and lose his soul?' is presumably to draw our attention to all those experientially familiar cases of people who have tried to gain the world and have, by failing to achieve a proper moral and spiritual relationship with God and their neighbours in ruthless and blinkered pursuit of material wealth or power, thereby lost their souls. In short, whether or not we do so will it that we should put the salvation of our souls before the pursuit of Mammon, it is a plain spiritual fact that our souls will suffer and fail to flourish if we neglect the truth of such observations.

Thus, though there are important factual truths of a historical kind about a religion such as Christianity which are literal, but not especially spiritual (such as that Christ was born in Palestine during Roman occupation), and also truths which are analogical or metaphorical rather than literal (that the kingdom of God resembles a priceless pearl or a mustard seed), there also seem to be religious truths which are both spiritual and literal, and which it is to a large degree the task of various religious analogies and parables to illustrate and explicate. (Indeed, it may be argued that it is also the role of the Catholic educator to perform a concomitant role with her students.) This task is similar, one might say, to the role of scientific models and metaphors in explicating, illustrating and giving human significance to our experience of the facts of physical and material nature.

But there is clearly a good deal more to knowledge than truth, and to possess knowledge is to have acquired more than a body of correct beliefs – of any kind – about experience. It was therefore a serious defect of the kind of empiricism which endured right up until the early part of the present century, not only to have construed knowledge in terms of the correspondence of human judgements to discrete items of sensible experience, but also to have regarded it as little more than the passive reception of just so many contingently connected sense perceptions. Subsequent versions of empiricism have therefore been at pains to construe knowledge as a matter of significant interplay between observation and theory, rather than simple inductive generalisation over observational 'givens' and, according to one major contemporary critic of classical empiricism, our beliefs about the world face the tribunal of experience not singly but as a body (Quine, 1952). So even if knowledge is more than just coherence, considerations of coherence do nevertheless enter significantly into the justification and evaluation of knowledge claims.

Religious knowledge and understanding

But then, religious knowledge and understanding could not be, any more than scientific knowledge is, merely a collection of disparate observations affirming the truth of this or that spiritual experience. In short, even if there are brute or irreducible religious experiences these would still need to be structured in terms of reasonable principles of religious or spiritual explanation and understanding, in order to have much significance for human affairs. Hence, to qualify as a way of understanding experience, religion also requires, just like science, some disciplined form of human enquiry through which the diverse deliverences of religious experience and intuition may come to constitute a coherent vision or explanation of humankind's relationship with God or the spiritual order. To this end, theology was formerly regarded as the queen of the sciences presumably because it aspired to this explanatory function with respect to what were once conceived to be the most exalted of human concerns. Nowadays, of course, theology is unlikely to be widely considered a science at all, precisely on account of a prevalent modern scepticism about the possibility of objective religious truth. But though theology is nowadays unfavourably compared to science as a way of understanding the nature of human experience, this often seems to have been on the basis of inadequate understanding of the point and purpose of theological enquiry – precisely, on a mistaken assumption that natural science and theology compete for the same explanatory territory.

Perhaps the most notorious instance of this general confusion of scientific and theological questions and concerns is the post-Darwinian controversy between proponents of evolutionary theory and religious fundamentalist supporters of the creation story of Genesis; in parts of the New World, for example, quite bitter disputes have arisen over the right of teachers to instruct children in certain well-trodden theories of the life-sciences in common schools. All the same, it is probably fair to say that few educated Christians would nowadays construe the story of Genesis as a rival natural scientific account of the origins of the universe, in direct competition with evolutionary theory. To be sure, Christians believe that God made the world but they need not suppose Genesis to be a literal description of how exactly God did this. Consequently, one may reasonably take the Genesis account to be metaphorical or allegorical rather than literally descriptive, in the same way that, one might argue, past scientific characterisations of the universe as a piece of clockwork, or present-day scientific talk of brain as computer, should be regarded as analogical rather than literal.

Putting matters thus, however, may well seem to suggest that whereas evolutionary theory gives us a detailed scientific picture of the mysterious ways in which God moves, what Genesis gives us is a kind of religiously inspired vision which operates more at a poetical or pictorial than genuinely explanatory level. Thus, the two versions' view of creation effectively renders one version, the religious account of Genesis, wellnigh redundant or, at any rate, without any genuine or serious explanatory work to do. But it seems that it entirely misses the point of the story to regard it as a sort of provisional non-literal explanation of the origins of the universe, which offers a merely charming poetic alternative to the scientific one. The significance of Genesis is not that of a simple-minded or figurative creation myth which tells the story of how the world came to be in pre-scientific terms, but that of a complex response to a distinctive *theological* problem which is also absolutely indispensable for proper Christian understanding of the spiritual nature and destiny of humankind.

A particularly pressing theological problem for any monotheistic religion is that of the widespread presence of evil in the world. This is not a problem for polytheisms which can, by a kind of divine division of labour, share out the responsibility for beneficent and malign divine acts between different deities who can also be assigned quasi-human virtues and vices. But the emergence of monotheism is more than likely driven by the idea that just as there is a discernible logic or pattern to the created order which seems to call for some sort of transcendent explanation, so there appears to be a discernible moral order by which human beings are able to tell what is right and just from what is wrong and unjust and for which some sort of divine or spiritual explanation also needs to be given. If, however, this moral order is also a reflection of divine nature, it is unthinkable that the divine should itself be exempted from the rules of justice it prescribes for humanity. This being so, it becomes difficult to conceive of divine nature in terms of the petty squabbles of minor deities characteristic of polytheisms. Consequently, it is more or less inevitable that the natural and moral order should come to be construed as the creation of a single unique God between whose judgments and actions there can be no inconsistency or conflict.

But this, of course, does raise afresh the problem of the presence of evil in the world in the particularly acute form of why the just as well as the unjust suffer; a problem addressed, more or less, in many of the so-called wisdom books of the Old Testament. Neither Ecclesiastes nor Job, however, can be said to deal satisfactorily with the theological significance of mortal trials and sufferings. Indeed there is some indication on the part of the author of Job, of a tendency to the dualist solution adopted by the Zoroastrian and Babylonian neighbours of Judaism; it is Satan, rather than God who is, after all, directly responsible for tempting and tormenting Job. Clearly, such a solution to the problem of evil is not readily available to any thoroughgoing monotheism; for if dualism is to avoid regress to polytheism, it cannot avoid laying the ultimate responsibility for evil at the door of God rather than at that of Satan who, if not acting autonomously, must be God's lackey.

It is to this problem that the story of the fall in Genesis may be seen as a genuine and serious theological response; the pain and suffering to which human beings are heir in this 'vale of tears' is a self-inflicted consequence of their wilful disobedience of and ingratitude towards God. The creation story is largely (though not wholly) a backdrop to the events of the fall, which sets the scene of God's beneficence to humankind in terms of both the creation of Adam and Eve and the provision of a paradise for them to inhabit in perpetuity. However, tempted by Satan, here a cipher for human weakness rather than a separate dualist deity, Adam and Eve succumbed to the urgings of their own perverse wills and brought all their sorrows, as well as those of following generations, on themselves. Thus, the evils, sufferings and injustices of humanity are almost wholly the result of original sin. That is, of a flawed nature which inclines humans to choose evil or disobedience of the moral law above goodness and obedience. It should be noted, moreover, that the flaw is not in God's design of human nature – for God could not but, in creating potentially good creatures, endow human beings with free choice between good and evil – but rather in what human beings have themselves made of their nature; thus, the wickedness of individuals is an occasion more for God's sorrow than his wrath or vengeance.

It is clear, of course, that this relatively early theological exploration of the problem of evil, as well as the solution it proposes, is tentative and in further need of refinement; but there can be little doubt that the Genesis account clearly indicates a need within Judaistic monotheism for new insight into and understanding of divine will and purpose of the sort encountered in the Christian revelation. In particular, it points to the absolute necessity of the Incarnation, since, if human beings have fallen by their own hand then they cannot, once fallen, raise themselves to the sinless state again. It is of no avail to try to heal the breach between God and humanity by the sending of divinely inspired prophets to reveal God's word because these are themselves weak and fallen; in short, humanity is redeemable by the personal action or intervention of God alone.

The difficult and complex issue of the Incarnation, of course, immediately gives rise to further theological problems about the personhood of God to which the orthodox Christian teaching about the Trinity is a direct, but also religiously controversial response. Indeed, the problems raised by the doctrine of the Trinity may also represent a theological price, so to speak, which more uncompromising expressions of monotheism – Judaism, Islam, Unitarianism – may be unprepared to pay. From the orthodox Christian perspective, however, any reluctance to pay it has clearly theologically higher costs for any coherent understanding of the Incarnation, or – if Incarnation is rejected – for seeing how God can be truly with humanity in any satisfactory religious or spiritual relationship. In this connection, then, enough should have been said to show why the working out in Christianity of the Genesis problem of original sin requires that certain theological, religious and spiritual truths should also, in due course, become historical ones: that the ultimate divine drama is one which must be acted out on the stage of the world by the Word made flesh. At all events, we may roughly see from this crude and amateurish theologising how religious enquiry can be understood as a rational attempt to address and reconcile certain objective problems about the nature of spiritual experience and truth, the character and provenance of good and evil – and, in the Christian religion, certain historical events of an extraordinary nature to which the fathers of the faith were witness – in a coherent general picture of human religious and spiritual experience.

From this point of view, however, it may well be that certain religions cannot be reasonably considered anything other than spiritual culs-de-sac – precisely because they fail to address problems of spiritual life honestly faced by other faiths. In this respect, the 'demythologising' and other reductive tendencies of so much modern professional theology – particularly (though not only) on the reform side of the confessional divide – must be as destructive and distortive of Christianity as the literalist tendencies of uncritical Christian fundamentalism. By the same token, however, it shows that the fundamental tenet of their faith that the Word was made flesh in human history, and that the battle for the salvation of souls is to be fought out on the stage of this world, means that for Christians, engagement in religious enquiry and reflection cannot be reduced merely to aesthetic sensibility or the expression of subjective personal feeling. On the contrary, far from religious commitment being some kind of surrender to unconscious impulses or subjective preferences, it must be an active search for knowledge of the way, the truth and the life of the very highest potential consequences for the salvation of the human soul.

Finally, of course, it is no part of the claims made here that the pursuit of religious knowledge and truth through religious or spiritual enquiry is all there is to religion, nor that Catholicism is the last word on either religious truth or Christianity in the contemporary labyrinth of religious belief and disagreement. Thus, there is an urgent need for both open and respectful dialogue with members of other faiths as well as genuine reconciliation with fellow Christians. My point for the moment is more that it cannot be a matter of indifference, of mere aesthetic sensibility, which religion people choose or, that having claimed to have found truth in Catholicism, they can seriously entertain it as just one belief among others; not, that is, if there is to be the same room for reason and enquiry in religion that there undoubtedly is in other areas of human life – as a reliable route to objective meaning, knowledge and truth. If it cannot be a matter of indifference to the central claims and purposes of Catholicism it cannot be a matter of irrelevance to the Catholic school where there may be a tendency to embrace the claims of the relativists and the 'meaning-makers'.

If Catholic education is to reflect these central and enduring claims to objectivity and their sustaining arguments then it must not shy away from embodying them in the teaching and learning within particular schools. Further, it must also bring them into the dialogue with the wider community, even where this may seem to be in conflict with the temper of the times.

NOTES

1. Rorty offers one of the most celebrated studies of the modern use of the term 'irony' in this collection.
2. This collection provides an interesting discussion of these issues from a range of perspectives – orthodox and otherwise.
3. This essay represents what would be widely regarded as a classic 'postmodern' assault on realist or objectivist accounts of knowledge and truth.
4. The second section of this paper reflects a number of ideas which I have pursued previously and published as 'Knowledge and truth in religious education', in *Journal of Philosophy of Education*, Volume 28,

Number 2, 1994. Other related papers concerned to defend a realist account of religious and spiritual knowledge and truth are my 'Towards a distinctive conception of spiritual education', in *Oxford Review of Education*, 20, 1995, and 'Rival conceptions of spiritual education', in *Journal of Philosophy of Education*, 30, 1996.

5. Haldane's contribution in particular offers some interesting insights on this.

8

THE NEED OF SPIRITUALITY
IN CATHOLIC EDUCATION

John J. Haldane

Introduction

By the time someone reaches college or university he or she will
already have a definite moral character. This may change, but for
the most part subsequent development will be in directions already
determined at earlier stages – the child is almost always 'father to
the man'. Even so, higher education should not neglect the
personal formation of students. In the past, particularly in small
institutions, there was a concern for the moral well-being of what
were perceived to be young people in transition to full adulthood.
One form – perhaps I should say one 'forum' – in which this
concern could be expressed was the individual tutorial. Tutors
thought of themselves as charged with the responsibility of helping
students form themselves, or as it might have been said in the last
century, 'cultivate virtue'. Now, however, reference to this way of
thinking would almost certainly be derided as paternalistic,
patronising and unduly 'directional', an infringement of student
autonomy.

It is harder, though, to deny that school teachers have
responsibilities to provide moral guidance for their pupils.
Sometimes it can happen that what is taught in schools, and the
general ethos that is created therein, undermine the attempts of
parents to inculcate one or other set of values. In recent years this
has been a problem in some larger cities where teachers have
pursued ill-considered philosophies against the grain of society and
of folk wisdom. Here, though, I hope I can set this danger aside by

assuming that where Catholic schools are concerned, parents and teachers are agreed on the importance of cultivating Catholic habits of thought, feeling and action. This may sound fine and comforting but it begs a major question, namely, what the relevant virtues are and what the end is that they help promote. The main issue to be considered, therefore, is the proper content of Catholic education.

Complainers and converts

In 1993 I was invited to contribute to a US/UK conference on Catholic schools which resulted in a publication about the contemporary Catholic school (McLaughlin *et. al.*, 1996). Much of the discussion at the conference revolved around notions of Catholic identity. Most of this took the form of reminiscences about childhood or complaints about the inadequacy of the Church. Let me say at this point that it is striking how much we Catholics complain. My conjecture is that this is often an expression of immaturity borne of an unreasonable dependence on the all-too-human aspects of the Church, and on a failure to distinguish between offices and their occupants. Over-clericalised and, historically, often tribal, Catholics tend to suffer from an inability to form an objective perception of themselves; and instead of getting on with things, they stay at home in their backyards and grumble about not getting out into the wider world. It really is an excuse to go on saying that Catholics are discriminated against in the professions, the arts, and in academic and public life.

For all the recent excitement about a return to Catholicism akin to that experienced between and after the two world wars – a 'Second Spring' or 'Catholic Moment' – it remains the case that in this century (and the last) English-speaking, cradle Catholics have contributed little to higher thought and culture. The great and oft cited figures such as G. K. Chesterton, Compton Mackenzie, Eric Gill, David Jones, Arnold Lunn, Christopher Dawson, Ronald

Knox, Evelyn Waugh, Graham Greene, Walker Percy and Thomas Merton, were *all* converts – as in my own field (philosophy) have been the leading Catholics thinkers: Jacques Maritain, Gabriel Marcel, Frederick Copleston, Elizabeth Anscombe, Peter Geach, Michael Dummett and Alasdair MacIntyre. So it continues: in journalism, John Wilkins of *The Tablet*, Clifford Longley formerly of *The Times*, Charles Moore of *The Daily Telegraph*; in literature, Muriel Spark and Alice Ellis Thomas, and so on – all are converts! Whatever it is that attracts these people to Catholicism, we must ask whether Catholic schools and colleges succeed in transmitting it to their own pupils and students. I fear they do not. In fact, I see evidence of their continuing to abandon those features of Catholic faith and culture that have attracted – and continue to attract – good and thoughtful converts.

At any rate there was much grumbling at the aforementioned conference. Indeed an auction developed reminiscent of the Monty Python 'Self-Made Yorkshiremen' sketch, with successive speakers outbidding one another in their accounts of the privation and cruelty of their upbringings. In the Python scene the recounted deprivations were material, but at the conference the miseries were those of having a Catholic identity. As well as suggesting an amusing parallel, this appears odd in two ways. First, it is somewhat difficult to believe that the reports were accurate and not the familiar exaggerations of group-therapy sessions. Second, this construal of the idea of Catholic identity is self-obsessively socio-biographical. Religious identities are more properly to be thought of in terms of founding scriptures, declared doctrines, authoritative teachings, established liturgies and spiritual traditions. Yet of these the conference participants had literally nothing to say. This omission may be construed as a real sign of a failed Catholic education (for further discussion, see Haldane, 1996).

It is worth comparing such views with that presented by another convert, this time a figure of the old (socialist) left. In 1979 Brian Wicker wrote a piece entitled 'Adult Education' for *The Tablet*. In this he describes his feelings at being admitted to the Church nearly thirty years previously, in 1950:

> One was joining something which put a strange gulf between oneself and the world as one knew it.... I discovered there were people about me who lived by vows (of poverty, chastity and obedience) so strange and extraordinary that in meeting them I felt I was moving into another world. Until then I had thought only remote people of moral genius, like Tolstoy and Ghandi, lived by renunciations as total as that in the modern world. Now I found they existed in absurd places like Birmingham or Peckham Rye. One could actually meet them. What is more, the ordinary Catholic in the street lived a hidden life by which he shared, in his own way, that amazing world. For example, by being solemnly committed to attending mass every Sunday without fail, whatever other so called 'commitments' he might have....
>
> (Wicker, 1979, p. 18)

I shall return to the difference between Wicker's appreciation and the attitudes of the conference participants in due course. But first let me say something very general about what ought to be the fundamentals of any Catholic philosophy of education.

Starting at the end

Briefly stated, the main point of a Catholic education should be to lay down the foundations of a good life and of a good death. The pagan Romans could say '*Mors ianua vitae*' (death is the gateway to life); yet these days many Catholics seem more disposed to say 'life the gateway to personal self-fulfilment'. The four last things: death, judgment, heaven and hell are in danger of being seen as unhelpful and perhaps removable intrusions from the Dark Ages. But life in the natural order is conditioned by death and human activity should be measured against this end. It is not morbid to think often of mortality when the point of doing so is to reflect back on one's present condition and actions. It might be said that those best love life who know its meaning, and since for the Christian a key to its meaning is the inescapable fact of death, no one can love life who seeks to deny its finitude.

It is within this context that a Catholic philosophy of education should be developed. Education is an activity or process. As such it is defined by its goal, what it aims to achieve. Chesterton had this in mind when he wrote that 'Education is only truth in a state of transmission' and immediately raised the rhetorical question 'how can we pass on truth if it has never come into our hand?' (Chesterton, 1910).[1] For Aristotle and Aquinas the theory of education belongs to the domain of practical reason, and both philosophers had a definite view of how such reason should proceed. First, define as best you can your ultimate aim; revision and refinement will come later. Next, ask what has to be the case for this to be realised: let us call this the 'ultimate realisation conditions'. Now consider what needs to be done in order to bring these about. Next, think of what is required in order to effect these intermediary circumstances – this last reflection introduces the 'penultimate realisation conditions'. On goes the reasoning, working backwards until arriving at the present situation.

When conducted with respect to any complex or distant goal, what this sort of exercise in reverse syllogistic usually reveals, is that the various enabling conditions are themselves many and complex, and the processes required to realise them may be many-staged and multi-dimensional. Once one appreciates this, and turns to consider the purpose of human life, namely communion with God, and the role of the Apostles and their successors in bringing people to this goal, it begins to become clear why the Catholic Church is a complex and multi-faceted institution. The destination may be mono-verbally described, viz. heaven; but the journey and the modes of transport reflect the complexity of the human condition

– a condition, it is important to recall, of inherited fallenness; that is, of sin.

The point of these reflections is to suggest that the traditional patterns of Catholic life and formation which those in their forties and older will recall, had their rationale in a definite and well-developed moral theology. Recalling religious texts from the 1950s and before, it is easy to form impressions of dull and doctrinal scholasticism, or of petty rigourism. Of course both may have featured. However, if one actually takes the trouble to look at this material there is much to be found that is both impressive and instructive. Moreover, it is dangerous hubris on our part to suppose that the fruits of two thousand years of doctrinal development and spiritual reflection can be discarded as outmoded impediments to religious well-being. Brian Wicker is no *Daily Telegraph* Tory, or even a 'New Labour' Tory; indeed he and others of the old 'new left' were frequently unwelcome critics of the political conservatism of the hierarchy. However, as the passage quoted earlier makes clear, he saw something sublime in the pre-Conciliar Catholic traditions of spiritual discipline and liturgical devotion. Yet it is precisely this order that the conference participants were keen to distance themselves from. Converts have generally had to overcome ignorance, indifference or hostility to the Church. Thus it is unsurprising that they are often better judges of what is good or bad than are cradle Catholics; nor is it surprising that they are frequently the best apologists for the Faith.

Three into one must go

Before moving on to look at some aspects of traditional spirituality there is a need to sort out some confusions about the nature of religion. As I have pointed out elsewhere (Smart and Haldane, 1996, Sect. 4) there is a marked tendency to distinguish and separate three broad approaches to religious belief: the spiritual, the historical and the philosophical. Those who follow the first emphasise experience, emotion and contemplative reflection; followers of the second concentrate on sacred Scripture and Church tradition; and those partial to the third favour abstract and general argument.

Part of what is implied in distinguishing between these approaches is that there is some kind of tension or opposition between them – or at least that they are in marked contrast to one another. This frequently emerges in people's characterisation of their religious attitudes. Currently, for example, there is a fashion for the spiritual approach, often under the description of personal renewal or integrative healing. Those who are drawn to this will often say that they are not tied to any Church or scriptural revelation but have a more personal or experiential understanding of religion. Such people are also inclined to regard philosophical theology as dry and overly rationalistic. The latter complaint is also voiced by the advocates of Scripture and ecclesial practice, but they take issue with the rootlessness and self-absorbed individualism of new-age spirituality. Finally, the philosophically disposed tend to be suspicious of the uncritical reliance upon emotion and similarly regard Scripture and Church as going far beyond what reason warrants. Readers may recognise themselves in one or other of these portraits.

Doubtless these tendencies reflect differences of personality types, and it is true that each approach appeals to genuine aspects of the religious. However, the division of religion into these three approaches is neither necessary nor desirable. Indeed, I believe that its effect is generally malign and that there is therefore a pressing need to reintegrate the spiritual, the historical and the philosophical.

As a general principle one should not presume that because one approach or form of understanding is available that others are thereby excluded. Not only may they be compatible but one may have to draw upon several or all of them in order to construct an adequate account and practice. Praying for the dead is a characteristic religious activity around which rituals and liturgies have been developed. This does not make philosophical questions about the possibility and nature of an afterlife irrelevant. On the contrary, the meaning of such prayer is given in part by the metaphysical idea that natural death is not the end of personal existence. So if there are philosophical objections to the ideas of disembodiment, reincarnation or resurrection then the point and value of the religious practice is threatened. As St Paul noted in writing to the Corinthians 'if there is no resurrection of the dead then Christ has not been raised... and your faith is in vain' (1 Co).

Similarly, although the 'god of the philosophers' is characterised in abstract terms, as a self-existent, eternal, immutable, omnipotent, omniscient, omnibenevolent, immaterial creator and sustainer of the universe, it is a serious mistake to sever the links between spiritual reflection, revelation and philosophy. Each has a part to play in the task of coming to know, to love and to serve God. In this connection consider St John's Prologue:

> In the beginning was the Word, and the Word was with God, and the Word was God... all things were made through him. And the Word was made flesh and dwelt among us, full of grace and truth. ... And from his fullness we have all received grace upon grace.

In the space of a few lines, John informs the Greeks and the Greek-speaking Jews of Alexandria that what the philosophers had long sought after – the Logos, or the ultimate account of things – has been with God from all eternity and is that through which all things were made; and that this very same Logos was incarnate in Jesus of Nazareth, 'the Way the Truth and the Life'. Thus are philosophy, history and spirituality united. To separate them would diminish each, for what John teaches is at once metaphysical, revelatory and a theme for meditation. A further example, this time from liturgy, supports the same conclusion. Gerard Manley

Hopkins (another convert) gives a fine English rendering of the eucharistic hymn traditionally ascribed to Aquinas. The first two verses run as follows:

> Godhead here in hiding whom I do adore,
> Masked by these bare shadows, shape and nothing more;
> See, Lord, at thy service low lies here a heart,
> Lost all lost in wonder at the God thou art.
>
> Seeing, touching, tasting are in thee deceived;
> How says trusty hearing? That shall be believed;
> What God's Son has told me, take for truth I do;
> Truth himself speaks truly, or there's nothing true.
>
> (Gardner and MacKenzie, 1970, p.211)

What is believed of the consecrated host rests upon the words of Scripture. The text itself is a testimony of personal and ecclesial belief couched in poetic terms and adverting to the philosophico-theological doctrine of the real presence.

Some religious believers take pride and comfort in the idea that their faith owes nothing to reason, historical testimony or doctrinal authority. Perhaps they believe that by treating their belief as a personal relationship with God they incur fewer troublesome burdens. However, such an attitude is quite alien to the central traditions of Western and Eastern Christianity (as it is to those of Judaism and Islam). The three monotheistic faiths are all religions 'of the book'; but neither value nor sense can be attached to the idea of discerning and trusting the word of Scripture unless it is possible to specify which writings and interpretations are to be accepted and which rejected. Every faith of 'the book' presupposes some sort of canon of authentic and authoritative Scripture, and one need only ask the question of how such a canon came to be determined, ratified and transmitted and how it would be defended against rivals, to realise the ineliminable role of reason and general understanding.

G. K. Chesterton said of philosophy that it is 'merely thought that has been thought out' and added that 'man has no alternative, except between influence by thought that has been thought out and being influenced by thought that has not been thought out' (Chesterton, 1950).[2] Holy Scripture together with the Creeds and biblical spirituality which it inspired are religious experience that has been thought out. Nothing less would be worth transmitting across the centuries, and nor should the religiously disposed settle for anything else. The spiritual, the historical and the philosophical are no more separable in reality than are the three sides of a triangle or, dare I say it, the three persons of the Trinity.

Religious knowledge and religious education

Accordingly, however Catholic education (at any level) proceeds, it needs to attend to the integration of these three aspects of faith. The ultimate concern on this occasion is with the spiritual, but the others are equally important and my sense is that we are failing in our educational task with regard to them. It used to be the case that Catholics knew that the Church placed great emphasis on reason and that theology was closely identified with philosophy. They were aware of the great figures of the Middle Ages, such as Aquinas and Bonaventure, and they knew in very broad terms the two main styles of argument for the existence of God: from the contingency of the world and from the order within it. They had some sense of the Catholic argument against the Protestant doctrines of the exclusivity of Scripture, and of salvation by faith alone.

Of course their knowledge in these matters was from testimony and they deferred to the expertise of others. But that is no disqualification. In general, think of how little of what we know, we are in a position to confirm by our own efforts. In any society there is division of labour by competence, and this is true also with regard to matters religious. Just as my scientific knowledge rests on the say of others whom I take to be (sufficiently) expert, so my knowledge of dogma is based on the word of those who have it from those who know. Certainly this assumes that someone somewhere does know or that the knowledge is set down and may be recovered, but it ill behoves a Catholic, as it would not a sceptic, to deny this. The following counsel of prudence may be recommended to all Catholics: 'Cultivate the habit of thinking that if the Church teaches it as a matter of faith and morals then somewhere there is a good case for it drawn from revelation, tradition or natural reason'. This may seem utterly obvious, but there are many who would regard what I have said as intellectually naive and as encouraging an attitude of docility. Well, the more I pursue questions of doctrine the more I am impressed by the richness of the Church's resources, and so far as docility is concerned, it is a virtue whose corresponding vice is ineducability. Better to be teachable than not!

Similar points of contrast may be drawn in relation to historic practice. It once was the case that Catholic children had developed in them a reverence for the sacraments and the liturgy. This effect was produced through a variety of means: by pious devotions, modes of dress and behaviour, stories of heroic devotion and so on. One benefit of these efforts was to prepare them for the idea that amidst the ordinariness of life there were channels of transcendence. It is much easier for a child to believe that God is present on the altar if the setting is physically special, if the demeanour of older children and adults is reverential, and if the priest later takes evident care to clean the vessels and consume the residue of the body and blood of Christ.

Talk of the Mass as a family meal encourages quite different ways of thinking. It is unsurprising when later in life those raised in the 'get-together-with-Jesus' style wonder why the Church should make so much fuss about restricting the Eucharist to Christians in communion with Catholicism. Again, they are liable to regard caution against participation in the religious services of other denominations as mean and prejudiced. It is as if having been taken regularly to McDonald's one were to be told that one's friends who eat at Burger King are not free to share one's meal, and moreover that one should not eat there oneself. This is liable to seem ' Burgophobic'. Yet the well-educated Catholic knows better. The Mass is not a religious service, nor is it a family meal, nor a community feast. It is an event in which heaven and earth come together, as mundane time and sacred time are united. In it the sacrifice of Jesus Christ, a Divine Person, is made really present – not re-enacted or remembered, but made actually present as a means of sacrifice by which our sins and those of humankind generally are atoned. He is the Messiah for whom the Jews longed and for whom many still wait, whose voluntary death opened the gates of heaven and who is presented to us as the priest speaks the words of consecration. Children cannot be taught this sacred doctrine all at once, but they should be taught it rather than the deflationary, desacralising account of the Mass as a devotional service akin to that of other religions.

It may be suggested that these recommendations would make Catholicism seem esoteric, supernaturalist and exclusive, whereas we should be celebrating the complexity and beauty of the natural order and opening children's eyes to the universally shared features of all religions. Certainly creation is wonderful, but in order to appreciate the extent of its glory one has to understand how limited are scientific and naturalistic accounts of it. The most compelling evidence for God's existence comes precisely as one realises that the natural order is not self-explanatory and that preternatural causes are effective in it. The 'supernatural', as Catholics should know, is not a scientific, quasi-scientific or metaphysical category; rather it is a theological one pertaining to the order of Divine Grace. This, not spooky magic, is what is made available through the sacraments. Furthermore, it is exclusive in as much as it is not generally available in all religions – unlike French fries in fast-food outlets – and in so far as it is freely and electively bestowed by God and is not an entitlement to all who feel benignly disposed towards the universe or to the ground of its being. If these matters have been confused or lost sight of it may be because too much attention has been afforded comparative religious education and too little given to Catholic religious knowledge.

The sacrament of the present moment

So on to spirituality; or rather a return to it, since it has been implicit in things said already, and the point of the section on the three approaches to religion was to argue that the spiritual, the historical and the philosophical-cum-theological are aspects of the same reality. Now, however, there is a need to discuss the character of spiritual development and question how it may be communicated to children and others. Earlier it was pointed out that activities and processes are identified by reference to the goals towards which they are aimed – not any old 'as it happens' goals, but their proper objects. The goal, in this sense, of spiritual development is union with God. Such union is in part a mystery, but to the extent that it can be understood it is well described by the great teachers and mystics of the Church. Those more familiar with modern ideas of spirituality might have expected a characterisation of the spiritual goal in terms of becoming a certain kind of person (a fully integrated one, perhaps), or of deepening one's understanding of reality. However, unless these are just elliptical ways of talking about union with the Divine Persons, then they are at best misleading and at worst plain wrong. Certainly, as the journey proceeds the traveller is changed and his or her understanding becomes more profound, but these are effects and not causes or constituent features of increasing proximity to God.

In the past when there was still a lively sense of the strangeness and dangers of unknown terrain, travellers sought out experienced and prudent guides, and where these were not available in person they studied any maps and topographical writings they may have left behind. Thinking, then, of human life as a journey towards

God, it is unsurprising that the Church Fathers and those who succeeded them often used the metaphor of the guide to describe one competent and willing to lead others along the way. In earlier days the names of the great Catholic spiritual writers and the titles of their works would have been fairly well known, even if most people had not read them: Augustine, *On True Religion* and the *Confessions;* Benedict, *Rule of the Master;* Gregory the Great, *Dialogues;* Catherine of Sienna, *Dialogues;* Catherine of Genoa, *Purgation and Purgatory;* Thomas à Kempis, *Imitation of Christ;* Ignatius Loyola, *Spiritual Exercises;* Teresa of Avila, *The Interior Castle;* John of the Cross, *The Dark Night;* Francis de Sales, *Introduction to the Devout Life;* and Jean Pierre de Caussade, *Self-Abandonment to Divine Providence.* At this point in the list it might have been added 'and one could go on'; but there are reasons to hesitate, one being the familiar feature of any list of 'greats' that it is a product of the judgment of time, and the nearer the past the less determinate the judgment. So let this list be left as it stands.

The title of this section is 'The sacrament of the present moment'. That phrase is taken from de Caussade and I will draw my conclusions about the role of spirituality by referring to his work (my knowledge of which I owe to the writings of Fr Benedict Groeschel CFR, 1987). Jean Pierre de Caussade was born in 1675 near Toulouse. At the age of eighteen he entered the Jesuit novitiate there and eleven years later was ordained a priest of the Society. In 1720 he was transferred to preaching missions, and in 1728 was sent to Nancy where he began work as spiritual director to a convent of Visitation Sisters. He left Nancy twice, in 1731 and again in 1739, and after tours of duty in various Jesuit houses he returned to Toulouse as spiritual director, dying there in 1751. Exactly a decade before his death he published *Dialogues on the Various States of Prayer* (De Caussade, 1931), but the works that contain his greatest teachings are the posthumously published letters to the Visitation Sisters, and the treatise known as *Self-Abandonment to Divine Providence.* I will quote from the latter to give the flavour of de Caussade's general guidance:

God still speaks to us today as he spoke to our fathers, when there were no spiritual directors or set methods. Then, spirituality consisted in fidelity to the designs of God. …Then it was enough for those who led a spiritual life to see that each moment brought with it a duty to be faithfully fulfilled. If the work of our sanctification presents us with difficulties it is because we do not look at it in the right way. In reality holiness consists in one thing alone, namely, fidelity to God's plan. And this fidelity is equally within everyone's capacity in both its active and passive practice.

The active practice consists in accomplishing the duties imposed upon us by the general laws of God and the Church, and by the particular state of life which we have embraced. Passive fidelity consists in the loving acceptance of all that God sends us at every moment. Which of these two requirements of holiness is beyond our strength?…. Not active fidelity, since the duties imposed by it cease to be such when they are really beyond our powers…. What excuse can we plead? Yet this is all that God demands of the soul in the work of its sanctification. He demands it from the high and the low, from the strong and the weak; in a word, from all, always and everywhere.

The passive part of holiness is even more easy, for it consists merely in accepting what most frequently cannot be avoided, and in suffering with love, that is to say with resignation and sweetness what is too often endured with weariness and discontent.

Perfection does not consist in understanding God's designs but in submitting to them. …They are God working in the soul to make it like himself. …The whole essence of the spiritual life consists in recognising the designs of God for us at the present moment.

Souls who walk in the light sing the hymns of light, those who walk in darkness, the hymns of darkness. They must both be left to sing to the end the part and the motet which God allots to each.

The more we seem to lose with God, the more we gain; the more he deprives us of the natural, the more he gives of the supernatural. (De Caussade, 1959, pp.3-9)

The meaning of the expression 'the sacrament of the present moment' will be clear. For de Caussade the search for God begins (and in a sense ends) exactly where one is at any given moment. No occult incantations, no esoteric diagrams, no strange exercises, no theatrical props, just a call to sanctity through willing service and acceptance. There is a striking contrast between this and many contemporary calls to spirituality. In, for example, a recent advertisement from a community of a well-established religious order which appeared in an issue of a prominent Catholic periodical: the advertisement featured a circular logo showing three joined figures stretching upwards towards a smaller circle in which a winding road or river heads towards the sun-rayed horizon, and the accompanying text read as follows:

SABBATICAL CHALLENGE FOR WOMEN RELIGIOUS

'Out beyond ideas of wrongdoing and rightdoing there's a field.
I'll meet you there.' – Rumi

- Experiential program; process-oriented
- Call to inner growth; self-empowerment, inner wisdom
- Supportive, loving community; safe environment to grow wholistically[sic]
- Surrounded and supported by a variety of resources

- Powerful, deep healing; loving integration leading to inner freedom

Jalal ad-Din ar Rumi was a thirteenth-century Sufi poet whose disciples formed the fraternity of Mawlawiyah, better known as 'Whirling Dervishes'. While not familiar with the writings of Rumi (the quote is taken from a work entitled *Open Secret*), I suspect that those women religious who respond to the challenge will receive rather different guidance from that offered by Father de Caussade to the Visitation Sisters – but I may be wrong!

Recall Chesterton's remark about education being truth in a state of transmission. Then ask what truths we know about the spiritual state and about how to advance it. Young people at school and college live in times where spirituality is often equated with pantheistic psycho-babble. This generally involves vague injunctions to be 'at one with oneself' and 'develop holistically' in accord with the unity of nature. Like the command to 'do something' these offer little direction and it is hard to think what they could exclude. De Caussade, by contrast, tells us exactly what to do: first, obey God's will as communicated through Holy Scripture and Holy Church; and second, within the structure this creates, accept what comes each moment as part of gracious providence.

The theology of acceptance is at odds with a culture that has extended the idea of consumer rights to the conditions of life itself. A few years ago commentators and politicians wrote of a 'dependency culture' in which people expected resources to come to them from the State. Now we are taught to be self-confident claimants to various moral entitlements. We have rights to be upheld: rights of ownership, of association, of free expression, of respect; in general, rights to fulfilment on terms chosen by ourselves. Ironically, since it wears the mantle of virtue, this ideology of entitlement undermines the notion of an objective moral order, for it treats subjective preferences as the determinants of value. Crudely, what is good (for me) is what I want. Any appeal by others to independent standards of right and wrong then appears as a threat to frustrate my efforts at self-fulfilment. It is, in other words, a violation of my rights.

This twisted logic of entitlement can be seen operating daily in discussions of abortion, adoption, care of the elderly, euthanasia, genetic therapy, human reproduction, sexual orientation and practice, and so on through the familiar list. We are left with the impression that young Catholics are often no better equipped to deal with such issues than are others of their age and general level of education. Given the riches of Church teaching and magisterial moral theology this must be construed as an indictment of educational practice. But I am not blaming the schools as such, for the explanation lies at an earlier stage in the failure to substitute sufficient lay expertise at the level of higher education in place of seminary clerics. In consequence, the current state of religious knowledge among teachers is often frighteningly limited.

There is little point, though, in continuing to condemn the failures of the past. The question is how to make our way forward to something better. One might try to begin with doctrine, or by retelling the story of the Church. Both are important, but before anyone will attend to these they must first be brought to the point of recognising that doctrine and Church form part of a single divine answer to a deep human need – the need to be united in love with an unfailing companion. This is the role of spirituality in education.

The guide identifies the destination and the starting point, and traces the route between them. De Caussade makes the point that we need travel for no longer than the present moment, and for no further than the spot on which we stand. Slow the pace of discussion to this, lower the volume of talk, and teach children to discern what the moment calls for – sometimes action to change the world, sometimes patience to accept it. With these habits acquired, it will quite naturally occur to them to ask what we know about God and of God's will for us. From that point on, education will construct itself in accord with the Aristotelian-Thomistic pattern of practical reasoning, working backwards from ends to means. I have faith that this will bring true happiness and contentment as well as other less important forms of success. Any education that could achieve this would be a great gift to future generations.

NOTES

1. Here it is especially helpful to see Part IV, *Education or the Mistake About the Child*. For a further discussion see Haldane, J. (1990), 'Chesterton's Philosophy of Education' in *Philosophy,* Vol. 65.
2. The section on *The Revival of Philosophy* is interesting here.

CAN THERE BE A CATHOLIC CURRICULUM?

Robert A. Davis

The Catholic curriculum: historical meditations

> It was barely visible: you had to look
> but everything showed him, even the crown of thorns
> in a wood-pigeon's nest
>
> John Burnside, 'R. E.'

In one sense the question with which this essay begins can be met with an unqualified affirmative. The origins of the modern curriculum can be traced, at least in part, to the late medieval and early Renaissance scholastic and humanist concern for the provision of a cycle of studies in which the educated mind acquired the means for coming to terms with 'reality'. For most of Western civilisation, this reality was *comprehended* by the divine truths of the Judaeo-Christian revelation and *apprehended* by the instruments of classical learning, the latter felt by many philosophers and theologians to function as a providentially ordained dispensation with a status little short of the truths of revealed religion (Fletcher, 1997). The general character of scholastic thought bred a synthesis of scriptural exegesis, patristics, and the discrete intellectual disciplines of late antiquity which established the educational diet of the schools and universities throughout Latin Christendom.

Scholasticism throve, however, not because of its attachment to the static, unchanging system of learning caricatured by its later detractors (Adamson, 1926), but precisely because it was born out of the essentially missionary dynamic of the Mendicant Orders whose engagement with a society in upheaval required a reform of the heritage of the ninth-century Carolingian educators. Methodologically, scholastic reform of older educational practices can be seen in the thirteenth-century renovation of the archaic processes of *questiones* and *responsiones* – structured questions and answers applied to the exploration of Scripture – and in the subsequent formulation of scholasticism's most achieved pedagogy, the *disputatio*, which evolved out of the older forms of the *lectio* and the *questio*, by the addition of the decisive contribution of the master, the *conclusio*. If the scholastic method thereby refurbished the teaching and learning styles of antiquity, it did so whilst maintaining a profoundly Christian sense of the individual's intellectual and ethical responsibility before God (Le Goff, 1988).

Curricular reform in the high and late Middle Ages involved a parallel emphasis on the formation of the individual mind through the union of reason and faith. The classical division of the *trivium* and the *quadrivium* maintained the presence in the school curriculum of the same seven subjects for something like a thousand years (Kristeller, 1972), but teaching friars faced with the varied and complex educational needs of the growing urban centres quickly recognised, in the words of Vergerius, that 'the choice of studies will depend to some extent upon the character of individual minds' (Woodward, 1963, p. 9). The pursuit of a validating authority for the content of the curriculum thus identified scholasticism not with fixity and permanence, but with a critical search for forms of communication which would uphold the truths of divine revelation sustained by reason in the context of the shifting intellectual and social frontiers of medieval civilisation.

The content of the *trivium*, in particular, became a controversial point of focus for the scholastic commitment to its own self-renewal in the name of reason. The foundational function of grammar remained relatively unaltered throughout the Middle Ages, but the teaching of the higher linguistic disciplines of logic and rhetoric was always potentially divisive, and can be said to have precipitated what might be described as the first great crisis of the Catholic curriculum from around the middle of the fourteenth century. The dilemma came down broadly to the question of human experience: should rhetoric concern itself simply with the ancient techniques of persuasion (following the classical models), or should it attend to matters of content drawn from the study of logic, moral philosophy, theology and the so-called 'new learning'? The conflict was, among other things, a generational one, because the champions of the new learning were younger men dissatisfied with the schoolroom models through which classical learning had been mediated to them, and for whom an appreciation of vernacular art and language was becoming increasingly important. Ironically, disputes about the *trivium* impacted very directly on the school curriculum because the key elements of the *trivium* figured prominently in the teaching of children aged between ten and sixteen. In the fourteenth century the spread of elementary schools attached to the chapels of guilds and lay associations complicated the linkages between the Church, the community and educational activity, enlarging further the potential for conflict between rival versions of the curriculum.

It was once a commonplace of educational historiography to simplify the pattern of change in late medieval and early Renaissance education into a series of polarities of old and new, logic and rhetoric, scholastic and humanist, contemplative and social, hierarchical and republican – even school and university. While it is certainly true in the words of Walter Ong that 'logic and rhetoric correspond to the basic polarity in life' and to acknowledge their shaping influence on Western culture (1971, p. 7), it is an oversimplified view which argues that at the dawn of the Renaissance a fossilised, atrophied scholasticism met a vigorous humanism in which were held the seeds of the modern, secular age (Seigel, 1968). Post-Enlightenment and sometimes anti-clerical histories of European educational thought make much of this imagined dichotomy, obscuring both the extent to which scholastic procedures interacted with humanist speculation, and the effectiveness with which a Christian humanist vision carried forward the best traditions of medieval scholasticism into the new learning and the needs of a burgeoning mercantile society (Cassirer, 1964; Blumenberg, 1983; Ullmann, 1977). The core of the humanists' *studia humanitatis* can be found in the library canon or 'reading list' of the reforming founder of the Vatican Library, Pope Nicholas V (whose Bull established the University of Glasgow in 1451), and included grammar, rhetoric, history and moral philosophy. Similarly, Aeneas Sylvius Piccolomini, later as Pius II (1458-64), the humanist Pope *par excellence*, in his book *Concerning the Education of Children* emphasised for the schools the vital importance to the *trivium* of philosophy, dialectic, prose composition, vernacular writing, and literature, for 'Literature is our guide to the true meaning of the past, to a right estimate of the present, to a sound forecast of the future' (Woodward, op. cit., p. 141).

From the perspective of the question with which this essay is primarily concerned, what is important about these initiatives is the clear confirmation they provide that an ecclesiastically sponsored curriculum of study not only endured through centuries of change, but proved itself adaptable, renewable and indeed instrumental in directing and interpreting that change. This is not to suggest that the development of the late medieval and early modern curriculum was a seamless process. Conflict, loss of confidence, fear of the unfamiliar, and still more culpable forms of reaction and repression undeniably inscribe the curriculum with what Ong calls 'the density of history' (Ong, op. cit., p. 7). Knowledge is invariably caught up in the discursive struggle by which power and authority distribute their influence and exercise their control over human affairs – but this is a feature of educational experience in all epochs and under every jurisdiction, whether sacred or secular. Too frequently the achievements of scholastic humanism are distorted or ignored in the service of a simplistically secular ideology of progress which represents the new learning as a breach with the past and as the beginning of an emancipatory separation of faith and reason presaging the enlightened, anthropocentric educational systems of the modern era which exist seemingly free from the dead hand of religious belief (Toulmin, 1990).

A subtler reading of the growth and development of its content and its purposes through the late medieval and early Renaissance periods shows that a creatively theocentric curriculum in dialogue with the wisdom of both past and present could maintain the truths of the Christian gospel without becoming isolationist or introspective. An incarnational theology indeed demanded engagement with the lived experience of the world, and at its best nurtured a curriculum that was Catholic in the fullest sense: committed to the Thomistic axiom that all knowledge is one, and wedded to the belief that the human subject is formed in mysterious contemplation of the symbolic order of being and the free self-disclosure of the loving God (von Balthasar, 1988).

The later, undeniable fragmentation of this vision of the Catholic curriculum, and the faltering of the existential accounts of knowledge and truth on which it was based, have complex origins. In part the consequence of divisions within Christendom itself, and also the result of far-reaching social and economic transformations, the demise of the scholastic and early humanist systems of knowledge and understanding has still deeper roots. Impulses within Renaissance humanist thought which sought a more detailed and authentic immersion in the pagan language and philosophy of the ancients began to alter the inherited categories of logic and rhetoric, reorganising the mental dispositions by which reality was approached and placing greater emphasis on individualistic concepts such as will and empirical observation. Shifts in the use of capital and property requiring the increased use of the written word at the expense of oral tradition led slowly to what Le Goff has termed 'The desacralisation of the book' (Le Goff, op. cit., p. 346). The invention of printing intensified this process by widening immensely the availability of the authors upon whose writings the operation of the curriculum depended, and by multiplying incalculably the rival versions of curricular planning circulating around the schools and universities. The consequent proliferation of competing ideas culminated in a fundamental assault on the central tenets of scholasticism by the new systems of classification championed by thinkers such as Rudolph Agricola and Peter Ramus. The major effect of these critiques was to create the spatialised epistemology which, in the view of many commentators, marks the irrevocable rupture with the Middle Ages and inaugurates the chief heuristic paradigm of modernity (Pickstock, 1998).

We see the older curriculum yield no more decisively than in the realm of human endeavour destined subsequently to be recognised as both the unimpeachable hallmark of modernity and the antithesis of metaphysics and religion: science. Behind the manifold forms of scholasticism lay the famous formula of St Anselm, *Fides quaerens intellectum*, faith itself seeking understanding. The younger men of the mid-fourteenth century who sought what they perceived to be a more authentic engagement with the procedures of classical enquiry steadily undermined the concept of authority on which the Anselmian formula rested, introducing a new emphasis on the search for proofs, and on the use of observation and experimentation. This shift in sensibility was brought about largely by social changes which saw the admission to the schools and universities of men drawn from a wider social base, with occupational links to manual labour and the mechanical arts. These scholars accorded a steadily higher respect to what they termed *scientia experimentalis*. They took their inspiration not from Aquinas but from Duns Scotus and Roger Bacon, establishing the priority of the will in the operations of theoretical and practical reason (Funkenstein, 1986), and installing at the heart of the curriculum an overarching concern for autonomous empiricism which would prove seminal for the rise of technology in the development of educational practice.

Once again, dominant secular histories of these dramatic transformations in the intellectual climate of Western learning have tended to present the rise of the scientific worldview and its incorporation into the curriculum as a fundamental leap in human advancement, freeing human thought from the shackles of superstition and obscurantism. This version of events was promulgated by the early apologists for the age of science and scientific method such as Francis Bacon and Robert Boyle. It still regularly finds its way into popular understanding of the history of science through the writings and broadcasts of influential and avowedly anti-religious propagandists such as Richard Dawkins (1995).

That the scientific revolution secured for (some) human beings a previously undreamed of access to the truths of the operations of nature, and that its technological applications have given us an astonishing capacity to control and manipulate our environment, are issues not in question – provided, of course, we recognise that the fruits of science have had embedded within them from their beginning the destructive spores of scientific hubris. What does require a more differentiated interpretation is the naive myth of human progress on which the dominant account of the rise of science is too frequently predicated. For the purposes of the present argument it is certainly important to recognise that the undoubted failure of the early humanist curriculum to embrace the scientific method contributed seriously to the damaging separation of faith and reason which led subsequently to the marginalisation of the Catholic worldview in the formation of the secular, Enlightened, modern curriculum. The experience of this separation, however, does not of itself imply an irremediable split between science and Catholic theology. Nineteenth- and twentieth-century educational innovations have shown that the division between faith and scientific reason is both unnecessary and heretical, and that the precise causes of the breakdown in the dialogue of Catholicism and the scientific revolution therefore warrant closer historical inspection. The failure of the Church at the supreme moment of historical opportunity to articulate a humanistic vision open to the operations of science, while lamentable, may in fact have stemmed not from a hostility to the extension of human reason, but from a more profound – even justifiable – quarrel with the anti-scholastic theory of knowledge and the intellect out of which the scientific method emerged and which continued to stamp it until comparatively recently (Alliez, 1996). Its dispute with these fundamental epistemological prejudices of modernity may in fact be one of the most valuable and radical challenges the Catholic mind has made to secular society.

Reformation thought deepened existing cultural and educational fissures by further discrediting scholasticism and by annexing aspects of scientific materialism to its anti-Catholic polemics. Some scholars have gone so far as to suggest that the rapprochement between Reformation theology and science, and the consequent recognition of science within the curriculum of Reformed schools and universities, contributed to the incredible commercial and imperial successes of the Protestant powers in the centuries which followed (Kennedy, 1988). Above all, the developments of the seventeenth century helped shape a later, stereotypical view that Catholic teaching was fundamentally inimical to science and that the eventual acceptance of the study of science and technology into the Catholic curriculum was forced upon Catholic institutions by the irresistible pressures of history and economics, and under circumstances of unease, suspicion and mutual incomprehension.

These early modern developments also completed the process whereby the concept of 'the Catholic curriculum' came to be regarded by educational philosophers (such as John Locke) as anachronistic and moribund. In their eyes, Catholicism had nothing to donate to educational progress, but was inescapably associated with authoritarianism and the repression of free enquiry. 'Science' in this context served, of course, only as an exemplification of all those new species of thought and reason with which Catholic belief was felt to be incompatible. This meant that at precisely the time something approaching a philosophy of education began to exercise the minds of the Enlightenment in the European centres of ideas, Catholic educational thought had been effectively banished, prohibited from influencing meaningfully the rationale of the emerging educational consensus.

The loss of vigour and direction of the great Catholic-humanist enterprise of the late medieval and Renaissance periods did not mean, however, a complete collapse of the Catholic vision of the curriculum, any more than the rise of science entailed the eclipse of Christianity in the schools and universities. One of the most important and wide ranging of the Counter-Reformation reforms of the humanist curriculum was that of the Jesuits – the *Ratio Studiorum* – completed in 1586 and ratified in 1599. Jesuit education, later destined to be the target of much Enlightenment scorn, demonstrated the enduring vitality of the Catholic curriculum and its potential for renewal. Characterised by a missionary zeal unknown since the heyday of the friars, Jesuit teaching not only recast the old humanism, but began the process of recontextualising it in a serviceably modern form, receptive to the best insights of the new learning (Scaglione, 1986). Loyola himself set forth an encompassing educational system from elementary to degree level, including a restructured version of the traditional curriculum based upon the Humanities (Grammar, Rhetoric, Ancient Languages and Literature), Logic (which included Mathematics) and Philosophy (Natural and Moral, Metaphysics, Theology, Scripture). The last of these divisions proved particularly hospitable to the new scientific learning flooding Europe and quickly became the principal mechanism by which the Jesuit schools acquired their unique reputation for training in the secular disciplines. Jesuit teachers became adept at absorbing and reframing secular knowledge and discovery, accommodating it to the philosophical scheme of their total curriculum. The Jesuit 'method' can also be said to have introduced many other features of teaching we are accustomed to seeing as peculiarly modern and secular – including timetabling, gradings, working in groups, homework and a system of annual examinations.

In the longer perspective, Jesuit education performed more than merely a maintenance function. Jesuit missionaries and teachers, and those countless others influenced by the witness of the Society of Jesus in education, were destined to bequeath to the modern age – and, ultimately, to the era of mass schooling – a coherent, credible vision of a Catholic curriculum of value and relevance to industrial society. This achievement, however distinctive its legacy, must be seen, nevertheless, in the wider context of developments in Enlightenment educational philosophy, with which Jesuit and broader Catholic practice had a deeply ambivalent relationship.

The Enlightenment as suppressor

As suggested earlier, strains within the ancient Catholic curriculum of study colluded at its demise, giving rise over the longer period to the dissociation of faith and reason in Europe's major seats of learning and the schools which fell within their orbits. Institutional Christianity, of course, retained a formidable hold over all types of formal education in Catholic and Reformed countries. Frequently education continued to be carried out under ecclesiastical supervision; scripture and divinity remained vital subjects of study and training; ordained ministers occupied key positions of authority; the influence of Latin remained pervasive. Neither alone nor in sum, however, did these factors amount to a Catholic or indeed Christian curriculum which would have been recognised by the scholastics or the early humanists. Increasingly, as systems of knowledge became more separate and specialised, the identifiably Christian or Catholic elements were localised to specific areas of the curriculum (heralding the coming of 'Religious Education'), confined to named disciplines, or assigned to courses of study deliberately designed for clerical formation. At the same time, classical learning, despite the almost uncontested preservation of its status in the education of the young, lost forever its links with an avowedly Christocentric metaphysics, assuming, instead, an aesthetic, moral and antiquarian character.

Enlightenment philosophers such as Diderot and Rousseau welcomed and hastened these processes in their desire to construct a rational curriculum aligned to what they believed to be the ascertainable and universal shape of human nature. The kinds of curricula they advanced were not deliberately irreligious, but what they offered, in effect, was an alternative religion, one based on the application of reason to the amelioration of the human condition, determined by a view of the human subject and his place in the cosmos disenchanted by history and empirical observation, and marked by the repudiation of much traditional custom and hierarchy. Enlightenment educational principles thus sought to embrace the autonomy of the individual and the diversity of human behaviour within a conception of 'natural' common experience from which might be derived proper orders of progression and right instruction (Gay, 1967). From the efforts to reconcile these paradoxical impulses there emerged the prescriptivism of a recognisably modern, fully secularised curriculum finally wrested from centuries of intellectual attachment to Christian belief. This is the vision of the curriculum to which the modern school is heir.

One of the most conspicuous consequences of the Enlightenment reformulation of the European educational project has been the steady retrenchment of explicitly religious and expressly Catholic accounts of the curriculum. Catholic education has been forced by the movements of history and ideas to temporise with the succession of Enlightenment versions of the curriculum over the past two centuries. One view of this process sees it as an experience of withdrawal and retrenchment, of

Catholic teaching gradually losing ground to the growth of the modern, technicist curriculum in even those societies where the Church succeeded in retaining a firm hold over educational provision until well into the present century (Hickman, 1995). A parallel process – albeit with slightly different emphases – can be seen in the history of the Reformed Churches' responses to curricular change (Humes, 1980). It may be, however, that this analysis is unduly fatalistic, excessively coloured by the teleological models of the Enlightenment itself, which strives always to write its own history. An alternative interpretation would see in the complex relations of Catholic truth and secular understanding a pattern of mutual critique and negotiation, the outcome of which is far from foreclosed. Indeed, if contemporary post-modern predictions of the unravelling of the Enlightenment settlement are to be believed, the insights of older traditions of thought may be ripe for revaluation (Lyotard, 1984).

The notion of a Catholic curriculum currently provokes a certain level of unease because it threatens to disturb the assumptions built into the latest, dominant version of the Enlightenment curriculum: the liberal-democratic model which, in various guises, has served industrial society through its period of grandest educational expansion for something like a hundred years. Never short of critics from inside its own positions, the liberal-democratic curriculum nevertheless enjoys an unprecedented status in the history of educational thought, having evolved a range of discreet school subjects derived from Enlightenment descriptions of the 'branches of knowledge', which commands enormous respect and sympathy and which has been imitated diligently wherever Western educational values have taken root. More importantly, the liberal-democratic model appears also to have developed a set of underlying core principles which now inform its growth and adaptation in the face of changing social, economic and academic needs. Whatever tensions may be felt in the processes of change and implementation, whatever struggles are evident in the outworking of its internal logic in specific historical conjunctures and local situations, the liberal-democratic curriculum presents itself as in many senses the final form of the curriculum for industrial civilisation. Classic theoreticians of the liberal-democratic model such as R. S. Peters and his followers expound its merits in essentially *ethical* terms (Peters, 1967 and 1973), employing a language which unites the forms of knowledge it seeks to transmit to fundamental concepts of the 'worthwhile'. A principled concern for what is worthwhile in the content of the curriculum shifts the emphasis of educational interest from the subjects of study undertaken by pupils to reflection on the underlying attitudes and beliefs fostered in the learner (Schofield, 1980).

The versatility of this version of the curriculum lies, according to its proponents, in more than simply its inherent capacity to embrace the ever-burgeoning fields of human knowledge which technological civilisation seems destined to generate – remarkable though this potential may be. Instead, it resides primarily in the key principle of validity (itself a characteristic Enlightenment notion), which harmonises epistemology, individual moral and personal fulfilment, and corporate identity and responsibility. Such breadth of vision is what provides the modern secular curriculum, according to Hamlyn, with its potential for pluralism – the sort of pluralism which permits the accommodation of religious and even expressly confessional belief within it (Hamlyn, 1978). Paradoxically, the scope for Catholic teaching within the modern curriculum is, in this account, attributable to Enlightenment traditions of tolerance which root the curriculum in an essentially open and liberal moral framework. This last, intrinsically recuperative move of the liberal-democratic thesis can quite readily be exposed as its culminating ideological gesture: passing off as natural, orders of meaning and signification that are in fact culturally constructed in the interests of prevailing systems of power and authority. Hirst's fulsome defence of the principles of rational enquiry which he sees embedded in the modern, secular curriculum has a similar effect, echoing Peters' argument and for the same apparently noble liberal ends. Seeking to avoid undue prescriptivism of content in the curriculum and its subordination to extrinsic ends, Hirst frames the justification of the content of education in strongly experiential terms, defending a view of knowledge as the pursuit of meaning, structure and intellectual organisation through the learner's acquisition of 'conceptual schema' (Hirst, 1974). This does not mean that the precise subjects of study are mere adornments to the development of the rational faculties, but it does lay stress upon the distinctive procedural features of the separate disciplines, and in so doing allies the curriculum to the great classificatory taxonomies of the Enlightenment through which it was believed the integrated individual might be formed (Bloom, 1964).

The experiential and pluralist nature of the modern liberal-democratic curriculum appears to open it to the claims of religiously motivated educators because of its celebrated concern for 'the whole person'. Almost all post-Enlightenment versions of the curriculum have been marked by a 'gap', a variously labelled 'space', the existence of which can be traced directly to the Enlightenment quarrel with *ancien régime* Christianity and the earnest attempts to retrieve from this some kind of moral or theistic absolute rooted in a reverence for the transcendent yet purged of the alleged abuses of institutional religion. Most of these efforts have been farcical, some tyrannical (Schama, 1989, pp. 831-36), but their educational legacy has been complex and enduring. The inscription of values at the centre of the secular curriculum has been inseparable from a concern with what has been repeatedly (indeed depressingly) configured as 'the spiritual'. An early defender of the British post-war educational reforms, Eric James, expressed the consensus view of the matter when he included as a criterion for measuring the effectiveness of the curriculum concern '[T]hat an area of study may contribute to the spiritual development of the individual' (James, 1949, p. 33). James' own explanation of the meaning of the term predictably retreats from openly religious definitions into 'the satisfaction of the highest intellectual, moral and aesthetic capacities'. A more recent gloss is still more apologetic:

> We may quite reasonably use the word spiritual to refer to such emotional aspects as aesthetic appreciation. By doing so we move away from the physical but we do not become involved in metaphysical speculation. We do not begin to ask such questions as 'What is God?'; instead we enter the areas of art and music.
>
> (Schofield, op. cit., p. 124f)

Embarrassment about the spiritual – stemming, undoubtedly, from a vague post-Enlightenment nostalgia for the sacred, an ill-defined sense that reason alone cannot minister human fulfilment – persists into the most recent statements about the overall aims of the contemporary curriculum and its aspirations for human growth (Scottish Consultative Council on the Curriculum, 1995; Scruton, 1990). In all of its manifold expressions, however, this intuition of spiritual absence – even hunger – refuses serious engagement with the outrageous possibility that the spiritual can only be meaningfully encompassed in the context of the liturgical community; a site where the language of the holy possesses genuine currency, and where spiritual development is not confined to the edifying effects of the arts, but is sought in the experience of the total curriculum and the access it affords to the hierarchy of God's creation. The implications of this narrowness of outlook are clear. Whatever its pluralist credentials, in the eyes of the liberal-democratic model, to be Catholic is to be outdated.

It must be appreciated that Catholic educational theory and practice have for the last century or so largely accepted the dominant propositions of the various inflections of the

Enlightenment curriculum. This was perhaps inevitable in view of the social and intellectual changes which have overtaken the Church in this turbulent period, amidst the increasing state sponsorship of education throughout the industrialised world. Local tensions involving specific areas of content or points of emphasis have been many, but they cannot disguise a process of conciliation which appears at face value to bear out the pluralist claims of the modern curriculum and illustrate its openness to difference and diversity. The Church has on the whole taken full advantage of the politics of educational tolerance, negotiating a position of acceptance which has on the one hand eschewed isolationism and on the other sought assiduously to highlight the positive contribution Catholic schools can make to educational attainment and civil harmony (McLaughlin *et al.*, 1996).

The position thus earned for Catholic schools in civil society is almost universally perceived to be an honourable one, and this must indeed be seen as a significant achievement for Catholics given the many brands of hostility they have had to overcome to reach this point. A balanced critique of the resultant compromise, however, calls for searching scrutiny of some of the costs involved for any residual notion of the Catholic curriculum that might have survived the secularising ideologies of the last two centuries. It can be argued that the price Catholic schools have had to pay for their accreditation as appropriate centres for the delivery of the modern curriculum is a restriction of their Catholicity to those features of school life where secular society is prepared to permit the manifestation of Catholic ideas – mainly worship, ethos and Religious Education (including sacramental preparation). Catholic schools have rightly won much acclaim in recent times for their ground-breaking work on ethos and identity, including an ethic of service widely imitated by non-Catholic institutions (Hull, 1982). They are also renowned in many countries for both standards of academic achievement and care of the individual pupil. Similarly, the teaching of Religious Education in Catholic schools is in many places acclaimed by religious leaders and pedagogues (O'Leary, 1983). In many respects, although the struggle to assert religious truths in an increasingly post-Christian world goes on, Catholic schools have accepted the basic terms that the liberal-democratic polity offers for their continuance, amongst which is a wholesale affirmation of the curriculum and the forms of knowledge of late technological society.

Some of the reasons for this concordat between Catholic education and the secular curriculum lie in the assimilationist tendencies which have marked Catholic intellectual life in the economically advanced nations of the developed world since the Second Vatican Council. In part a justifiable reaction to the conservative neo-scholasticism of the first half of the century which sought to galvanise Catholic thought for wholesale opposition to modernism, assimilationism has emphasised Catholic engagement with the world and aimed to establish dialogue with the key centres of intellectual activity in secular society (Gleason, 1995). At the level of schools, the assimilationist movement blurred the distinctiveness of Catholic identity, to project an image of the Catholic school as progressive, caring, academically respectable and wedded to the secular goals of material progress. This was especially the case where Catholic schools had an important role in the education of social élites or of targeted groups among the disadvantaged (McLaren, 1986). Assimilationism meant doing the same things as secular schools, only better. In an era when, for example, certain Protestant evangelical schools rejected the teaching of evolutionary theory, Catholic schools were able to distance themselves from scriptural fundamentalism and mainstream their teaching and learning in the sciences. Recognisably a positive outcome, what was overlooked in this action was that Catholic affirmation of the theory of natural selection derived from a much larger theology of Creation, and a Catholic anthropology, which were rarely taught to anyone outside a seminary. The necessary rejection of neo-scholasticism, moreover, entailed an unfortunate loss of a perhaps poorly formulated but nevertheless crucial principle of curricular integration with which the pre-Conciliar twentieth-century Church had set out to address the cultural crisis of the age and restore a much-needed sense of unity to intellectual endeavour.

Towards the possibility of a Catholic curriculum

The near total abandonment by Catholic curriculum theorists of what Maritain called 'integral humanism' is reflected in many recent otherwise laudable defences of the merits of Catholic education. These for the most part either pass over the curriculum in silence or else make reassuring statements about the normative content of all that is taught in Catholic schools outside the RE department. Bryk and his colleagues go so far as to state that 'Contemporary Catholic educational philosophy actually shares much common ground with postmodern social thought' (Bryk *et. al.*, 1993, p. 321), and relate this to the Catholic school's theological scope for 'enculturation', which means a positive disposition towards the cultural forms of specific social and ethnic groups. Upholding the dignity of the human person is certainly a fundamental tenet of the enterprise of Catholic education, and this of course means respecting difference. But it must surely also imply a much deeper process of reflection on the content of what is taught and the framework of knowledge and understanding in which that content inheres. Many Catholic schools in the British Isles, for example, are famous for their resolute defence of the rights of the unborn, yet no one seems to ask if the presuppositions of technological instrumentalism by which the teaching of science subjects are driven are somehow implicated in secular society's attitudes to the unborn. Catholic teaching has always argued that issues of value penetrate all systems of knowledge regardless of the local circumstances in which these systems are 'enculturated'.

The fear of seeming backward and reactionary also inhibits a more radical analysis of the curriculum taught in Catholic schools. There is an understandable reluctance to appear 'deviant' or censorious in ways which might be seen as reminiscent of the infantile prohibitions of the Index. The academic credibility Catholic schools have earned seems sometimes a fragile thing, under constant scrutiny by libertarian watchdogs and opponents of denominational education. The young Terry Eagleton urged, in the 1960s, the rejection of the concept of a Catholic curriculum, insisting that notions of Catholic history or science were delusory and damaging because they harked back to an era of social and intellectual regulation which the post-war reforms had swept away (Eagleton, 1967). Patrick Walsh has since suggested in fairly modest terms that the Catholic school can reasonably aspire to what he names 'A Contemplative Curriculum' in specific subject areas such as history, the arts and even science, but only if the construction of such a curriculum is assisted by canons of taste and judgment extrinsic to the school and to Catholic tradition (Walsh, 1983). Walsh writes stimulatingly about prospects for the study of 'science as food for the soul' and 'history as piety', but in his historical survey of Catholic educational policy since 1965, James Arthur rightly finds himself perplexed by the lack of 'substance or concrete application to the content of the Catholic school curriculum' in the few specific proposals Walsh makes. Arthur acknowledges that 'adherence to Catholicism should make a difference to the focus and content of the curriculum in Catholic schools' (Arthur, 1995, p. 174), but can find little worthwhile detail in the submissions to emerge so far from consideration of the issue, principally because it has not yet received the depth of investigation by theologians and practitioners which it requires.

If this assessment is correct, then it confronts Catholic educators with an urgent task: envisioning a theology of the curriculum which reconnects the content of what is taught and learned in the contemporary school to a unified, coherent Catholic philosophy of knowledge, what Newman termed 'the skein of thought', upon which all sound learning is predicated. It invites all those involved in the development of the curriculum to match the efforts of recent years which have been devoted to the formation of the Catholic ethos with equally rigorous scrutiny of the detail of what is taught in the subject areas for which they are responsible. The dangers in such an initiative, incorrectly implemented, are manifold. Rehabilitation of an authentically Catholic curriculum must not be seen as retreat from the complex challenges of modernity; it must not lead to a 'remnant' mentality. It needs to be a dynamic affirmation of the truth claims of Catholic anthropology, shared in charity, humility and dialogue with the surrounding polity. It must avoid any suggestion of academic surveillance or exclusivity, and offer, instead, the questing intellect supported by the fruits of the tradition, exhibiting all that is best and most open from the deposits of Catholic learning and from the recovery of the rich humanistic pedagogy of the evangelising orders.

What might such a revamped Catholic curriculum look like? Walsh's comments on the specific disciplines and Groome's definitions of distinctiveness (Groome, 1996) are certainly very useful here. In keeping with the synthesising spirit of the scholastics, the shape of the Catholic curriculum would have to be determined from the inside, moulded by the Catholic scientists, mathematicians, linguists, historians and teachers of all kinds whose witness generates the life of the Catholic school. It would have to be a theologically informed – a Christocentric – curriculum, suggesting that the initial staff development priority would be renewing the covenant between Catholic teachers and the theology of their faith; a restoration of the bond between the subject areas and the integrated mission of the Catholic school, too frequently, nowadays, shunted into the (unduly capacious) mental spaces of the Religious Education department.

Walsh bravely cites science as one of the key disciplines where the Catholicity of the curriculum could be affirmed. He calls for a celebration of 'the intellectual fecundity of science', highlighting its utilitarian centrality, and its embodiment of rationality in action – features which, properly contextualised, he avers, 'nourish... the child's sense of wonder and admiration at our universe and God's' (Walsh, op. cit., p. 8). He mentions in passing the contribution such an approach to science can make to 'ecological consciousness', and here, quite inadvertently, touches upon what is probably one of the more problematic elements in the implementation of a Catholic curriculum: its adversarial potential. A Catholic understanding of even secondary school science could conceivably seek to contest some of the underlying paradigms of the subject in the name of a responsible and loving regard for God's universe. We might dispute, for example, a materialist account of the life sciences and their increasingly instrumental definitions of the living organisms in general and the human subject in particular. We might wish to encourage pupils to reconsider usually unexamined prevailing models of biological systems such as 'the food chain' – with its unspoken elevation of hierarchy and predatoriness – in the light of alternatives such as 'the web of life', with its emphasis on co-evolution and interdependence (Clark, 1993). Similarly, sociobiological and evolutionary psychological interpretations of human behaviour and the descriptions of consciousness on which they rest – progressing largely unchallenged through the academy and filtering down steadily into schools – might be countered by examining more dynamic, interactive explanations of the phenomena of personhood and relationships. Above all, in our society's dealings with technology the science curriculum ought to be one of the key locations for interrogating the values which are at work subtly redefining the boundaries of the human and binding us ever more problematically to the products of industrial culture. The moral implications for this area are vast, but then so also are the resources on which we have to draw to explore the topics with which it is populated.

If science is the 'hard case' for the Catholic curriculum this must not mislead us into believing that there are 'soft' areas which are effortlessly amenable to the Catholic mind. The tendency to see the arts, for example, as a domain of study with self-evident affinities to the claims of religion merely repeats the Enlightenment aestheticisation of religion criticised above. The Catholic curriculum would certainly articulate a cogent theology of the imagination (Harries, 1993), and it would give due prominence to those works of the imagination which express the Christian sensibility. But a meaningful engagement with literature, music, the fine arts would soon encounter the struggle with ideas, with the intractability of language, with moral and existential dilemmas, with the reality of human joy and pain, that the arts exist to document and mysteriously transfigure. Such an engagement could not be reduced (and rarely was in Catholic history) to approved reading lists or confessional affiliations (Sheed, 1954). It would affirm a James Joyce alongside a Graham Greene, embrace the transgressive alongside the orthodox in the name of the unity of God's truth. The point is, of course, that a fully humanised, strong Catholic curriculum would be unafraid of addressing these profound concerns, assured yet attentive in its exploration of the achievements of human cultures, stoutly opposed, perhaps, to the disfiguring nihilism of post-modernism, but equipped to enter the darkest recesses of the modern condition.

Patrick Walsh's depiction of 'history as piety' postulates in unfortunately all too abbreviated a form an approach to the study of the past predicated on the encounter between the living and the dead. What lies behind his version of history taught in the logic of charity is a commitment to the meaningfulness of the past and our relationship with it. The Catholic history curriculum is not a chronology of events – not even 'Catholic' events – and still less a mere vehicle for the acquisition of skills, but the manifestation of our obligations to those who have gone before us, a covenant of memory which binds together past and present in the mutual confirmation of human purpose (Carruthers, 1990). This undoubtedly extends to commitment to another moral imperative which ought to play an informing role in the teaching of all of the humanities in a Catholic school: a concern for justice which opens the curriculum to the voices of the marginalised and the oppressed wherever they are to be found, and which provides a vital link between the broader curriculum and the aims of Religious Education. The synergy created by such a combination of elements can make the Catholic curriculum a potent tool for releasing into the experience of teaching and learning a critical intelligence – what Groome describes as a 'sacramental consciouness' (Groome, op. cit., p. 111) – which questions all knowledge by the light of Gospel truth, which is liberal and dialogic in the fullest senses, and which preserves the synthesis of faith and learning that promises full humanity in Christ.

Conclusion

This essay began with a consideration of the past, and it concludes with the presence of the past, completing a circle of reflection, perhaps, but abstaining from undue speculation about the future. The question with which the essay opened is one which surely must be put before the next generation of Catholic teachers, in full awareness that their responses may differ from those offered here, but urging upon them serious exploration of the issues it throws into relief. The essay has tried to show that it is a question which, for complex historical reasons, is now rarely discussed in Catholic education. But many hitherto unspoken questions are now being asked of Catholic schools, including that of their continued existence in the next millennium. In at least addressing the controversies which lie behind the question, the next generation of Catholic teachers will demonstrate their willingness to be attached to the genealogy of Catholic learning and may even possibly find answers which replenish the schools in which they serve for dealing successfully with all that lies ahead of them.

INSPIRATION, TRANSFORMATION
AND THE HOLY SPIRIT

James MacMillan with James C. Conroy

Introduction

This paper offers a view of inspiration as the opening up of the self
to the creative possibilities of being 'with' God. In doing so it
recognises the richness of the Judaeo-Christian tradition and the
provisionality of all our strivings. It represents the insights of one
who comes to these matters as a creator of music rather than as an
educationalist. It articulates a particular way of looking at the self
with God as a meditative resource to Catholic educators.

Being a composer I am frequently asked to reflect about my
music. Inevitably the question of inspiration arises. How did the
ideas come? What made you think of that? How do you start
formulating your ideas? These questions are deceptively simple and
yet frighteningly enormous. They rank alongside the 'meaning of
life' question in their ability to inspire terror and humility in any
composer rash enough to attempt a response. Most of the time it's
easy to hide behind answers which tackle the abstract nature of
music. Most composers, myself included, devise methods of
channelling attention towards impressive-looking charts complete
with complicated note rows, Fibonacci series and Shenkerien-style
structural analyses.

Music is, after all, the most abstract of all the arts. At a
fundamental level it needs no point of reference other than itself,
other than its own substance, its own methodology and technique,
its own explicable parameters. And yet these questions, whether
posed externally or internally, keep coming.

During a recent television interview the somewhat acerbic host, Muriel Gray, proffered one such question. Recognising that spirituality was now an issue of current debate again in the discussion of a lot of contemporary music, she was nevertheless keen to explore the matter from her own secular perspective. Did I, as a composer, think that religious piety sat uncomfortably with freedom of artistic expression? Did I not think that the greatest artistic challenges were faced from within a spiritual void, involving a struggle which relied on no emotional or religious crutches, thus the artist could forge his or her own sense of meaning without falling back on any received traditional and therefore probably false sense of meaning?

As a semi-automatic response, the words 'divine inspiration' had slipped unguarded from my lips and were sitting there, exposed and vulnerable, awaiting the inevitable avalanche of ridicule to be heaped upon them. It failed to materialise. My interrogator was surprised by the response, which she described as non-conformist and, in its own way, avant-garde. Then it struck me that the engagement between theology and culture, between religion and the arts, is now such a faded memory for most people that a whole generation has grown up without an understanding of the true meaning and implication in the word 'inspiration'. And when a creative person comes across this definition for the first time, it is a discovery made with undisguised delight – a recognition of a primal truth that has lain hidden for a long time.

On inspiration

The true, spiritual meaning of words like 'inspiration' and 'transformation' has been obscured by the layers of transient trendiness which pass for much cultural debate nowadays. A childlike pleasure accompanies the realisation that inspiration, from the Latin *inspiratio*, means 'in-breathing', an arousal or infusion of an impulse or illumination that impels a person to speak, act or write under the influence of some creative power. Divine inspiration is understood as that charismatic supernatural influence which moved and guided the prophets of the Old Testament period in revealing God's will to Israel and the attendant writing of the word. The Christian tradition understands that the Spirit of God has been profoundly involved in the actions and communication of these prophets and authors.

Over the years I have scanned Scripture from a composer's perspective, looking for clues as to the true nature of human creativity, of artistic fecundity; clues as to the significance of the eternal interaction between the Human and the Divine; clues to the religious artist about the significance of the full and active engagement of all one's human faculties – the cerebral, the aesthetic, the critical, the emotional, the visceral, the carnal and the corporeal; clues as to how all this should be open to the will of God; clues as to how one can become a channel for the divine will without diminishing one's own God-given free will. Some of these clues may be unveiled in a couple of crucial passages from Scripture. In Genesis, God presents his limitless love for humanity in the gift of Creation yet, at the same time, invites Adam, the archetype, to make his own sense of this new world. God provokes Adam into calling on his, that is Adam's, own imagination in naming the constituent elements of his world. Humanity's inner creativity is being *inspired* to express itself in the face of God's immeasurable love (Genesis 2: 18-23). Here is the interaction, indeed it might be suggested, the interface of God's will with that of human beings.

The creativity implied in the story of Adam's Rib has many resonances for composers who, through the centuries, have always taken fragments of material, consciously or unconsciously, from elsewhere and breathed new life into them, creating new forms, new avenues and structures of expression. Whether these fragments are taken from liturgy, from plainsong, from folk-song, from self-quotation, from allusions to other sources, from traditional cadential formulae, from half-remembered melodic shape, from a dimly perceived harmonic resonance, from a distant pulse of rhythm – they are all like embers of an old fire, extracted and gathered up, and wafted into a new flame. Indeed, one of my own pieces is entitled, *Adam's Rib* (1994/95) and is simply an acknowledgement of this eternally regenerative process in music as it develops through the ages; 'This at last is bone of my bones and flesh of my flesh'.

An even more crucial New Testament passage from St Luke is linked, like a mirror image, with the extract from Genesis, through a text by Jeremy Taylor (1613-67) that I once set for choir and organ – *On the Annunciation of the Blessed Virgin Mary* (Heber, 1822).

How good a God have we, who, for our sake,
To save us from the burning lake,
Did change the order of creation;
At first he made
Man like himself in his own image, now
In the more blessed reparation
The Heavens bow:
Eternity took the measure of a span,
And said,
'Let us like ourselves make man
And not from man the woman take,
But from the woman, man.'

In St Luke's account of the Annunciation, it is not just Mary's fecundity that is inspiring to a creative person. A more powerful and more pertinent metaphor for the religious artist is the balance between, on the one hand, Mary's independent free will and, on the other, her openness to the power of the Holy Spirit. There is something in the instinct of an artist or a composer, or any creative person, or any Christian for that matter, which is inexorably drawn to the idea of Mary's 'vesselship' – the notion of providing oneself as a channel for the divine will. This is not, of course, to negate the individual's human will. The Incarnation came about through Mary's free and rational acceptance of God's plan for her. Similarly an artist or a composer who thinks in real and meaningful terms of a divine inspiration would be mistaken in underestimating the full and active participation of all one's human faculties. It is a mistake to negate our human dimension and experience. It is through the interaction of all that makes us human – our intellect, our intelligence, our emotion and our physicality, our universal experiences of joy and despair, our flesh and blood – with the breath of God which brings forth creative fruit (for an artist – new work, new art, new music). Jesus himself was at once flesh of Mary *and* the Son of God.

This is why many have said that to be an artist, to be a Christian in fact, is to be spiritually or paradigmatically female. The Dominican, Gilbert Markus (1995), sees this in the marriage-motif of the New Testament, in which the Bride makes herself ready for the coming of the Groom. '[This] is the sexual and reproductive metaphor of God's relationship with humanity, both collectively and individually. The [ultimate] paradigm here is Mary, whose son is also the Son of God.' Mary who was receptive to God; Mary who was filled by God; Mary who bore God's son. Mary is the paradigm of our receptivity. Mary is an extreme version of all of us – a model for all creative people, an image for Christian educators and an example for all Christian believers.

The Christian believer is paradigmatically female: receptive of the seed of God's word. Receptive of the potency of God, the believer is waiting to be filled, longing to bear the fruit which will result from his or her union with God, to bring Christ to birth in our own life stories.

We come closest to Mary's example of receptivity, longing and patient openness to God in our own religious contemplations. For these silent, introspective searches we are required to give up *time*.

Prayer and contemplation are undeniably a kind of sacrifice. That is why we are so reluctant to put time aside. There is, even at the heart of the most committed Christians, the fear of inspiration since, on this view of inspiration, there is an implicit invitation to relinquish control of our time, of our structures, of ourselves. Inspiration, in this sense, need not be associated with any particular forms of liturgy and worship, nor need it be seen as the prerogative of particular groups of Christians who have the bounty of exclusive means of communication with God. Instead it may be regarded as an acceptance of our potential to be stretched, deepened, challenged and changed. The very notion that human beings may be changed embodies a sacrificing of some part of the self; the self that exists at this moment and with whom 'I' might be comfortable will, inevitably, be altered. The fear that this realisation induces, however dimly perceived, is an entirely understandable phenomenon. In the Annunciation it is clear that Luke regards Mary as embodying both fear of change and of the unknown as well as the recognition that change is inevitable. Mary's 'blessedness' like Hannah's (1 S 1:16ff-2:1) is bound up in her preparedness to be open to God. Again, as Luke has it, her soul magnifies the Lord and [her] spirit rejoices in God…'.

We know that her response to the Annunciation was an inspired and radical vision of a new life, a new revolutionary moral universe. We see this in the Canticle of Mary, the Magnificat, where as a good Jewish girl she was able to take the words of Isaiah and transform them into her own vision. A vision in which the world as we know it is turned upside-down, inside-out, where the proud are scattered, where the mighty are deposed, where the poor are exalted and the rich and powerful are turned on their heels. Through the breath of God Mary is inspired to see a new world. Her eyes are opened to a frighteningly radical overturn of everything that is accepted – an end to tyranny and oppression. The world is changed through Mary's vision. Through Mary's example we learn to see beyond the apparently obvious and predetermined paths of human behaviour. In Mary's example we see that when the breath of God moved through her she was made 'God-like' in her potential to love.

The patristic writers talked about *deificatio* in connection with the breath of God, in that its influence makes us divine. We begin to see things like God, to behave like God, like Adam when he engaged his inspired imagination to name the animals and other things in the Garden. The breath of God becomes our breath. No wonder we are terrified of being changed by our contemplations. Because along with the unbelievably joyous upheaval in Mary's life, the Annunciation also brought the shadow of the Cross. The recognition, right at the heart of Luke's infancy narrative, that all joys carry their own ambiguity; that her soul would be pierced by a sword (Lk 2:35).

Music also demands our time. It unfolds its narratives in time with an authority that will not be hurried. Something essential to our lives is sacrificed to music. Whether we are performers, composers or listeners we need to give something up, something of ourselves, something of our humanity, our 'flesh and blood' – our time – to learn its intricacies, to communicate its depths in performance or in its very inception itself, and in our serious hearing of it. Being openly receptive to the transforming power of music is analogous to the patient receptivity to the divine that is necessary for religious contemplation.

I have for a long time seen music as offering a striking analogy for God's relationship with us. As McDade (1994, p. 2) has it, 'music may be the closest human analogue to the mystery of the direct and effective communication of grace'. I would go further and suggest that music is a phenomenon connected to the work of God because it invites us to touch what is deepest in our souls, and to release within us a divine force. Music opens doors to a deepening and broadening of understanding. It invites connections between organised sound and lived experience or suspected possibilities. In the connection is found the revelation, a realisation of something not grasped before. Such 'seeing' offers revelations about human living and divine relationships that can effect changes in our choices, our activities and our convictions. Music allows us to see, like Mary, beyond to what lurks in the crevices of human-divine experience. Rowan Williams, in a sermon for the Three Choirs Festival, said

> To listen seriously to music and to perform it are among our most potent ways of learning what it is to live with and before God, learning a service that is a perfect freedom.... No one and nothing can compel our contemplation, except the object in its own right. In this 'obedience' of listening and following, we are stretched and deepened, physically challenged as performers, imaginatively as listeners. The time we have renounced, given up, is given back to us as a time in which we have become more human, more real, even when we can't say what we have learned, only that we have changed (1994, p. 248).

Mary learned to live with and before God. She was not commanded or forced from on high, but the breath of God entered her and she was stretched, deepened, challenged and changed. As a composer asked about inspiration I am drawn back to these pages from Luke's Gospel. I find inspiration in Mary's Magnificat, which is one of the most set texts by composers throughout the ages, and in the story of the Annunciation, apparently one of the most painted scenes of the Scriptures. Artists are pointing us towards these two events in St Luke. There is obviously something momentously significant in their ubiquity throughout musical and artistic history. There is equally something momentously significant in Mary's central presence at the heart of these things. She is not only an example and a model for all Christianity but in this is the embodiment of what human beings experience only dimly; that we live with the ambiguity of limitation and creative possibility in constant tension. She opens the door to the very heart of God. And in the silence of my own contemplation, in that necessary stillness where all composers know that music mysteriously begins, the following words from sacred liturgy have lodged themselves in the womb of my soul, trapped in a scarlet room, gestating gently with a tiny, distant pulse: 'Hail Mary, full of grace....'

And of the school

These meditations and reflections on the 'in-breathing' of God open two connected insights into what might count as the nature of Catholic education. The first of these is concerned with what it is that teachers and administrators in Catholic education believe themselves to be doing; the second concerns the ways in which the Catholic school offers its students, not only opportunities to meditate, pray and worship but also the possibility of being inspired.

The Catholic school system, which of course may not be confused with Catholic education, is to all intents and purposes as attentive as any other part of the State-funded education system in Britain to the contemporary language of Performance Indicator, Attainment Target, Assessment and Efficiency in education. While this may seem enormously important in the current politico-economic climate it behoves Catholic educators to recognise these for what they are: fleeting and transient measures of our own insecurities. The justification for a Catholic school, the very reason for existence is rooted, not in such shibboleths but in the inspiration of God; the sharing in God's creativity. Many Catholic educators make valiant attempts to construct a view where there is no incompatibility to be found between this world of targets and the possibility of creative openness. No doubt there are ways in which this may be empirically tested but in the absence of appropriate and reliable evidence there still appears to be some questions worth asking. The most important of these is whether or not openness as a receptive disposition to the world and to the 'in-breathing' of God is enhanced or stultified by strategies which are themselves exercises in foreclosure. In recent curriculum constructions directed towards what is generally referred to as 'spiritual development' (Burns and Lamont, 1995; Dorset Education Authority, 1992) spiritual creativity has itself been reduced to a kind of cipher of civility; a 'spirituality of civics'. Teachers in Catholic schools have then an 'awesome' task in recognising that this opening up of themselves carries with it the acknowledgement of the ambiguity which survives right at the heart of a Christian education system. To manage an institution which has no rootedness in the openness of creativity is to have, what Buber (1970, p. 93) termed a *golem*; that is, an 'animated clod without a soul'.

As suggested above there is a second, related issue which is focused on developing an understanding *of* and *in* individual students in both their listening to and their making and playing music as creative acts; drawing them into the creativity of contemplation in a context which normally eschews the reflective moment in favour of activity. This 'activity', it should be acknowledged, is frequently generated by the students themselves so that they can avoid the invitation to enter into their own souls creatively. While nostalgia about the meditative qualities of education in previous generations is to be avoided, it is the case that the speed of image and impression, the quantity and volume of 'sound and fury' provides a very real challenge to the creativity which comes from contemplation. The emotional entering into the possibilities which music offers can be a lonely journey for a child or young person unless they are offered appropriate space. This space is not limited to time or place; it is rather more fundamentally concerned with attitude. In creating such an ontological space the Catholic teacher and the whole school offer the possibility of raising students into full consciousness; as Swanick has it, 'aesthetic means to feel more powerfully, to perceive more clearly [and] its opposite is *anaesthetic*' (1980, p. 112).

PART TWO
Catholic Education – Outside-In

CATHOLIC EDUCATION IN SCOTLAND: A PHENOMENOLOGICAL APPROACH

Malcolm L. MacKenzie

Introduction

Scotland, according to Brown, McCrone and Paterson (1996), is a figment of the imagination. This is not a joke but an intellectually persuasive analysis of the meaning of national identity. A nation is to be defined not only in terms of geography but in respect of the consciousness of its people, a consciousness to be understood by an analysis of its history, symbols, rituals, art, language and discourse as much as by location, economics or the decisions of governments. The late Enoch Powell was heard to state in a public lecture at Swinton College in 1960 that a nation existed if, and only if, people thought it existed.

This analysis leads us into complex and contentious matters. Ireland and Cyprus are islands. That does not make them nations. They are places where competing consciousness leads to violent, perhaps irreconcilable differences. To put it another way, one might say that the social construct of reality of different groups of people in those islands, their phenomenology, is so different as to produce conflict.

Of course geographical reality changes over time. It would appear that in the distant past South America was joined to Africa and that the British Isles were part of Europe. However, these changes took place over such vast expanses of time as to be almost unimaginable. That is not the case with consciousness. People's perceptions and ideas, their 'social construct of reality' (Greenfield, 1975) can change very quickly. This is particularly so in the modern (or post-modern?) world where the processes of information technology and globalisation have accelerated the speed of change to a point which is almost frightening (Shane, 1977).

To return to that 'figment of the imagination' – in spite of its promised Parliament, Scotland is not a nation state. Sovereignty, at least for the time being and under the proposed legislation (Great Britain. Laws and Statutes, 1997), will remain with the Westminster Parliament. If Scotland is not a nation what is it? Most Scots apparently see themselves as Scottish rather than British although they are British nationals. Brown, McCrone and Paterson overcome this problem by describing Scotland as a civil society, that is, a group of people with a strong sense of identity who nevertheless belong to a larger 'nation'. Whether the aforesaid nation can survive a predominant other identity among a section of its population the future will tell. Of course Scots have a sense of belonging to different groups. Some, like this writer, see themselves as British, Scottish and Highland with perhaps a dash of European thrown in. It may be that some *of a certain age,* who remember the Second World War, have a predominantly British consciousness, while the younger generation feels very much a Scottish even an *exclusively* Scottish, identity. This may explain the humiliating defeat suffered by the Scottish Conservative Party in the British General Election of 1997. That party which had been perceived (whether rightly or wrongly) as an English party, became displaced in Scottish consciousness, with catastrophic electoral consequences.

Identity, therefore, is an extremely difficult concept to pin down, whether applied to individuals, groups or nations. It has become a major theme in political, sociological and cultural writing. Thus Brown, McCrone and Paterson identify a crisis of identity and suggest that 'the eagerness to talk about identity is symptomatic of the post-modern predicament of contemporary politics' (op. cit., p. 190).

Individual identity

According to Hall 'There has been a veritable explosion in recent years around the concept of identity, at the same moment as it has been subjected to a searching critique' (1996, p. 2). The critique has indeed been 'searching'. So much so that any explorer of the literature might well be advised to have a wet towel handy for wearing around the head when perusing it. It is fascinating that social scientists, in pursuit of this elusive concept, have rediscovered psychoanalysis. R. D. Laing, thou shouldst be living at this hour! Hall, quoting Freud, invokes the concept of 'identification', even, the Oedipus complex, in pursuit of 'the novel repertoires of meaning' now surrounding discussions about identity. Because of its relevance to our argument about Catholic education it is worth quoting what Hall says about the Freudian concept of 'identification':

> In common sense language, identification is constructed on the back of a recognition of some common origin or shared characteristics with another person or group, or with an ideal, and with the natural closure of solidarity and allegiance established on this foundation. In contrast with the 'naturalism' of this definition, the discursive approach sees identification as a construction, a process never completed, always 'in process' (ibid.).

The 'process' aspects of identity are central to much of our analysis of contemporary culture. Hall's phrase that the nature of identification is 'lodged in contingency' should be borne in mind by those who see identity as a fixed, timeless characteristic independent of social, cultural and economic change.

So far as the individual is concerned the matter can be put quite simply. A person may have several identities, which may change in the course of one's life. We may negotiate our identities in relation to our changing environment. One hears echoes of 'Dr Jekyll and Mr Hyde' which may prove the truth of the assertion that in his analysis of the individual in relation to an essentially Scottish culture, Stevenson was well ahead of his time. The opportunities for assuming different identities and the range of choice available (rather like a supermarket) have increased enormously in contemporary society. If one thinks of gender issues, sexual orientation, political allegiances, life-style, the range of socially acceptable choice is enormous.

Of course these changes, which some have called post-modernist (Harvey, 1990), are anathema to many people who find them both morally disturbing and frightening. The response to the stress caused by cultural ambiguity can take a number of forms. The world-wide retreat into fundamentalism in religion may be one of its manifestations, noted from Afghanistan to the American mid-West. This is both a dangerous and inappropriate response for world religions. Fundamentalism is not only frequently associated with intolerance and fear of ambiguity but its incapacity to enter into discourse with other groups, to maintain the complex level of communication demanded in contemporary society, can lead to the religious faith which reverts to it becoming a sect or a cult, isolated and out-of-touch, especially with the young. Such a response is ignorant of the subtleties contained in Hall's point that 'identities are constructed through, not outside, difference'.

The fundamentalist response to the contemporary 'identity crisis' can also be seen in an alarming retreat into nationalism and tribalism. One might say that the return to Balkanisation has been most noticeable in the Balkans, although the Middle East and Ireland provide obvious examples. The current attempt in Ireland to reverse the process is of enormous international significance.

The mobilisation of identity

In a presentation to a seminar organised by the Scottish Educational Policy Forum held in Moray House Institute of Education on Friday 27 March 1998 on the theme *Education Policy-Making in Catalonia and Scotland*, McCrone invoked the concept of 'the mobilisation of identity'. He gave, as an example, the post-war discovery of oil in the North Sea, which it can be argued reinforced Scottish consciousness and played a considerable part in the Scottish National Party's electoral success in the 1974 General Election, in which the slogan, 'It's Scotland's Oil' figured prominently. Whatever one's views about that example, an examination of 'mobilisers' is a useful task for those concerned with identity. So far as the British people were concerned, the threat of defeat and invasion in 1940 was a 'mobiliser'. It may explain why the sense of British identity is still strong among those (a diminishing band) who remember the Second World War. It might be worth making the pun that it is a 'moot' point whether the Scottish Parliament will mobilise Scottish consciousness to the point where independence becomes inevitable or whether the Scottish people will feel so relaxed at having achieved a Parliament that the Union will be strengthened. The future of Scotland may well hang on the answer to this question. Of course, one of the greatest mobilisers of all is the education system. That is why politicians are so interested in schools and why, in recent years, they have become noticeably interested in the curriculum. To ensure that the young adopt the identity of the 'good citizen' or 'skilled worker' is a goal of government and it must be said that these are neither ignoble nor inappropriate goals. It also explains why the Catholic Church is anxious to maintain denominational schools, on the basis of the 1918 settlement, presumably to ensure the preservation of the identity 'good Catholic'. Whether a last ditch defence of Catholic schools is the exclusive and best way to maintain Catholic identity or whether other matters need to be carefully examined is a question which this discussion must now address.

Catholic education: roots and routes

I should perhaps state here that I am a Protestant, an active member of the Church of Scotland, an ecumenical Christian. The thrust of the argument of this chapter is that the Catholic Church and the professional educators among its adherents should seek ways in which change and adaptability, an outward- rather than an inward-looking approach can best fulfil the mission (used in the managerial/organisational sense) of Catholic education. Indeed, it might be suggested that such an approach is the only way to fulfil that mission. Of course, some might argue that for a non-Catholic to engage in this debate is sheer effrontery. It is hoped that this response will not be evoked and that it will be appreciated that this is written out of a very real and genuine respect for the Catholic tradition and for the contribution which that tradition has made to Scottish life and culture. To make it clear that my views are more than that mere 'personal opinion' which abounds in public, popular discussion, the argument is related to the current debate about identity. To take this analysis a stage further and into a theological context, a correspondence may be detected among the ideas of sociologist Stuart Hall, Jesuit priest Joseph M. O'Keefe and the American Quaker theologian, Parker Palmer.

Hall argues that identities are constantly in the process of change and transformation, that they multiply across different 'often intersecting and antagonistic discourses, practices and positions'. The following quotation from Hall will lead us into the argument from a theological perspective.

> Though they seem to invoke an origin in an historical past with which they continue to correspond, actually identities are about questions of using the resources of history, language and

culture in the process of becoming rather than being: not 'who are we' or 'where we came from', so much as what we might become, how we have been represented and how that bears on how we might represent ourselves. Identities are therefore constituted within, not outside representation. They relate to the invention of tradition as much as to tradition itself, which they oblige us to read not as an endless reiteration but as 'the changing same' (Gilroy, 1994): not the so-called return to roots but a coming-to-terms with our 'routes' (op. cit., p. 4).

The distinction between roots and routes as well as the notion of 'the changing same' have a remarkable affinity with some of the ideas put forward by O'Keefe (1998) and Parker Palmer (1990). Both O'Keefe and Palmer see a threat in America (and no doubt, by implication, in other countries) to a sense of community, to the 'public' aspects of human existence, characterised by a retreat into individual, often selfish isolation. Both are talking about a loss of public and, as a consequence, spiritual identity. Palmer describes a world denuded of public places, in which individuals leave their offices in a neglected downtown city area, for detached, intruder-protected homes where all contact with any individuals or groups who could be characterised as 'different' is avoided. His vision is of a nightmarish, almost Wellsian world of 'The Time Machine' in which an effete élite are afraid to venture forth. He contrasts this with Christ's concern for those who are on the margins of society, for the outsider, and indeed Christ's injunction, as in the parable of the Good Samaritan, to abandon what modern social psychologists might call in-group/out-group animosity.

O'Keefe laments the end of 'common space' (he talks about the town and village common) and a retreat into a culture of nostalgia or narcissism represented by the attempt to pursue roots (often imaginary) rather than routes and an absorption in 'self', perhaps as an attempt to discover an ever-elusive identity. It is worth noting that both Palmer and O'Keefe see such characteristics of contemporary culture as indicative of a spiritual malaise, or even death. O'Keefe describes the situation as one of anomie. Both theologians, building an ecumenical bridge in terms of analysis and recommendations, are concerned with the needs of the stranger and of those whom Palmer describes as being 'on the edge', while O'Keefe reminds us of the Church's 'preferential love for the poor' (op. cit., p. 17). In more political terms both are concerned to rebuild a sense of community and the public aspects of social and cultural life.

In stating that the contemporary 'crises of identity and diversity will not be met by an unthinking return to the past', O'Keefe was presenting an argument not dissimilar to that of Hall, who is from a very different tradition indeed. A similarity of analysis can therefore be seen in the work of thinkers writing from very different standpoints. It is not in the interests of those devoted to Catholic education to ignore it. It is from this conceptual view that the practical, policy solutions to some of the very real problems facing Catholic education in Scotland will be found. It is to some of these problems that we now turn.

The 1918 Concordat

The year 1918 was a 'landmark date' (Jones, 1992) in the history of Catholic education in Scotland. The Catholic Church voluntarily transferred its schools to the new education authorities created by the Education (Scotland) Act, 1918 which, unlike previous legislation, allowed the Church to retain control over the appointment of teachers, particularly with regard to those teachers' religious beliefs and character. As Jones has it, 'For the Roman Catholic Church it was and has been ever since, a vital concession' (ibid., p. 105).

Concession might not be the term most appealing to the leaders of the Catholic Church in Scotland. It can be argued that what was offered by the Act was not a concession, with the patronising overtones of that term, but a recognition of the crucial place of Catholic education in Scotland since the coming of Christianity.

The concession was, it might be argued, a Concordat between the Catholic Church and the people and government of Scotland, one which can not now be unilaterally discarded without inflicting great dishonour on all the Scottish people. Yet the 1918 Concordat is now in great danger and is one of the most obvious, but by no means an exclusive site of the crises of identity facing Scottish Catholic education. What has happened to bring a debate into focus now which, apart from a brief period in the 1960s, appeared to have ended?

Before proceeding it is necessary to explain the reference to the 1960s. In 1964 a Labour Government under the leadership of Prime Minister Harold Wilson was elected on a platform which included the reorganisation of secondary education on comprehensive lines. The theory and practice of this policy had been argued out in the Labour Movement for many years previously (MacKenzie, 1967). Essentially the policy was based on the premise, as the Report *Secondary Education* (Scottish Education Department, 1947) stated, that the common school was the appropriate way for a democratic society to organise its education and one, furthermore, in harmony with the Scottish cultural tradition. To socialists, this was an appealing philosophy. The comprehensive school would be a mechanism for weakening social class and ethnic barriers in pursuit both of equality of opportunity and social equality. But what about religious barriers? If a 'common culture' (Williams, 1958) was a goal of socialism, what possible argument could there be to retain denominational schools? In 1965 the Government circular (Circular 600) requesting local authorities to reorganise their secondary schools on comprehensive lines did not propose rejection of the 1918 settlement. Yet the possibility of such a threat did exist, certainly in the minds of some Labour MPs. The political consequences of such a retreat from 1918 ensured that the Wilson Government did not go down this road (Jones, op. cit.) although it was certainly 'in the logic of the comprehensive ideal'.

There the matter rested until recently when it has re-emerged in public debate. There are a number of possible reasons which can be adduced for the return of the issue, viz., the prospect of a Scottish Parliament, falling school rolls, the shifting sands of identity and, paradoxically it might seem, a loss of confidence in the comprehensive school extending to public education itself.

A Scottish Parliament

'There shall be a Scottish Parliament', states Section 1(1) of the Scotland Bill (17 December 1997). In this phrase alone, without reference to the detailed sections of the Bill, lies a potential threat to Catholic education. A cynic might argue that the new Parliament is not a Parliament at all since sovereignty will remain at Westminster but a fulfilment of the late John P. McIntosh's devolutionary dream (1968) in which a Scottish Assembly effectively becomes the top-tier of Scottish local government, with one of its main concerns the strategic management of the Scottish education service. Under such a system, and the climate now created, everything in the education system is 'up for grabs', to be revisited anew. Thus, public figures now feel it possible, in the currently popular term, to 'think the unthinkable' without worrying too much about the consequences. Indeed there are many advantages to be gained from setting the policy parameters now and putting down markers for the future. Two recent examples which can be cited are Lord Mackay of Ardbrecknish, a Tory peer who, in the House of Lords, called for an end to separate Catholic schools, and Labour MP John Maxton (the bearer of a famous name, not to be discounted in Scottish culture) who also drew attention to the advantages of a policy of integration. Let there be no doubt, integration has re-entered Scottish political discourse. It is likely to remain in that discourse. It has been given added point by what is probably the most important development of all in Scottish education since the war; the decline in population.

Falling school rolls

The implications of the fall in the birth-rate have been the subject of discussion for many years (Briault and Smith, 1980; MacFadyen and MacMillan, 1984). In 1995 the Accounts Commission stated that it made no economic sense to keep open schools with surplus capacity in Scotland (pp. 4f). The political and local conflicts which can arise when a school closure programme is attempted can be seen by a study (Campbell, 1996) of what happened in Strathclyde Region following publication of their policy document *Adapting to Change* (1986). As Briault predicted, 'save our school' campaigns started with angry, placard-bearing demonstrators appearing outside local government offices or even, as Glasgow can recently bear witness, inside Council debating chambers. The closure issue in respect of Catholic schools in Glasgow has been commented on by Jones.

> Closure rows arise because Glasgow's Catholic schools, mostly located in working-class housing estates, are acutely afflicted by problems of falling birth-rates in, and population shifts away from these areas. But merger with a non-denominational school is absolutely unacceptable to the Catholic Church, which regards Christian teaching in non-denominational schools as non-existent (op. cit., p. 105).

It can be seen therefore that opponents of the 1918 settlement are in a position to argue that mergers and amalgamations are now an accepted part of public policy and in such circumstances the maintenance of separate Catholic schools is an unacceptable charge on the public purse. In other words, opponents can argue that denominational schools are a luxury Scotland can no longer afford. Such arguments, one predicts, will be reiterated and grow in force. At the same time the comprehensive school 'ideal', so prominent in the 1960s, is now itself under serious threat.

The comprehensive school

Falling school rolls; concerns about school discipline; curriculum reforms such as Higher Still (in Scotland) which involve more resources and closer links with further education; the alienation of boys from education in the phenomenon known as 'laddism' (Halsey *et al.*, 1997) have all contributed to questions being raised about the future of the 'all through' comprehensive school which caters for the twelve to eighteen age-group. This form of secondary school organisation is not a mere administrative convenience but a social and educational ideal enshrined in the famous Circular 600 of 1965 and in the writings of many distinguished commentators. Most recently, Benn and Chitty have drawn attention to the success of the comprehensive school in Scotland.

> However, if evidence is needed to show that the more comprehensive a school system is, the better it does in terms of some of the 'standards' that those opposing comprehensive education so often use, Britain has good evidence in Scotland (1997, p. 471).

Optimism about the future of the comprehensive school has been expressed by head teachers such as Tony Gavin, Head Teacher of St Margaret's Secondary School, Livingston, who argued that this form of organisation could deliver the Higher Still national unified post-sixteen curriculum framework reform, given proper support in terms of resources.

Nevertheless, at the same conference at which Gavin spoke, Iain Ovens, Principal of Dundee College pointed out the largest single group pursuing Higher Still qualifications will be in further education. The interface between incorporated further education and colleges and the State education system will soon become one of the main areas of management tension (and opportunity) in Scottish education. It is indeed difficult not to foresee the emergence of new diverse structures which will inevitably challenge the 'all-through' comprehensive arrangement. With such a challenge and in face of an inevitable demand for more diverse, flexible structures, the place of the Catholic comprehensive school can no longer be assumed or guaranteed. The resolution of the matter, however, will lie not only with debates about structures and resources but with the perceptions of the Scottish people. The growing sense of Scottish identity, reinforced by the creation of a Scottish Parliament, will support groups, institutions and organisations which resonate with it. Those which do not, which become displaced in Scottish consciousness, may suffer the same fate as the Scottish Conservative Party in the 1997 General Election. The survival of identity in response to the changing consciousness of the Scottish people requires communication, not isolation; empathy not defensiveness; the sending out of scouts and emissaries rather than placing the wagons in a circle. This demands what Hall calls 'the radically disturbing recognition that it is only in relation to "the other" that identity can be constructed or maintained'. It is to the nature of that relationship and its policy implications that we now turn.

Towards a resolution: the contribution of Catholic education to Scottish life and culture

The mission of Catholic education must be and must be seen to be more than the preservation of Catholic schools, without prejudice to the importance of that goal. It must include a contribution to the spiritual dimension of Scottish culture as a whole and to closely related issues such as the raising of levels of attainment and educational management.

From the coming of Christianity until at least the Education (Scotland) Act 1872 the spiritual dimension was prominent in, even lay at the core of Scottish education. The Christian Church, whether pre- or post-Reformation, laid the foundations of Scottish education and is the source of that international reputation for excellence (whether deserved or not) which that education has enjoyed. Whether in the doctrines of the Catholic Church or in the idealistic scheme of compulsory education as the basis for a theocratic state put forward by Knox (1561), the moral, spiritual element in Scottish educational thought has been historically significant. In 1947 the Report of the Advisory Council on Education in Scotland, entitled *Secondary Education*, stated that:

> The term 'Christian Democracy' holds its own ambiguity: yet better perhaps than any other it summarises the ideals that have governed our thinking about the task of the secondary school (op. cit., p. 6).

Reacting to the horrors of war, not least to the barbarities of the Holocaust, the Report described the child 'as an end in himself', thereby defining education not in terms of religious dogma but firmly based on the worth and dignity of each person. The role of religious thought in contributing to the aims and practices of education in relation to the kind of society we wish to achieve must be reaffirmed in the modern world as it was by the 1947 Report in the immediate post-war era. It is here that Catholic thought, communicated to a much wider community than the Catholic Church in the form of publications, seminars, conferences, use of the media, inter-institutional collaboration, etc., has a very significant contribution to make. Some such contributions, of course, already take place. The speeches, writings and contributions to policy of a number of Catholic educationalists such as McGettrick have contributed to the general debate in Scotland on educational values. Such public communication of ideas backed, one hopes, by influence in the 'corridors of power' will demonstrate to the Scottish people an engagement with the needs and aspirations of all and the capacity of Catholic thought to contribute to acceptable solutions. This will demonstrate itself in areas of current concern to which the word 'practical' can readily be applied, for example, in the growing interest in management in the education service.

Management in education

Management training in education is the latest and most important contemporary educational shibboleth. Scottish Education Minister, Brian Wilson, MP, announced (23 December 1997) plans for a Scottish Qualification for Headship which would 'help ensure that all the headteachers possess the leadership qualities which their position requires'. At the time of writing work is nearing completion on a qualification that will be ready for national delivery in the academic session 1999/2000. A Development Unit for the Scottish Qualification for Headship has been set up. Conferences have been held to discuss the publication *Consultation Paper on a Scottish Qualification for Headteachers* published by the Scottish Office education and Industry Department (SOEID) in August 1997. No doubt, in the future, a qualification in management will become an essential prerequisite for those aspiring to headship in Scottish schools.

Yet underlying these developments and assuredly given impetus by them lies an international debate about the nature of management itself. It is to this debate that Catholic thinkers can and should make a major contribution. There are some obvious ways in which this can be done; others are more subtle. For example, as long ago as 1969 Catherine Lindsay drew attention to the importance of the pastoral tradition in Catholic schools in dealing with discipline and behaviour issues. The religious, pastoral and values dimension promoted in and beyond Catholic education may be seen in the work of Catholic educationalists like Conroy, editor of this volume, and his colleagues in St Andrew's College. In a society increasingly worried by ill-discipline, notably bullying in schools, the pastoral dimension to Catholic thought and practice has a significant contribution to make to all schools. However, I wish to draw attention to a more subtle area in international thought to which a Catholic perspective will give added value. Growing attention is being directed to the place of spirituality in management. From some utterances and official publications one might conclude that some leaders of Scottish education are just beginning to catch up with scientific management and Taylorism and are oblivious to the 'shifting paradigms' (Bush, 1995) which characterise the 'cacophony' of contemporary thinking about management (Bacharach and Mundell, 1995). In a world of chaos theory (Peters, 1987) and ambiguity models (Bush, 1995), to attempt to found management training exclusively on a competence model is truly to build one's house on sand. This theme is so enormous that it demands volumes, not a conclusion to a chapter. In pursuit, however, of the theme of the relationship between spirituality and management, reference is now made to the work of the American writer Terence Deal (1995). Deal writes about organisational behaviour and, in his analysis of organisations, has emphasised the place of ritual, metaphor and spirituality. The place of metaphor in understanding organisations has also been given wide currency by Gareth Morgan (1997). The thinking of Deal will, one expects, strike a chord with those who look at organisations from a Catholic perspective. They will not find it difficult to agree with Deal when he suggests that 'we need a reminder that spirituality, belief and faith are not issues that progress and modern people have moved beyond or outgrown' (op. cit., p. 113).

In saying this, Deal is not uttering a pious, religious platitude. He is talking about how organisations must be understood and run in the modern world. He is as hard-nosed in his analysis of human needs and behaviour as any manager dedicated to management by objectives. According to Deal the most effective way to improve organisational effectiveness is through the reincorporation of spirituality into organised human activity.

It is now recognised that organisations are not governed by

scientific laws which, once understood, can lead to those who purport to understand them providing infallible training courses, with measurable outputs, in terms of individual and organisational performance. The attempt of the *Theory Movement* in the United States to do this, laudable though it may have been, was effectively torpedoed by Greenfield in a paper first delivered to an international management audience in Bristol in 1974 (Greenfield, 1975). Modern management stresses the person, not management rules and laws, and is more inclined to focus on the cultural processes in which the individual operates, seeking a virtue in its very ambiguity, than the now abandoned attempt to create scientifically proven management principles. Only those who are totally out of touch with modern thought see management training exclusively in terms of techniques which the trainer, backed by proven scientific theory, can impart to the trainee. People who claim to do this, and they abound, would find a more appropriate use for their talents in selling snake oil from the back of a wagon!

Deal, having studied such eminently practical operations, with no obvious link to spirituality, as the construction of the Polaris submarine, writes that 'in every organised activity it is important that people believe in what they are doing, share a common heritage and faith – and dream together' (op. cit., p. 112).

It seems to me that this analysis provides an educational and managerial argument for the retention of Catholic schools. He is, of course, not using the term 'faith' in a religious sense, more in terms of shared purpose. Nevertheless, we now know that successful organisations have a culture which ensures the motivation and commitment of all involved in the enterprise. The acquisition by managers of skill or the passing of examinations based on box-ticked outcomes does not ensure this. If we are to raise levels of attainment in all our schools; eliminate ill-discipline and bullying; overcome cultural alienation such as 'laddism'; counteract the effects of poverty and deprivation, especially among an underclass (Murray, 1990); ensure that appropriate innovations do not suffer from what

Hoyle called 'tissue-rejection', then we need to look at what people like Deal are telling us. His is an exciting vision which reminds one of the thought of Palmer and O'Keefe quoted above, not to mention Hall. Deal concludes the essay from which the aforementioned quotations have been taken by writing, 'to become fully human, Western industrial man, and his non-Western brother insofar as they are touched by the same debilitation, must learn again to dance and dream' (op. cit., p. 133).

I have spent some time on Deal because it is my contention that to preserve and indeed enrich its identity, Catholic education must reach out to Scottish culture by making the contribution which it is capable of making to the great currents of thought of our time. It can help us resist a retreat into narrowness, loss of vision and an understanding of management thought which it would be charitable to describe as anachronistic. Catholic thought and practice can also help internationalise Scottish culture and resist an inward-looking nationalistic perspective which is in itself a threat to that very Scottish identity that it claims to advance. To do this an ecumenical approach is needed but this in turn brings with it its own perceived dangers.

Ecumenism: the baby and the bathwater

There are, perhaps, biblical overtones in the notion that to gain your identity you must first lose it. It is remarkable that from perspectives as diverse as Christian and neo-Marxist comes a view of identity which echoes the notion that self-realisation depends on relationships with others. Of course there are perceived dangers in such an analysis, which one might call 'the baby and the bathwater' syndrome. To the traditionalist the attempt to preserve identity by working and communicating with others can imply the abandonment of that which must be preserved. It is a common theme, for example, in the European debate which has changed the very nature of British politics. To some, British identity will be lost in closer union with Europe; to others, it is the only way to preserve it. To the traditional Catholic it might appear that the name of the baby to be thrown out with the bathwater is Jesus. This is not the argument of O'Keefe or of this chapter. Given goodwill and proper management, there are a vast number of ways of collaborating based on positive outgoing approaches to others which can enrich the mission and tradition, not only of Catholic education but of other, very different approaches. Since this chapter calls itself 'phenomenological' it is going to conclude with a personal statement by the author which justifies the use of the first person.

In February 1998 the University of Glasgow and St Andrew's College, Glasgow sent a proposal for merger to the Secretary of State for Scotland. The merger document was based on many months of hard work and negotiation. The fear that the highly respected Christian ethos of St Andrew's College would be lost as a consequence of merger was naturally expressed by some parties in the negotiations. The merger document seeks to put in place management and administrative structures which will 'ring-fence' that ethos and ensure its survival. Yet in terms of identity, the merger offers much more than that. It provides an opportunity for teaching, research, publications and conferences which can demonstrate to the world that, given good will, an ecumenical approach can work and perhaps even offer help to some of the world's most intractable identity problems, for example, in Ireland. The ecumenical aspect is a broad one. It includes non-Christians such as academics who base their work on a Marxist perspective. The interaction of ideas among Christians (Protestants and Catholics) and non-Christians seeking to address fundamental problems in education, such as alienation, low attainment, management, the role of parents and communities, could provide an environment so rich that people would wish to visit it from all over the world. In such an environment, to which Scottish Catholic education would make a visible, powerful contribution, Catholic identity would be enhanced and internationalised. That is my vision and my hope.

On a final, highly contentious issue, previously referred to, I wish to make clear that I would not favour the abandonment of the 1918 Concordat without the agreement and wish of the clergy and laity of the Catholic Church. I would, however, welcome some positive steps in an ecumenical direction, even on an experimental basis. In her recent study of Lagan College, Belfast, Wicklow (1997) offers some interesting insights into the possibilities of schools founded on ecumenical priniciples. I would like to see similar schools in Scotland, especially in the west of Scotland, a culture which more than the rest of Scotland has historically been blighted by religious bigotry. Such steps in ecumenism would not threaten the identity of Catholic education but would, on the contrary, demonstrate its tolerance towards and love of all the people of Scotland. If such a school or schools existed in areas of deprivation they would demonstrate that love of and concern for the poor which O'Keefe reminded us was one of the key missions of Holy Church.

The search for identity discussed here, along with the policy implications of such a search, if brought to fruition, will make a great contribution to the creation of a Scottish society whose people are enabled to 'dance and dream'.

THE PRIMACY OF RELATIONSHIP:
A MEDITATION ON EDUCATION, FAITH
AND THE DIALOGICAL SELF

James M. Day

Introduction

This chapter began as a lecture intended for a particular audience: Catholic educators in Scotland. While reflecting a highly confessional approach it was at the same time informed by years of professional work and research both inside and outside Catholic educational institutions. It had as its objectives both the offering of a critical outsider's perspective on an issue of central importance to Catholic education and the building up of community with others whose involvement in education was in some way informed by a sense of Christian vision and commitment. These objectives are also part of what structures the larger book of which this chapter is but one part. In keeping with its original intent the tone remains discursive and somewhat conversational, highly personal yet professionally informed. In the sections which explore actual case stories much of the reflection is couched in the present tense since the people involved continue to live and act within the present.

These reflections emanate from the experience of being a psychologist and educator, trained as a clinician and researcher in developmental psychology, formed in the classroom, in counselling and research interviews, in the practice of educational administration, and in collaborative evaluations of students, teachers and administrators. A considerable portion of this experience has occurred within Catholic contexts: from psychological testing work in Catholic primary schools, to work as a counselling psychologist in a Jesuit university, to a professorship at Louvain.

There have also been consultancies in Catholic primary and secondary schools, training courses and workshops in the psychology of human development and the psychology of moral education with personnel from Catholic youth movements, religious orders and schools; and research on moral and religious judgment with Catholic adolescents and young adults. This work has largely been in the United States and Belgium, but has additionally included numerous contacts with British, French, German and Swiss educators. This in turn has been broadened by membership in the International Association of Catholic Educators, where lively annual discussions occur on matters of the kind this book undertakes to consider.

It would be unfair to go further without mentioning the huge influence on my thinking that my Catholic students, research 'subjects' and clinical clients in these contexts have been the subject of extensive discussion and without these conversations writing this essay would have been unimaginable. Finally, it is important to note the influence of those many hours spent on retreat in Catholic houses of worship, prayer, public service and personal reflection. From Jesuit residences, retreat houses and chaplaincy contacts in Pennsylvania and the Catholic Worker House in New York, to St Edmund's College Cambridge, the Communauté de Charité at Les Houches, France, the Fraternité du Bon Pasteur in Brussels, and Montserrat in Catalonia, Spain; all of these places and the conversations therein have inspired my reflection and have touched my life and thought in a profound way. Thus, this chapter will offer the perspective of an outsider, with origins far from the Catholic tradition, enriched within my own religious way by Anglo-Catholic worship and practice, looking in at education as it has been known to me in those Roman Catholic environments which have been so kind as to grant me access.

Grounded in a view of psychology as the study of human

relationships, and drawing from narrative accounts of educational experience, this essay attempts to show that the quality of education is a function of the quality of relationships established in the educational process, and that a crucial aim of education is the development of responsivity as a foundation for learning and responsibility. Finally, it is proposed that a psychology of education centred in an appreciation of relationship provides a potentially rich perspective for thinking about the meaning and value of Christian faith for education, and more particularly, for what a Catholic education might, at its best, make possible.

Reformulating the equation: how relationships count in learning

I want to move now to how psychology matters in this, and to some preliminary pointers as to why we should emphasise relationship as the key ingredient in educational work. To do so it is helpful to begin with a conversation – part of an interview I was having with a young woman named Sharon. At eighteen, she has recently graduated from secondary school, and is thinking about becoming a teacher. In our conversation I asked her to tell me more about her view of schooling, what learning means to her and how this affects her thoughts concerning an educational career:

Sharon: Well, of course it should be about learning, that is what we're there to do. But don't you think schools should be, I mean, that they should be concerned with everything there is to learn?

James: Everything?

Sharon: I mean, there's what you learn officially, and then what you learn about how to learn, which I think some schools don't really get to, and then there's the context, what makes the learning possible.

James: Let me see if I am following you. There's an official curriculum, then there's something that succeeds or not in helping students to learn about their own learning, maybe learning how to learn and keep on learning, and then there's the environment of the school, which affects the first two. Does that get at what you're saying?

Sharon: So I'm saying, you learn some things officially, let's say maths is the perfect example, something that appears to be just what it is, something that is untouched by the school itself. Mathematics is certain computations, certain approaches to figures and facts; addition, multiplication, subtraction, division and so on, algebra, geometry, trig and calculus, everywhere, it doesn't matter what school you're in. But whether you *feel* anything for algebra, whether you could *love* it, say, or really *want* to learn it, that is something else entirely. Maybe that's your particular nature, or your innate ability, or maybe it has to do with something else.

James: Something else, such as?

Sharon: Such as your ability to love anything, your ability to feel that anything counts, your feeling about whether you count – that's kind of funny, but it feels right to me. Do you see what I mean?

James: That you're more likely to care about counting if the math counts as something important to you, personally. And maybe that you matter, as a recognised participant in the learning process. Something like that.

Sharon: Yes, you know, I had a decent teacher of math before algebra. Someone who knew the material, had a comprehensible style, could get a point across, illustrate equations satisfactorily and so on. And I got some preparation for algebra out of it. There were some things, at least, I didn't forget, when I had to make use of the subject. But then I had a teacher who *loved* algebra, and made me feel it meant the world to him that I could come to love it too. He made algebra into a wonderland, and me into an algebra fanatic. Algebra, everything about it, became fascinating, everything about the world was involved in it, algebra was suddenly important to other things that mattered in the world. You could just feel that when you went in there.

James: Into the classroom, or ...?

Sharon: Yeah, there, but really, what I mean was in the *relationship*. Every day, I know it wasn't me, just me and not the others, because you could see how hard they also worked, what they got from it, how they still talk about him. What I mean was in the *contact* with him, how he cared about us, how he wanted us to succeed, how we could talk with him after class or in the study period, how he was a person, see, and not just a teacher. For me, that was learning, and not just algebra. But when I do think of algebra, I think of him. I see his face, I hear his voice, and when I get stuck on a problem in mathematics, or maybe even a problem, you know, in life, I think of how it was he talked with me. I hear his voice as I think the problem through, it's like I talk with him about it. Anyway, everything counted where he was concerned, he believed I could learn the material, he took my questions seriously, he let me be real and not just a computer. And that made a difference for all of his students. That, that was learning. I measure everything in every kind of school against that now. And it won't surprise you to hear that this experience has influenced my thoughts about whether or not to become a teacher.

At this point I was quite engaged in the conversation and was thinking about the distinctions which formed Sharon's initial point of departure; how she talked about 'objective' material, then what could be called metacognition – learning about learning, and then about the environment of the school. I asked her if she was willing to revisit this theme, in light of what she had gone on to say; she was happy to do so:

James: I wonder if you could tell me, then, if you could elaborate on what you said at the outset in terms of what you've added about these teachers of yours, and the contrast between them.

Sharon: Well, now I'm kind of nervous, because I'm thinking that maybe I contradicted myself. I mean, that it doesn't seem so separate to me now, what is algebra and what was the relationship. What is mathematics, and how or in what way I learned it. I think I'm maybe kind of confused about this, though I think the factors I mentioned are still important.

James: The confusion is...?

Sharon: That, well, for me algebra is the way I lived it, or hear it, or replay it in my mind. To me, algebra is what it felt like to learn it with Mr Norton, and though I know the subject well, I can use it to my personal benefit and teach it to others as a subject, I can't say that my thinking about it or my sense of its importance are at all independent of him. I tried to explain this once to my father. I was telling him about what a difference this made to my life, how it just made the school different for me, and better than it had been before. I told him about how Mr Norton had taken the time to work with some of us after school, in advance of an exam, how we learned the algebra but also, really, ended up talking about ourselves and what it means to us to learn. And he, my dad, said I was in love with Mr Norton, which isn't true. My friend Alice said that doesn't matter, that my father is jealous or something, but maybe my love for the subject does, and she says anyway that I clearly seem to like myself better, and to be doing better in everything in my life since I started loving algebra. Maybe Mr Norton as a person made algebra lovable because of how it was just to be there with him and us. But I think, anyway, that love is involved there, that when you care for something, when you believe in it as I have come to feel about algebra, there is a kind of love involved. Maybe a love like this, some kind of deep appreciation, some kind of seeing the thing in its several dimensions, seeing its uses yet being in awe of what remains beyond you about it – what it is you still have to learn ... maybe that is, I don't know, part of what education, at its best, *could* be. And maybe in that sense I can love algebra, or even I think sometimes other people – isn't this kind of weird?, because of the way Mr Norton treated me in his class, and kind of gave algebra to me as a gift.

Recalling our teachers, recalling ourselves

It is something of a truism to suggest that most people would like to have had a teacher like Mr Norton, perhaps especially, such a teacher of mathematics, whatever the branch. It is equally probable that a considerable number of educators can recall some teachers who have helped us to love the world, and in it, each other, through our love of something we have discovered together with those teachers, in school. I would wager that many of us read this story with a measure of envy; we'd like to have had a teacher we could tell others about in such glowing terms.

At the same time, I would expect that Sharon's story could arouse other kinds of feelings; feelings of scepticism, anxiety and in some sense being unnerved as we enter into her story. She makes us think of other teachers, teachers we've forgotten or would perhaps prefer to forget, teachers who, as one interviewee put it, 'are all caught up in making you feel how small and ignorant you are when you compare yourself to their knowledge; how insignificant, how inconsequential, how you, as a student, may just come and go, but the subject, lofty, above you, pure and untouchable, will remain long after you're gone'. Some of us, perhaps, know how it was, as students, to have felt that we were a nuisance, a non-presence, to have experienced ourselves as mute, cut off, far away from those things we were to be 'learning'. Some of us may rarely have heard our voices, as students, in our classrooms, rarely have felt our passions connect, never have felt that the knowledge or the room or the school we went to were really ours. Another recent high school graduate put it this way when speaking of the school he had come from:

> It was a good school, by reputation, and there were some brilliant teachers there. But I swear to you that when I try to remember them, I just see marks, abstracted markings, on a blackboard. The school was very invested, unofficially, as far as I know, in making us feel beholden to them for everything, and made us grateful by convincing us of our stupidity, or our impertinence or triviality. You get some poets in our school, you know, some people who publish poetry in literary reviews later on. But what they write is really haunting. For them their school days were days of darkness and alienation. Reading their poems makes you think of how it felt to be there; cold, anxious, and alone.

What use is to be made of these accounts and our possible feeling responses to them, now? I suggest that we return to Sharon's words, and see how they might be reread to our benefit.

Sharon's story: algebra as a narrative of relationship

It's important to note, as a beginning, that Sharon's account is a narrative account. The information she imparts is conveyed in the form of a story. According to Sharon, you can't understand algebra, as she understands it, unless you hear the story of which it is a part. She tells us of certain characters: herself; a previous teacher of mathematics; Mr Norton; her father; Alice, her friend. One could argue, plausibly, that algebra, itself, is one of the characters here. In the 'who, what, when and where' of Sharon's story, algebra figures as a character with a life of its own; something that can be loved, that is not exhausted by its uses, that remains other, with something potential yet to be given, embraced or otherwise understood.

Having acknowledged that Sharon's account is a story, and having identified some of the characters in this account, let me turn for a moment to the themes in Sharon's tale. There is learning; her rendition of the goals of learning and its place in the school, how it functions relative to the factors in the school environment. There is math pre-Norton; a time when Sharon had not had the kind of learning experience she describes having occurred with Mr Norton. There is love, and belief, and relationship. While she struggles somewhat in defining it, Sharon is resolute about her claim that what she has come to feel about algebra is a kind of love. At one point she speaks of algebra as though it might be a person. Her criteria for love are these: that you respect the thing in its own right; that you see its being larger than any set of uses to which you could put it; that it remains something larger than its instrumentality; in your commitment to it you discover that it, as well as you, grow larger and more capable than either of you had been before. Algebra takes on what we might want to call a human, even a sacred character; it is irreducible to the sum of its parts, it is knowable only through fascination, desire, respect, commitment and responsible use, it remains something other and mysterious that, if approached properly, will give us more than we could otherwise ever hope to understand about it. Its being loved is the condition whereby it yields both its secrets and its powers. Its being loved is the possibility of its being known – if in knowledge we permit wonder, uncertainty and a respect for our limitations to become part of the formula. What we don't know, what we lack, what we desire but come to cherish in order to have – algebra stands as a metaphor for our longing and our inability to know, save for the relationship we enter with the thing we want to understand.

Mr Norton, the father, Alice – who are they in the story? If Sharon's account is reliable, and there is no reason to think it is not, Mr Norton is a teacher who is simultaneously very demanding, caring and extremely competent. His love for algebra is at once an exacting and a profoundly inviting one. For if this is an accurate reading of Sharon, she is talking about a teacher who at once threw open the world of algebra as a vast and majestic other, and brought out that way of speaking which, from the student, is the voice of her desire to be part of the other he would reveal. Mr Norton sets the students free to find what it is they will never know; they will not know 'the' definitive algebra when they walk away from his class; neither algebra nor Mr Norton, nor they, themselves, will be transparently and conclusively captured and contained when the course is over. But in setting them free, in connecting algebra to their desire, Mr Norton gives a different kind of gift; for he introduces to his students the possibility that knowledge doesn't have to be a matter of possession, but of respect, of relationship. A student departs Mr Norton's class believing that education could be about love, that the best way to appreciate something, even to find out how it should best be used, is through your love for it, in its mystery.

It's not clear that Sharon's father understands this. From the account, however, we can suppose or imagine that he regards Sharon's talk of love and algebra as having something to do with a transient phase; it is particular to Sharon's emotionality. She is talking this way because she has a crush on Mr Norton. Meanwhile Alice, comforting and practical, says not to worry too much about Sharon's dad, but to look at the outcomes for Sharon, who now loves algebra and should accept that it is legitimate to do so, and finding love with mathematics has helped her to feel better as a person and as a friend. Look to the consequences, Alice seems to be saying in the story; this may be weird but there's nothing wrong with it – in fact, the benefits are abundantly evident.

To this point we haven't sufficiently explored Sharon's place in the story. She's important, of course, we've acknowledged that without her we could understand neither Mr Norton's special role nor the algebra he helps her to discover. But in some way, up to now, we've neglected her.

Let's return to what Sharon says about counting. According to her, one counts more effectively if one counts oneself in the process. Where I am counted as an important part of the equation, she seems to be saying, I am more likely to take mathematics seriously. Where my voice can be heard (you'll recall her several points about Mr Norton as a listener) I listen more effectively. Where the classroom and the subject are mine, I will give more to them, and I will learn more of what it is there is to learn. When those things can indeed be mine, where I can love them and speak them and be heard in what they mean to me, I will want to give them to others, I will want to share what I have, I will have something to give and I will want others to know how wonderful it is. Where I am a person, and not just a consumer, a role, an instance of the enrolment figures, not, as she puts it, a 'computer', I will learn something, and I will treat that something as sacred. I will feel better about myself, I will want to give to others, I will let them, also, be. And I will believe that this process is reproducible. I will have faith in this way of learning.

In the interpretation of what Sharon's narrative offered here 'faith' becomes central. But faith in what? – In Mr Norton? – Yes, in a way, she believes in him. She trusts him, respects him, she can go to him and into his room and feel that she is at home there, that she has a place there, that her voice can be heard. She believes that this will continue. There's something about this that has moved her to test the limits of her competence, to go beyond what it was she previously thought she could do best. Because of him she has come to feel better about mathematics, herself, and the world. She believes, in the sense that she finds in this way of being a person, that it is worth the risk, worth the effort, worth the disappointment she will find in discovering that not everywhere is the world Mr Norton has helped her know and love and be part of. Through this process Sharon is building faith in herself; locating a voice and calling it her own, naming what she sees and believing she is worth listening to. Her own voice and that of Mr Norton will continue to be formative in the conversation that composes her mind; in hearing them she will continue having a place to speak, to be part of the process, the subject, the world. His responsivity has helped Sharon to respond herself, to her desire to know, her need to be heard, to speak and be one of the makers of words.

She has faith in another sense, too, suggested earlier but not spelled out. She has faith that the wonder and the process of loving something as a way of knowing it is preferable to other ways of being in the world. According to Sharon, she measures every other aspect of school, at any school that is, by what it is she has learned with Mr Norton about algebra. She has become a person, in a richer way, in the process of this experience. She can appreciate algebra, love the world, feel better about herself, and love other people more effectively because of this experience. She can give herself away now, because she has a self to give.

Sharon tells us, in part, how this has happened, how this has developed. She enters into the experience with Mr Norton, she comes into relation with him and with the subject matter and with herself and with others in new ways. As she works through problems in algebra, or in other arenas of her life, she appropriates the methods she has acquired in the classroom. What does this mean? That Sharon appropriates the strategies of equations and sped-up calculation to effect new balances and analyses of her relations with others in the human world? That's not what she tells us. Instead, she tells us something very different. She tells us that as she approaches a problem in algebra or in other relationships in life, she allows herself to treat that problem as worthy of engagement through her employment of a dialogue. She talks to herself, she hears Mr Norton's voice in her head, she reconstructs the problem in terms of a discourse that she has learned to speak with him. Through what Mr Norton has said and encouraged her to say, she allows her voice to sound, she turns to 'his' voice in relation to 'her', and, through dialogue, the problem is engaged and worked out.

Before moving on, it is essential to say something we might at first take to be an obvious part of who Sharon is as a character in this story. Sharon is a girl. We need to pay attention to that. She's a girl who feels that before Mr Norton she wasn't taken seriously in her school. She's a girl speaking of her deepest convictions and getting put off by her father. In his 'given' understanding of what his daughter's meanings could be, he competes with the male teacher, and dismisses his daughter's claim on truth as a misplaced crush. She's a girl, Sharon, who like other girls, in the transition from adolescence to adulthood, is struggling to know her own voice, to honour relationship, not to give up connection for the attractions and powerlessness so many of us would insist are part of womanly femininity. Her peers, we know from considerable research, are in trouble, at risk, most of them declining in self esteem, many depressed and engaging in behaviours of self-destruction (see also Brown & Gilligan, 1992). For adolescent girls, primed for discovery and caring for what they know, we educators too often are those who thwart, demean and abuse. We haven't learned what we need to learn from them.

Problem-solving dialogue and the self

Particular problems in mathematics, like other problems in life, are, like algebraic equations, multifactorial processes, in which no constituent member of the equation can be understood apart from the others; in which any given variable has meaning only because of the role it can play in the world of numbers that has been arranged. The mind, Sharon's mind, is not independent, not an information-processing machine, chewing up data and, on someone else's schedule, spitting out on command. It is, rather, structured in the form of dialogue, self-talk, drawing its form and effective in its activity only according to its capacity to speak, to hear its own voice and to count that voice meaningful. It needs to play a role in the learning process that it can make explicit in the form of conversation, talking its way through problems, always addressing itself to another. It is a self that knows itself through the words it is capable of speaking, through the voices which sound in its field of being, as the speaker whom others address, in the stream of a story in which it is both the subject and the author of the terms. The self is, in other words, vocalised into being, spoken into its identity, played out in the theatre of its life, where its roles are both marked and inscribed by its voice(s) and the speeches and roles of others. To speak of education as the transmission of something fixed, unchangingly true, without further need for discussion, or, on the other hand, as a process that produces atomistic, independent selves whirring freely in a universe of their own autonomy, is to leave the actors stranded, the stage bereft, the person outside of the parlance.

At this point then it may be said that we learn in relationship, to ourselves, to our teachers, to our colleagues in every part of the school. We learn as a function of whether we are heard, or misheard, or closed out. We regard our education in terms of the relationships we have formed in its course, and we remember it fondly or not on account of the kinds of relationships we have had as part of it. Learning, I have tried to show, is a relational process, in which even the most 'objective' of things to be known, like algebra, mean what they do to us in accordance with our capacity to let our desire for them be known and engaged. We learn by loving, or in spite of it, and the difference is consequential. In the first case we feel good about ourselves, our teachers, and the subject at hand, and we want to share that feeling and the related knowledge with others. In the second case we get by, we prove our point but remain distant both from the thing we are supposed to understand, and the self, or selves, as fields of dialogue, through which we might understand 'it'. We are distant from what it is we hunger for. We resent our teachers and our schools, and, if we should become teachers, we often, even with the best of intentions in mind, even with the intention to correct what was wrongly, we feel, done to us in the process or our own schooling, reproduce the ill effects of the learning environment of which we have been part.

The stories we tell about what it is we know, what it is we want to learn, and how it has felt for us to be engaged in the educational process are well worth listening to; that is another point of these reflections. We think and act and make our way in story form, according to the roles we are allowed, according to the ways we have come to sound to ourselves, to the voices and dialogues we know. Our learning, then, is embodied, the objects of our quest are incarnational. When we talk about educational experience we feel something physical. We see faces and hear voices as we speak. The notion of education as the imparting of a truth apart from the way we experience it is false, dangerous and corrupting. To tell our students that there is a truth apart from their imaginings, questions and participation in the community of those who make the consensus that we call the truth is to tell them that the truth of their experience doesn't count, that they are not worth counting on, and invites them to opt out of the commitment required for learning to occur. To pretend to a knowledge that we don't have, and to tell the story of 'the thing' to be learned, without discussion or permission for mutual construction, is to demean ourselves and our students, and to fly in the face of what we otherwise might learn from them. It permits us to go on dividing ourselves, keeping us distant from one another, locked up in the cold, alone. (See also Belenky *et al.*, 1986, Brown & Gilligan, op. cit.; Bruner, 1986; Cupitt, 1991, 1992; Day, 1993a, 1993b, 1993c, 1991a, 1991b; Day, Naedts & Saroglou, in press; Day & Tappan, 1996, Tappan, 1991; Tappan & Brown, 1989; Wertsch, 1991; Witherell & Noddings, 1991.)

Fides ex auditu

What might this have to do with a Christian education? Is there anything about what I have tried to outline today that would be of consequence in relation to the development of faith? Is there anything that might matter here with regard to our identity as 'Christian' educators and schools? Is there something our faith has to offer in the light of Sharon's story and the view of education which the interpretation offered here attempts to underscore? Is there something Sharon's narrative brings to our appropriation of faith for education, some way to recover, or renew, or reread the text of our faith in order to be more effective as educators?

I will remind you that I come to all this as a psychologist and as an educator, as a fellow traveller in the world of signs, and that I carry no priestly authority. Like most Christian educators I come to the Christian story through my experience as a participant in it. I have no metaphysic to offer.

Perhaps, paradoxically, that is part of what I *can* offer, saying words from my experience of them, and saying there is a great deal I do not know. How, after all, given what I have said, could I possibly present 'the conclusion', the definitive story, about education and faith? That would, on the terms I have offered, be both ridiculous and offensive, since what has gone buffers a claim that truth is participatory, conversational, for the long term. The terms of truth are still being worked out, and they are structured, through words, in relationship. As for learning, that comes, at best, through love. I learn something in so far as it can be brought into the scope of my vocabulary. I appreciate that learning when the words I speak taste good in my mouth. That there is no metaphysic, no knowledge, of algebra or of the Christian faith, save through those in relation to whom we learn to talk about it, feel about it, and embody it, does have, I think, some tangible consequences for how we might speak about Christian education. We never come to know what 'the Christian faith' is. Rather we come to think it important, valuable, inspiring, worth the time, and so on, through the practice of it with other persons. I don't identify Christians by some abstract criterion that comes from reading metaphysics, or by embracing an ideology. Neither do I live a Christian life, or offer a Christian education, by reading or teaching theology or ethics or the like. If what I assert has any merit, it is in its emphasis on the lived relation as the pedagogical fulcrum; when I address you as someone valuable and come to know what you think in terms of the person you are, perhaps then I will have something to offer you, perhaps then we will learn something of value.

Neither in faith nor in education is it possible to get very far where the starting point is abstraction. It isn't possible to know a Christian life by reading philosophy about it. Instead to be Christian is to live in a world that is infused with stories, words and performances, some of which, in the course of contact with them, get appropriated as 'Christian'. From there they come to mean something, to appeal or offend, to inspire, move to action, incline the person to a sense of wonder and respect, or not. Indeed, we hear words used in different ways. Other persons, other speakers, invite us in or close us out of what it is they have to say. They offer up text-like performances which we make sense of in story form, and it is through the stories we tell to ourselves, in the form of dialogues that we hear and reproduce from interactions with each other, that the 'truths' of our faith become 'known'. We employ these words as practices, and, through engagement with other people, come to decide that these words make sense or that they don't. Words get reworked, we hear them anew, we stop suddenly and find ourselves mouthing familiar words as if for the first time, in light of new contacts, new employments, new relationships in which the words can or cannot be used. We live from what we have known *in relation to*, outside of that there is no reality. And reality, as I have tried to accentuate in this essay, is something wordy, physical, full of emotion. We are what we are to others first, we become a combination of what they say about us, and what we come to feel about them, in the multitude of conversations where we find ourselves in speech. Our churches are like our parents in this regard. How we feel about ourselves, and about what they say,

No need for 'C.E'

depends on what we experience there. Faith is how we feel about the relationships we are in, where the words of faith are first heard, before it is a belief or an ethic or a practice that we call our own. And however much this faith becomes owned we are thrown back, continuously, into the stream of words and touches and faces and feelings in which it has come to be part of our vocabulary. According to this view, faith is living, anti-ideological, never determinable as a metaphysic. Christian faith is a relational practice. It's something we're invited into, not as a museum but as a living conversation.

Suffer the little children, and let them come unto me. *Fides ex auditu*... Now I see dimly...In the beginning was the word. I want a plan and I get a metaphor, seeking a strategy I am given a story, needing to assure myself of my virtue I am told to hesitate before throwing my stone, knowing whose side I am on I am challenged to love my enemy. Where have I seen thee? In the least of these.... Wanting an abstract principle far off and in control I am given a person, born as a baby, cared for by a mother, someone with a face, who asks questions, grows weary, has need of his friends. Wanting an all-powerful, triumphant God, I am given a man historical, hanging on a cross, waiting to die.

In this reading of the Christian story, there is a most peculiar message: that in being vulnerable I may understand that in being responsive I engender responsibility, that in listening I give the word speech, that in uncertainty, I will be received, and that in dying, in giving myself away, in accepting that I am the time of my life, I will taste eternity; I will be reborn.

This central paradox of Christianity returns us to an understanding that to teach we must surpass all of our certainties, that to achieve perspective we must be engaged in our desire, that to hear we must be permitted to speak, that to become responsible we must have been responded to. It remains for us to think about some of the resources and obstacles that the Catholic tradition in education provides to making this 'way' of education possible.

From the inside, seen from without

It lies well beyond the scope of this chapter to consider both the defining characteristics of Catholicism, the distinctiveness of Catholic experience, and what makes Catholic education at once Catholic and special. Readers would be well advised to turn elsewhere for such resources (see, e.g. Bryk, 1993; Dolan, 1985; Greeley, 1990; McBrien, 1980; Rohr & Martos, 1989; Schreck, 1984 and Tracy, 1982). What is offered are some personal reflections that seem to me pertinent as to what, from the inside, viewed from without, would appear to be resources for a relational education within the Catholic tradition. Additionally, I wish to suggest that there are some obstacles which present a real challenge to the commitment to relationship in education in those Catholic environments I know best. My task here is not to undertake the question of whether these obstacles are to be found *solely* in the Catholic context. Such a comparative task lies beyond what can be done here, and would require an entirely different point of departure – namely, a rigorous empirical study of a variety of religiously and non-religiously inspired educational environments, the development of hypotheses and the development of criteria for testing them, more than one analyst of the data which would be collected, and more. What matters here is that over the course of years of experience certain features of Catholic education seem to me particularly striking as resources or, alternatively, as obstacles. As we shall see, in some cases, what might well be or become a resource has the potential to become an obstacle. On then, to these admittedly personal observations.

Firstly, it is almost a truism to state that Catholic education has a history of close association with particular communities: communities of faith, religious communities within the Church, neighbourhoods and/or ethnic communities. Each of these networks potentially serves to remind educators of their rootedness in relationships which transcend the particular 'business' of 'education' as a method or profession. They serve, moreover, to demonstrate to students, that whatever their expertise, teachers in such settings hold in common with their students a vision that may bond them in a covenant that is relationally more profound than a simple or conventional provider-consumer contract. Many of Catholicism's religious orders have spawned their own particular visions of how this relationality is to be lived in the educational process. Of course it is also true that some students regard this as so much antique jargon because in their experience it merely adorns brochures designed to attract parents and convince them their children are really getting a Catholic education, but in some cases does little to influence educational practice within the walls of the school. Teachers who are inspired by such visions often feel isolated and ineffectual in their schools, because relationship is not to be regarded, according to their school authorities and colleagues, as being expedient to the 'business' of their schools. In some cases the relationships that might be enriched by such visions of community are often obstructed by another element of Catholic education that seems to me striking, namely, an often cruel attachment to hierarchy and rigid notions of authority. The attitude that 'it's not for *us* to say, *they're* the ones who know, or who will make the decisions' is nowhere so prevalent as I have met it in Catholic educational institutions, at all levels of study and ranks of prestige. Something apparently deeply ingrained in Catholic consciousness inclines people to be keenly aware of their place in a distinct hierarchy that is seen as something not to be challenged, even where it is regarded to be unfair, ill-informed or abusive. The degree to which silence reigns in such circumstances, and how much of what matters to the pedagogy of places remains unspoken in public forums related to them is a matter of both surprise and anxiety. There is at once a relational prerogative and tremendous institutional disincentive to realise it in some Catholic contexts, and here there may too frequently be seen a greater tension between official discourse and how the ideology embedded in that discourse was lived with so little protest or open discussion on the part of community members.

Second, the sacramental element in Catholicism would appear to be well adapted to a relational emphasis in education. When a community of learners is brought together to bear witness to a drama of the most crucial existential proportions on a regular basis, and to share in the grace it is supposed to offer, there is a potentially very healthy levelling and renewing effect for relationships. Regrettably, the sharing of sacramental processes is all too often either isolated from the mainstream of community discussion about pedagogy, or a matter of rote obedience with little carry-over to daily decisions about how relationships are to be lived within the school or university.

Finally, and perhaps curiously, it seems to me that the tradition of saints and of Marian spirituality offer much to a relational perspective for Catholic education. The saints offer numerous examples of lives transformed through relationship, lives that inspire on account of relationship, and lives which rearrange the hierarchical structures that often impede relationship; they defy obstacles of social class and ethnicity and speak of a vision of community in which all might find a place, a voice, a spirituality. This seems to me part of the genius of the Catholic tradition – a knack for diverse mediational practices and figures, which provide an enormous variety of cultures and personalities with the means to identify with someone who became wise and holy. Frequently, however, the appropriation of these devices is perverted – the truth is already known because 'they' already said it and they were holy, so…, or through a kind of doublespeak in which all are supposed to have a calling but some are holier than others and always will be so. The Marian element in Catholicism seems a particularly fascinating case in point of what I've just tried to suggest, and recent studies (e.g. Carroll, 1983, 1985; Greeley, 1977, 1988, 1990; Stanford, 1988; Zimdars-Swartz, 1991) show that the figure of Mary is especially compelling to a great many, including young people, in our day. This figure serves at once as a symbol and tangible reminder of how important the feminine is in Catholic spirituality and religious practice, and serves to balance other elements in faith experience. Mary's importance is constantly relational in the Catholic tradition and is appealing to young Catholics today. She invites a new look at devotion as part of the heart of educational practice, and at the roles of boys and girls, women and men, in pedagogical theory and action. Too often, of course, she has been misused in this regard, and instead of a relational resource has become a kind of impossible standard remote from the immediate experience of students and teachers.

In exploring these possibilities and models it is important to note that I am keenly aware of how many students in Catholic schools and universities are not Catholic. I do not for a moment assume that the renewal of relationship as the central focus of Catholic education can exclude the experience of non-Catholic students or teachers within it. That would hardly make sense given my stance as a writer, looking in from outside the Catholic world.

Conclusion

As an outsider looking in, and working from the inside out, I am at once struck by the enormous resources which exist for relationship in Catholic educational contexts, and the same time, concerned about the misappropriation of those same resources, and, indeed, by some of what I have found to be all too frequently stifling of relationship in certain attachments to rigid structures of authority and tradition in a way I have rarely seen elsewhere.

I hope that this brief essay may be of some value to those who care for relationship, for education, and for the Christian faith, both inside and outside the bounds of Catholic institutions and communities.

SPIRITUAL EDUCATION, RELIGION AND THE MONEY CULTURE

John M. Hull

Introduction

This enquiry about the future development of Christian education must begin with the character of money. From there it goes on to questions of culture; because money generates a certain spirituality and the spirituality of money is a principal factor in the creation of this culture. The third stage in our enquiry will lead towards religion, which challenges the supremacy of the money culture. Next, we shall deal with self-deception, since the most familiar coping strategies used by Christians in managing the culture of the money spirituality are forms of self-deception. By then we will have reached the point where we can consider the formation of children and young people within our school system, and so we will pass finally to the question of the curriculum and how far this may contribute to a Christian spirituality for tomorrow's world.

THE SPIRITUALITY OF MONEY

The global power of money has reached proportions today which were unimaginable even as recently as one hundred years ago. The very survival of whole species of living creatures depends almost entirely upon their monetary value. Nature's law, the survival of the fittest, has given way to the law of human society, the survival of the most financially interesting. Scope for investment has taken the place of adaptation to environment. Perhaps it should rather be said that money has become the all-pervasive environment to which the species must adapt in order to survive. Money is the very air we breathe. The diminishing habitats of the animals are the products of financial exploitation of the world's resources and an animal species will only be able to restrain the forces that threaten to destroy its habitat if that species itself is of sufficient investment interest to pose a countering financial power. Only money restrains money.

The impact of money is seen not only upon the survival of the species and upon the environment but is to be found in our own human relationships, our inner emotions, what we think we are and what we should pursue. George Simmel divides his great book *The Philosophy of Money* [first published 1901] into two sections, the first dealing with the objective character of money, and the second dealing with the subjective or the psychological impact of money. It is striking to note that both in the objective and the subjective senses, money is similar to God. For example, money is not an entity like other entities but is the entity which represents the value of all other entities. It is that commodity which enables all other commodities to be related to each other; it is the purely generalised value of all specific values. Through money, entities are lifted out of time and space. Before my apples go bad I dispose of them, turn them into money, which will resist the ravages of time, inflation permitting. While my apples will deteriorate if bounced around too much in too many container vessels, my money will slip easily, in a mere second, from one part of the globe to another. God also must not be regarded as a thing amongst things but as that reality in whom all things whatever are grounded, in whom all things subsist, the Being who is regarded as the ground of all particular entities and thus as the power of Being itself. Invulnerable to time and space, God is nevertheless involved in both space and time, unapproachable in his own essence as being the most general of all universals, the supremely transworld reality; God is nevertheless accessible through the particular, as sacramental theology describes.

From the psychological point of view, God is that which attracts our ultimate longing, that concern which has no rival, is unconditioned. Similarly, the fascination of money is such that those who long for it become possessed by it. It preoccupies the imagination and although it is only of value as a means to many ends, it becomes the supreme end in itself. Money is the outstanding fetish of our society, and like all fetishes it manifests a concentrated erotic or numinous power. Just as God, when moved from all contexts in life and history, reified into mere language, becomes a magic talisman, charged with potency over the imagination, acting like a virus in a computer file, so money, when cut off from its use-value, itself becomes charged with the fascinating power of pure holiness.

Jesus certainly understood the subjective similarity between God and money when he told his hearers not to lay up for themselves treasures upon earth, for 'where your treasure is, there will your heart be also' (Mt 19:21). The striking parallel drawn by Jesus between God and money suggests the very similarity, indeed the exchangeability, to which I draw attention. 'No one can serve two masters' (Mt 19:24), but the one you do serve will indeed become your master and (if it is not already God) will take upon itself the attributes of God. People worship money, and have some dim realisation that they are indeed worshipping money.

When people within a money culture worship God, they do not always realise that the God may be the personification or the reification of money. The religious content itself has become invaded by the character of money, so that, as St Paul said, we have 'exchanged the truth about God for a lie and worshipped and served the creature rather than the Creator' (Rm 1:25), (see also Hull, 1996a).

Culture

In kinship societies, human relationships are shaped by marriage and descent. Society is arranged in family groups. In societies based upon domination, sometimes called 'tribute societies', human relationships are dominated by military might. But when societies are based upon human relationships as mediated through money, we have a radically different type of culture (Wolf, 1982, p. 76). If you consult the various dictionaries of industrial relations, you will find articles on culture creation (Huczynski, 1987, p. 55). There are techniques for deliberately changing culture, and Britain in the past twenty years has passed through a significant process of culture creation. It has become customary to contrast the service culture with the enterprise culture, and it is certainly true that the latter is not particularly interested in service, since the enterprise which it nurtures is primarily enterprise in the generation and the multiplication of money. Most of the serious books on money emphasise its power to create culture (Marx, 1976; Thompson, 1961; Vilar, 1976; Sohn-Rethel, 1978). I have already referred to George Simmel who emphasised the freedom and adaptability of social relations that money introduces. If the medieval lord of the manor demands that the serfs or peasants should render their due to him in honey, they have no choice but to keep beehives. But if the lord will accept a financial equivalent, then the peasant is free to rotate his crops, to innovate in fresh forms of production (Simmel, 1990, p. 286). Money is one of the most brilliant inventions because it leads to such incredible adaptability. Money makes free association more widely possible, since through paying my subscription I can support many causes and distribute my energy and commitment in a far more diverse way than would be possible if I myself had to be personally present at everything I supported.

The former Professor of Greek at the University of Birmingham, George Thompson (1961), has shown the impact of the very first money upon Greek culture and philosophy from the seventh century BC. Nancy Hartsock (1983) has described the close connection between the exercise of masculine power in the realms of sexuality and finance. The most insightful of all the western critics of money was Karl Marx, who analysed the close connection between money, shopping and industry, developing a parallel between industrial production and cultural reproduction.

W. F. Haug (1986) has traced the history of modern shopping, showing how it happened that one was no longer buying merely the commodity but the ethos, the image, the lifestyle. The commodity becomes an extension of the self, and even the body becomes a commodity, as is clearly shown in the history of the cosmetic industry. A particularly significant aspect of the culture-creating power of money is to be seen in the rise of the symbolic commodity. In the nineteenth century, industrial production was aimed at the satisfaction of human need. It was a matter of satisfying consumption. As the power of industrial productivity increased, it became possible to make far more things than people could consume, leading to gluts on the market. In the twentieth century it has been possible to overcome this to a certain extent by shifting the focus of the commodity from need to desire. My needs are limited but my desires are endless; I am satisfied with just so much food, my feet will not wear more than one pair of shoes at a time, but my imagination conjures up world upon world of desirable things. So it is that the traditional economic distinction between use value and exchange value must now be supplemented by a third type of value: symbolic value (Bauxrillard, 1975).

Now we have reached a stage where only a few pockets of resistance remain against the all-powerful penetration of money. Any structure of human relations which is not available for the free transformation into money values and thus available for the generation of wealth is an obstacle and must be removed. Now, by investing in the National Lottery, for a mere £1 a week you can buy a little bit of hope, a little bit of excitement, a little bit of meaning for your life.

Religion

There are several areas of human life which still stand as pockets of resistance against the domination of the money culture. One of these is the freedom and spontaneity of human sexuality, without which love would give way to universal prostitution. Another pocket of resistance is created by children. Very young children are immune to money; they live in simple trust and dependence for their daily bread upon those who love and support them. It is in this sense that they represent the Kingdom of God and its values. Those of us enmeshed in the money struggles of adult life can no longer easily find such innocence (Mt 18:3; 7:9-11). A third pocket of resistance (and this list is not intended to be exhaustive) lies in religion.

The Bible of course was written in a pre-industrial age. Nevertheless, a growing awareness of the impact of money upon human spirituality can be traced through its pages.

> Ho, every one who thirsts, come to the waters; and he who has no money, come, buy and eat! Come buy wine and milk without money and without price (Is 55:1).

> You know that you were ransomed from the futile ways inherited from your fathers, not with perishable things such as silver or gold, but with the precious blood of Christ (1 P 1:18, 19a).

Jesus spoke more about money than about prayer. When he held up a coin and asked whose image and inscription was stamped upon it, he drew a parallel between coinage and human personality (Mk 12:14-17). A human being is like a coin, stamped with the image and inscription of God. When human life becomes coin-shaped, it is relatively easy for one image and superscription to take the place of the other. Almost without our realising it, the image of God is replaced by the image of Caesar and the coin-like character of human life moves from the symbolic area into increasing literalism.

Against the money culture Jesus poses the culture of loving self-sacrifice:

For the Son of man came not to be served but to serve, and to give his life as a ransom for many (Mk 10:45).

Once again we notice the financial metaphor of the ransom. The Kingdom of Heaven is like a merchant who seeks precious pearls and at last finds one of great price. The Kingdom is like a man who ploughs his field and who finds buried treasure (Mt 13:44ff). It is always the same – the values of the Kingdom are expressed in financial terms, but are the opposite to them; they cancel them out by presupposing an alternative culture.

For you know the grace of our Lord Jesus Christ, that though he was rich, yet for our sake he became poor, so that by his poverty you might become rich (2 Co 8:9).

Consider your calling, my brothers and sisters, not many of you were wise according to worldly standards, not many were powerful, not many were of noble birth; but God chose what is foolish in the world to shame the wise, God chose what is weak in the world to shame the strong (1 Co 1:26-27).

… a thorn was given to me in the flesh … three times I besought the Lord about this, that it should leave me; but he said to me, 'My grace is sufficient for you, for my power is made perfect in weakness' (2 Co 12:7-9).

So we see that the values of faith, of grace, of love stand against the corrupting money values and offer us an image of a new kind of society, a Kingdom of God, in which money will become our servant to enhance our solidarity and our freedom, and no longer our master and our God to turn us into its own image. Religion itself, however, is ambiguous. God and money are so easily interchangeable. Rival theologies jostle against one another within the spirituality of the money culture. The prosperity gospel assures us that God favours the rich and has rewarded them with their money, whereas the gospel that emphasises the bias of God, towards the poor and the needy believes that God 'has filled the hungry with good things, and the rich he has sent empty away' (Lk 1:53). Which theology is correct? To what extent has our own spirituality been invaded by the ambiguity of theology? Christian theology has no privileged realm of escape, no magical haven of protection within which it can be safe from the penetration of money values.

Self-deception

At this point it becomes necessary to have a theology and a psychology of self-deception. Money itself is full of guile and deception, transforming itself from one shape into another with astonishing versatility. The money culture becomes almost invisible as it surrounds us so completely. We no longer notice it and our imaginations are so possessed by it that we can no longer conceive of an alternative to our complete dependence upon it. It is through self-deception that honest and trustworthy people maintain their self-respect in a money culture (Christian Aid, 1994, Chapter 6). We do this in many ways (McLaughlin and Rorty, 1988; Via, 1990). Our language itself conceals the truth from us by telling us alternative stories about our culture and ourselves. People talk about the enterprise culture, which is, in fact, a money culture. People talk about the generation of wealth when what they mean is making money. People talk about the danger of setting one's heart upon material things when the danger lies not in material things which may be beautiful and useful, but in setting one's heart upon anything other than the true God. It is the love of money, not materialism, which is the blight of our culture, and those who contrast the spiritual with the material are merely distracting us from the central issue. We are to find our spirituality not as an alternative to our materiality but within it. St Paul said that we were to present our bodies as a living sacrifice to God and thus to achieve the transformation of our minds (Rm 12:1).

Self-deception disguises us from ourselves, and it does this by taking hundreds of tiny steps, each one of which is barely noticeable by itself. Self-deception uses selective attention to screen out unwelcome knowledge and inconsistent facts. Self-deception puts things into compartments, so that one part of my life is not in touch with another part, so that I myself become fragmented into several persons. Self-deception results in a loss of integrity, since in order to deceive myself I must reduce effective communication between one part of my mind and the other. Self-deception functions through refusing to spell out in detail the implications and consequences of our actions. Self-deception thrives upon vagueness and upon distraction. Self-deception is one of the major coping mechanisms used by people who live in a money culture situated within a world of wretchedness and poverty. Self-deception is pleasant because it enables us to maintain our self-esteem, and it is innocent because it succeeds in its object, which is to deceive us about the very fact that we are deceived (Fingarette, 1969; Elster, 1983).

Spiritual education

If the general outline of my argument so far is accepted, it becomes possible to interpret many features of the growing literature on spiritual education. Here I try to illuminate four of these:

1) Spirituality is often regarded as the cultivation of the inward. There is a great deal written about inner feelings, although I have not yet discovered what outer feelings might be. There is a great deal about the inner journey, about discovering self-transcendence and so on. I shall describe this feature of the spirituality literature as the introversion of spirituality (see Slee, 1992).

2) There is a tendency, to which I have already referred, to contrast the spiritual with the material. The spiritual is thought of as being located in the mind, in ideas, in heavenly aspirations and in so-called spiritual realities. Against this, I try to adopt an incarnational model of spirituality, one which emphasises the word made flesh, and this tendency could be called the materialisation of spirituality. By this I mean to suggest that we should not seek to make the spiritual more spiritual but should rather seek to make it more concrete, more earthly, more in touch with the content and structure of our bodily lives (see Davis, 1976).

3) There is a tendency to root spirituality in a sort of universal anthropology, to speak of the capacity of human nature to transcend itself through imagination and art and so forth. Spirituality is regarded as a characteristic feature of the human species in contrast with the other animal species. This anthropologisation of spirituality distracts us from the specific historical and social characteristics of spirituality as we know it today. It suggests that spirituality is somehow immutable and perennial, whereas spirituality, as I have tried to show, is fluctuating, ambiguous, driven by technology and economics and susceptible to profound and often rapid social change (see Hull, 1996b).

4) Spirituality is aestheticised. Its locus is to be found in the beautiful, it is to be pursued by cultivating our finer feelings, our more insightful perception; it is to be located in poetry, in music, in the arts and in all the finer flowers of what we call the higher culture.

The latter feature turns spirituality into a pursuit of the refined classes; it becomes a privilege available to the few, something which middle-class families can provide for their children in order to enrich their children's lives. We may call this the aestheticisation of spirituality. It should be contrasted with that spirituality which acknowledges the reality of human pain, which seeks to bring human beings out of their own pain into a shouldering of responsibility for the pain of the world (Chopp, 1986; Lamb, 1982). These are some examples of the kinds of false emphases which I detect in the literature of spiritual education, and I believe that these can be understood as various kinds of evasions, self-deceptions and cultural productions attributable to the money economy. They represent various forms of what I have called the spirituality of money.

Spiritual education is that education which seeks to inspire children and young people to live for others. Spiritual education seeks to recreate solidarity through participation in the lives of others. This is to be distinguished from moral education partly because of the quality of inspiration. Moral education has to do with the concepts of duty and obligation, of right and wrong. It enables children and young people to develop moral judgment and to distinguish the character of justice and so forth. The spiritual education to which I refer is inspirational and thus practical. It is focused upon achieving a transformation of life in the direction of mutuality and sharing.

Before we take this any further we must pause to reflect upon the impact of the spirituality of the money culture on children and young people. I have already pointed out that early childhood, very early childhood, is a haven of use values as opposed to exchange values. Young children sometimes try to bite a coin only to throw it away with disgust. It's no use. Those who take so-called 'rational economic man' in the market-place as the fundamental characteristic of human relationships have already revealed their choice of values. It would be more faithful to our species if we took the first relationship between mother and baby, or that between the young infant and its first adult carer as the model of our true humanity (Hartsock, 1983, p. 41). This is a model of dependence and inter-dependence, in which the rationality of the agreed price gives way to the mutuality of exchanged powers. Who is more powerful, the mother or the baby? Weakness and strength are here exchanged and become complementary. This is the way we 'win strength out of weakness' (Hb 11:34). It is not the same as the satisfaction produced by having got a good bargain.

Children quickly learn, however, that amongst adults money is regarded as the secret of happiness. This awareness does not usually become mature until the secondary school years (key stages 3 and 4). Now money begins to function as the universal expression of good will, which just because it is universal and no longer individualised obliterates goodwill itself. My fourteen-year-old, instead of choosing or making a present for his friend at school, gives him a five pound note. The five pound note is passed on from friend to friend on birthdays. It is convenient since nobody has to bother; it is absolutely equitable since the value of the five pound note is stable, and it doesn't actually cost anyone anything. The former National Curriculum Council published some guidelines on economic and industrial awareness as a cross-curricular theme. These referred to using 'giving' in order to help pupils to understand the character of economic transactions. The curious thing is that when this happens, giving itself becomes invisible. Instead of giving, we have circulation, that being the only form of giving which is intrinsic to the character of money.

It is symptomatic of our spiritual situation that giving becomes a way of teaching the nature of money, by way of illustration. 'Schools should consider ways of teaching pupils to ... know that buying, selling and giving are ways of exchanging goods and services' (National Curriculum Council 1990, pp. 14f). It is suggested that children should 'examine money in circulation at a simple level, e.g. banks, shops, post office' and should 'discuss ways in which things are exchanged without money and why, e.g. gifts and "swaps"' (NCC, 1990, p. 15). It would be more illuminating for children if they were helped to see the contrast between giving and circulating. Giving is not a way of exchanging goods and services.

Give to anyone who begs from you, and do not refuse anyone who would borrow from you (Mt 5:42).
Freely you have received, freely give (Mt 10:8).
I was hungry and you gave me bread (Mt 25:35).
Thanks be to God for God's unspeakable gift (2 Co 9:15).

The spirituality of the money culture and the spirituality of the culture of grace confront each other.

With students aged sixteen plus, everything has become instrumental. Recently a chemistry teacher from one of our well-known independent schools told me how he tried to help his students to respond to the wonderful beauty of chemical structures. One of the students said 'You're sad, sir'. 'No', he replied, 'You're sad, because you don't understand the beauty inside things.' For this student, the only sensible pursuit in life was to use everything as a means to an end, that end being the securing of money through getting a well-paid job. Everything is looked upon as instrumental in terms of its examination and career prospects, and that in turn is based upon the belief that money gives the golden touch that transforms life. The point is that if you haven't got any, it does. Nevertheless, as King Midas discovered years ago, as the universal means it destroys the very ends it pursues.

These values which are the internalised product of the money culture are in conflict with the pockets of resistance of which adolescents are often so keenly aware. As the young child's sense of reciprocal fairness, the idea of taking turns and the idea of fairness give way in middle and later adolescence to a sense of universal justice and to increased appreciation of the nature of human communities, the outrageous invasion of human values by the money culture is often seen quite starkly by our young people, sometimes indeed hidden under a mask of cynicism, but often flashing out in moments of real indignation. I have already referred to the word 'sad' which is such a significant expression in the current vocabulary of young people. My wife and I received several phone calls from the troubled parents of a student in his first year at university, with whom they had lost contact, asking if we could find him, deliver letters to his assumed address and so on. The student was not my student; I had never met him or his parents. We took the phone calls with courtesy, as anyone would have done, and ran around to the house with the messages.

> 'Why don't you just tell them to get lost?' asked my twelve-year-old.
> 'Because everyone who asks you for help has a right to be heard,' my wife said.
> 'That's sad, Mum!' was the reply.

To be 'sad' is to be burdened with values of solidarity and mutuality, to care for things in themselves, to be pathetic in one's failure to adopt lines of action which are obviously and immediately in one's own self-interest.

It was only a few days later that my twelve-year-old, the same one, said:

> 'Sarah thinks I'm sad!'
> I asked why.
> 'Because she says it doesn't matter if the tropical rain forests get destroyed because we don't live there and I say it does matter.'

Our young people are also keenly aware of the fragmented character of the spiritual life as expressed through religion. Graham Rossiter and Marisa Crawford (1994), the Australian Catholic educators, have written about this with considerable insight. They point out that whereas most adults still comprehend Christian spirituality as a more or less coherent tradition, which they accept or do not, regard themselves as within or outside, for many young people this sense of the unified character of a spiritual tradition has waned. They have adopted a pick-and-mix approach to the spiritual traditions. They are often quite open to religious ideas and actions, interested in these ideals and the people who have lived in accordance with them, but have a certain independent attitude toward them. They can take it or leave it. They don't mind learning about such subjects and are often quite interested. Here and there, where there is something which they feel has an affinity or an identity to offer, they accept it, but they seldom identify completely with a religious tradition. On the other hand, there are those few exceptions who become totally engrossed and even fanaticised by the integrity of a particular tradition. These aspects of adolescent spirituality today are consistent with the notion of identity diffusion as outlined by Erik H. Erikson (1968) and by the sociologists Peter Berger (1979) with his concept of 'the heretical imperative' and Robert Bellah (1970) with his contrast between compact and complex religious symbolism.

My own interpretation is that this fracturing or complexification of the traditional spiritual houses is at least partly the product of the impact upon them of the money-culture values, to which they have responded ambiguously, becoming increasingly divided and disjointed in the process. This brings us to what Jürgen Habermas (1975) described as the great legitimation crisis of our culture: so great is our technological might that we can make anything, except meaning. Our societies need to generate meaning in order to induce people into the pursuit of wealth, even in the face of the discouragement of knowing that only a few can succeed. The only sources of genuine meaning are, however, the ancient spiritual traditions, and these are being eroded by the very processes of the money culture. Consequently we have a crisis.

Spirituality across the curriculum

If we take seriously this analysis of the conflicting spiritualities of our culture, in the light of the suggestion that truly spiritual education is that which inspires young people to live for others, we will find that this makes a considerable impact upon the curriculum and indeed upon the structure and values of school life. There is within each subject a subject for death and a subject for life. The deeper you go into the meaning of the subject, the more this dichotomy emerges. This is an example of spelling-out as a technique for dissolving self-deception. For example, it is not sufficient in teaching chemistry and physics to draw attention to the wonder, beauty and design of nature. This is certainly an important aspect of spiritual education, in that it draws attention to the beauty of things in themselves rather than as means for the generation of wealth. However, one must pass on to consider the character of the human exploitation of chemistry in relation to the environment and particularly the unequal distribution of the world's resources. If this second part is not added on, we are left with the spirituality of the aesthetic.

A similar distinction could be made with respect to religious education, where we should distinguish that form of religion which promotes the quest for universal peace and justice from that form of religion which builds up individual and group identity in a tribalistic way by excluding other religious traditions. This latter type of religion is what may be called religionism (Hull, 1996c). Thus one can ask of a Christian education curriculum whether its major emphasis is upon Christian-ness or upon Christian religionism (Hull, 1995).

The relationship of this approach to the teaching of economics and business studies is rather obvious. Just as there is no private language so there is no private money. Language and money are forms of social life. Is the collective, social and interpersonal character of money recognised and affirmed in the teaching of economics and business studies or is the assumption always that money is a private matter where individuals freely choose on the open market, thus establishing what are called market forces? In the teaching of history, does the curriculum tend to emphasise the history of 'our people' or does it enable young people to identify with and form a vision of a global community? A spiritually inspiring curriculum would tend to emphasise what Eric Wolf (1982) has called the story of the people without history.

I will not attempt in these closing remarks to enlarge upon the contribution which the specifically Christian curriculum might make to spiritual education, nor will I try at this point to offer a Christian theological rationale for this approach. It is sufficient for the present to promote the concept of a spiritual education which consists of the two-step approach: out of one's own pain into the pain of the world, out of one's own happiness into a wider joy. This is a vision to which men and women of all faiths, and those whose vocation in education is inspired by the values immanent within the human species alone, may all contribute together. It is worth adding that the way in which money as both an object and a language is viewed by Catholic educators and Catholic education may ultimately determine not only the future direction and purpose of Catholic education, but its very existence.

14

CATHOLIC EDUCATION: AUTHORITY AND ENGAGEMENT

Alex R. Rodger

A personal prologue

This chapter attempts to provide a particular phenomenological perspective on an experience of Catholic education, albeit from without that tradition. Given that the faith by and in which any individual lives, consciously or otherwise, will radically influence the views that person holds about virtually everything else, it is important to place the author in his personal context. I write as an ordained Baptist minister, as an educator and as a human being who is happily a Christian believer, but cannot avoid the sense that to be Christian is more important that to be a Christian. To be accurately described as the latter is no guarantee of the former. This is a quite simply a matter of shell and inner reality.

Although I am deeply involved in the work of a particular Church and a particular denomination, I have little interest in institutional religion – both loving the Church that brought me to faith and hating its frequent obscuring of the truly good news that the Christian faith conveys. My interest is in the living faith that changes people and helps them towards living more fully as God's children. I am constantly challenged by the radical implications of the words, 'The sabbath was made for man, not man for the sabbath' (Mk 2:27).

I do not believe that educators or religious believers (far less politicians) are always consistent in their thoughts and practices about religion in education. People discuss religion and education from a position of membership of particular institutions and their views and arguments are frequently based not only on such group loyalties but also on the forms of language and discourse available within the group or institution (Wittgenstein, 1938). In seeking understanding across convictional gulfs, therefore, it is as important as it is difficult to attempt to find procedural agreements which will make for productive discussion and lead to cooperative action for the common good.

As to the common ground on which believers of different hues, and unbelievers of different kinds, may meet in order to seek ways forward which do justice to all, I propose what is known as the golden rule. This principle is enshrined in many religious and non-religious stances for living in both negative and positive forms. Roughly it can be stated, with general agreement, as, 'Do to others as you would have them do to you' (Mt 7:12). As will appear below, the application of this principle – particularly if its spirit is also observed – can enable us to see where change is called for and motivate us to accept it, even where it is unwelcome.

Responding to pluralism

In any open, liberal and democratic society, there is an implicit social contract which is necessary for its well-being and for the protection and preservation of the rights of groups and individuals within it. It is foundational that for all to get some of the benefits they seek from education (or from other social agencies), all must accept that they cannot get all of the things that they might wish (Rodger, 1982). So, for example, a believer of a particular kind might be expected to recognise that in order to protect her children from any proselytising or indoctrinatory intention within the school, she must agree that other people's children should also be protected from any such intention on her part or on the part of those who share her outlook. Thus, while a Christian might wish that it were possible for her faith to be proclaimed without hindrance to all people in order that they might share its benefits, she would accept that, since this same opportunity cannot be available to all, it cannot be available to her either. All that she could legitimately ask in this situation is that her faith be honestly represented on the same basis as the faiths of others.

There are clearly educational and cultural grounds supporting the view that Christianity should be given a more extensive treatment in the schools of our society than is the case with other faiths as a consequence of both historical and, more particularly, present societal circumstances – although this could, conceivably, change (Scottish Office Education Department, 1992). But this more extensive treatment cannot legitimately be conjoined with a different intention. For example, it would be illegitimate, and certainly less than Christian, to seek to ensure that the public schools in an open society, which are provided for the children of all citizens who wish to send them there, should espouse, advocate and proclaim a particular faith, simply because it happened to be the majority faith. (The question of denominational schools is a separate one and will be touched on later.)

It may, of course, be argued that the great commission to make disciples was entrusted to Christians and that, therefore, they must do so at every opportunity and in every situation. It is worth taking a moment or two to reflect on this. It is to be remembered that the great commission was entrusted to the Church – the followers of Jesus – not to society or to the school. Consequently, the obligation to discharge the great commission should be shouldered by the Church from its own resources rather than the Church expecting that a society which is ambiguously Christian should ensure that this commission is carried out. This would be to expect the State to side inappropriately with certain members of society and against others. Further, the great commission is an invitation, in fact an obligation, to service not to privilege, to persuasion not to power, to influence not to compulsion. It is surely the case that a first principle of taking a particular stance for living seriously is that, where it involves the proclamation of a particular message, the implications of the message demand concomitant behaviours of the proclaimer. In other words, the message must be reflected in the method. This puts an inescapable obligation on the messenger to ensure that no means of advancing the gospel will be used which might themselves contradict that gospel. Can those who hear a message realistically be expected to take it more seriously than those who proclaim it? Finally, in this regard, it is worth reminding ourselves when we appeal to our rights and privileges, that our model is a saviour who was crucified because he would not appeal to legitimate power, and that he was prepared, when the people of Gerasa wished him to leave them in peace, to do so (Mk 5:17f).

At this point some of my fellow Christians object to the position being put forward. 'What about the lordship of Christ?', they ask. 'Is not the Christian teacher of religious education under an obligation to seek every opportunity to proclaim the faith and thus to see the religious education classroom as an evangelistic opportunity?' I do not believe this to be the case. And this is not because there is any situation in the Christian's life in which she is not under the lordship of Christ. On the contrary, it is precisely because of such an allegiance that, within the classroom as outside of it, the Christian teacher is under an obligation to do to others as she would wish that they would do to her, given the circumstances were reversed. Our basic respect for people of other convictions, and their children, requires from Christians – as Christians – the kind of respect and voluntary self-restraint which, in that situation, is the best witness that they can make to the lordship of Christ. Of course, I recognise the tension that this creates in the Christian, as in any other person who, from a religious or non-religious stance, has deep convictions that she would wish to share. There is all the difference in the world between failing because of unwillingness to speak a word for Christ and voluntarily refraining from doing so because, in the circumstances, that seems to one to be the best way in which a faithful witness to Christ's lordship and obedience to his commands can be expressed.

The creation of a common ground, in which different faiths may be presented for understanding, but no faith be advocated for adherence, by all is an implication of wholehearted membership of the open society envisaged here (Macquarrie and Taylor, 1995). This is not, as is sometimes supposed, to favour an uncommitted, or neutral, stance. It is to advocate the stance of impartiality. And these are different in respects which are crucial to this discussion. The position of neutrality is a stance adopted in an attempt to avoid being committed to any particular position. It expresses no view of its own, either because it has no view of its own or because it wishes to avoid the consequences of acknowledging the view it holds. The position of impartiality, however, is very far from being value free and neutral. It is, in fact, a very strongly value laden position. It takes a definite stance in relation to certain fundamental values, one of which is a refusal to be partial – that means, a refusal to take the side of one interest group against other interest groups as a contribution to ensuring that the interests of each group are considered fairly. To be impartial is to be committed to values and to be loyal to a community which embraces the interests of all who will be affected by our decisions and actions (McPhail *et. al.*, 1972).

This position of impartiality is a main part of the common ground to which I referred earlier. Where people's interests differ in the public space, it obliges them to seek negotiated agreements with regard to practice by reference to those values which are shared by all parties to the discussion, rather than to impose the specific claims of particular groups on the whole community, when significant numbers of that community do not share that interest. This is a principle of fairness rooted in respect, itself rooted in good will, and is akin to a significant number of fundamental principles without which no community can order its affairs in a way which has due regard to the needs, rights, interests and feelings of all its members.

It is tempting to jump straight from this point to a discussion of the question, 'What does Roman Catholic education contribute to the wider society?' That would be premature. It is important, first of all, to consider, however briefly, the prior question, 'What is Roman Catholic education for?'

What is Roman Catholic education for?

There is, of course, a considerable variety of views as to the proper goal(s) of Catholic education. Rather than make any attempt to provide a description, let alone discussion, of that whole range, here I will be extremely selective, with the sole intention of illustrating the existence of positions which are clearly radically different, though equally held by Roman Catholics. This will serve as a stepping-off point for the next stage of the discussion.

The goal of Roman Catholic education is often expressed in such terms as, 'To make good Catholics', a view which is sufficiently ambiguous to fail to give any specific indication of what its advocates have in mind. The only certainty is that it means a number of significantly different things to different advocates. During a television interview some twenty years ago, when asked why the Scottish Roman Catholic hierarchy would not agree to the 'integration' of denominational and non-denominational schools, Cardinal Gray offered an interesting riposte. He suggested that the task of Catholic schools is not to educate young people for a job; it is not to educate them for life; it is to educate them for eternity. This perspective offers what certainly appears to be a significant alternative to that which is concerned with the making of 'good Catholics'. Haldane offers the view that 'the main point of a Catholic education should be to lay down the foundations of a good life and of a good death'; which he considers can be best effected through 'scriptures, doctrines, authoritative teaching, established liturgies and spiritual traditions' (Haldane, 1997, p. 4). Whatever one makes of this, it certainly sits ill with any simultaneous intention to invite or encourage those of other convictions to send their children to schools whose goal this is. Price offers an interestingly different emphasis, when he writes that 'the aim of a Catholic school is to integrate the development of the person around a love of Jesus Christ and of their neighbour... to help pupils/students to achieve complete dignity as persons in a relationship with Jesus Christ and with each other' (Price, 1993, p. 11). It is interesting to speculate how close or how distant these views are from each other in their practical implications; or how compatible they might be with the view expressed by a Catholic colleague that 'The goal of Catholic education is not to produce good Catholics, but to produce good human beings'.

An outsider to this discussion ought not to be thought perverse in failing to have any clear and precise notion as to what it is that Roman Catholics conceive their education of their children to be aiming for. This is, of course, not something which separates Catholics from the wider educational community. Nonetheless, where a faith community attempts to define a position and use it as a basis in arguing for specific claims, it would seem reasonable to expect clarity and a measure of consistency, if not precision. The import of this seemingly trivial point is that it is no longer possible, if ever it was, to argue confidently from 'The Catholic view of, or aims for, education'. For these are inescapably plural, without the prospect of any authoritative pronouncement being able to render them otherwise.

This is a very important instantiation of the general truth to which Conor Cruise O'Brien was alluding when he wrote, a number of years ago, 'A very wise and experienced priest, the late Monsignor Pádraig de Brún was once asked what people believed – in the remote Kerry parish where he spent much of his time – about life after death. He replied, "They believe three things, simultaneously. They believe what the Church teaches, about the immortality of the soul, the resurrection of the body, reward and punishment. They also believe that when you are dead you are dead, like an animal, and that's that. And finally they believe that the dead are there, under the ground, watching the living, and plotting malevolently about them'" (1974, leader article).

If this pluralism – or anything approximating it – exists within the Roman Catholic community, and if it is neither realistic nor wise to assume that the clock can be turned back, the Church faces a radical challenge which, it seems to this writer, is at the same time an opportunity. For the same circumstance which requires the Church to recognise the pluralism which inhabits its own members, also invites it to recognise that its own membership shares with the population at large a feature which is pervasive of and fundamental to its being. This feature is the inescapable awareness of the modern world that all attempts to frame final articulations of the truth are, not only doomed, but misconceived. The ancient prohibitions of idolatry have their modern counterpart. A Church which is willing to recognise this openly will be strongly placed to accommodate and affirm within its bounds people at different stages of their faith development (Fowler *et. al.*, 1992); people whose experience and education lead them to different articulations of the faith they yet regard as the 'same' faith; people whose interests and preoccupations shape their valuations and actions in relation to different aspects of the rich panoply of faith; people whose circumstances so place them as to enable them to recognise and embrace what others will deny and even anathematise.

Now, such a proposal may not be easily distinguishable for some from what they would regard as abandonment of any givenness in faith, any objectivity in truth, any ultimates which do not yield before the vagaries of intellectual fashion. It is appropriate here only to allude to the argument that, in an age when relativity is recognised as a more comprehensive truth in relation to the physical universe – and the earth does not, by that acknowledgement, become any less supporting of the weight we place on it – we should be similarly bold to embrace the fact of the relativity of all our knowing, without the panic fear that we shall fall into the abyss of relativism, where nothing is supported by anything. Gillis offers a helpful understanding of this from within the Catholic tradition in suggesting that 'the truth remains absolute. However all expressions that attempt to describe truth are themselves relativised' (Gillis, 1993, p. 59). It seems to this writer, however, that just such a generous and disciplined embracing of truth incarnated in the human world has always characterised the Roman Catholic Church when she has been true to her deepest inspirations, as manifest in the reflections issuing from the Second Vatican Council. This remains the case, although a more nervous approach has been adopted by ecclesial authorities in an age where many, sensing the weakness of the unrepresented truth, are more bold in their impatience with the custodians of truth 'authorised' for the community. It is here we are or may be offered an opportunity to understand how Roman Catholic education may contribute, in a distinctive way, to the wider society of which we all are part.

The contribution of Roman Catholic education to the wider society

Where a Catholic or other denominational or religious school is a genuinely religious community, much good can be expected. However, it is often the case that religion, particularly in its institutional form (a religion) is susceptible of losing touch with its originating and sustaining spirit and that, when this happens, it suffers from goal displacement. This means, quite simply, that the values for whose advocacy and expression that institution has come into existence become subordinated to those values which are regarded as vital to the survival and progress of the institution itself. This does not affect only religious institutions, but it does affect them and, when it does, it always results in a loss of the institution's proper *raison d'être* and of its spiritual vigour – even though its absence may be substituted by an increase in human activism. Its reasoning is more likely to be driven by a calculating spirit, directed to its own advantage, than by its originating values – especially when adherence to these could be costly in whatever terms have come to matter more to the institution. When such a temptation is resisted and a school is moved by its faith and its associated values, the benefits are literally incalculable. For then the notion of a religious community becomes an operative and regulative ideal.

It is not, in the main, the schools which need to hear and heed this caution; or so it seems to me. It is the Ecclesiastical Authorities which, in their urgent concern to protect the interests of the Church, can act in ways which suggest that it has lost sight of the abiding – do we not claim, eternal? – spiritual values for the sake of whose observance (even before their furtherance) that Church, or any Church exists – or it fails in its primary loyalty.

Not least among the above mentioned benefits is a shared allegiance to a cluster of core values which serve to define the community's identity and govern all its doings. Not every set of values can provide such benefits. A community which aligns itself around and by values which originate in a sense of their givenness and their transcendence is a community which is always *en route* to a goal. And, although that goal will never be reached in this life, it sets a constant direction and provides a reliable inspiration. Consequently, a dynamic of growth, within an agreed understanding of what growth may mean, is provided. Here we touch the fundamental context of faith within which such a community exists.

The Catholic school, therefore, is inevitably a witness to the fact that education is, consciously or otherwise, premised on certain assumptions about the nature and significance of human life (Congregation for Catholic Education, 1988). There is an explicit conviction that human life in this world is not, as it were, 'self-contained' or self-explanatory. There is also an awareness that there exists an inescapable relationship between what human beings believe about the universe, their place in it and how they should live their lives. This is true of any educational process which is to be capable of giving a coherent account of itself. The question, 'What is the purpose of education?', or, 'What is education for?', can only be answered in terms of some conception of what it is to be – and to become more fully – a human being. In many schools this question is kept alive by the presence of, and the insistent questions raised by, religious education. However, in the largely secularised State education system, there is little that requires that question to be constantly put to every part of education other than, and only perhaps, where it is the specific interest and concern of some members of staff. In theory, wherever educators reflect on the nature of their calling, such questions ought inevitably to arise. In practice, such questions have often been rendered 'invisible' by the formation of minds, through education and other influences, which are impervious to whatever does not fit within a narrowly empiricist frame of reference. While this bears witness to the power of education in the formation of minds, it also carries with it its own salutary warning. Certain kinds of education will so form minds that they are capable of seeing only what can be accommodated within a preconceived frame of reference. Education can thus function as an initiation into agnosticism. It is a direct consequence of its very existence that Catholic education poses a fundamental question about the goals and nature, not only of education but of human life.

Where the impulse of that education is genuinely educational in its intention, it carries with it an openness to transcendence, in several senses. To the transcendent God, obviously: but also, by that very fact and its conjunction with the conviction that human beings are made in God's image, to the fact that transcendence is constitutive of human nature taken seriously. The not yet – and never here – completed being is, by his very nature, faced with the call to grow; to move beyond any existing condition towards what is imperfectly discerned, yet carries with it an authentic call to learn how to become more fully what one is. Implicit in this is the openness to transcend any and every current understanding of the world; any and every achieved maturity or condition of character; any and every pattern of relating to the world, to other people and to the transcendent reality who is, at the same time, immanent in every aspect of the mysterious universe we inhabit. This human vocation is both personal and social. Thus, together with its implications for individuals, it bears on the organisations in and through which faith is expressed.

Catholics in dialogue

Now, far from claiming that such a recognition is in the sole possession of Catholics, or of religious people in general, it is demonstrably true that such intuitions of possibilities are present in the experience of many who claim no religious allegiance or, indeed, explicitly disavow it. At a time, then, when there is a renewed interest in matters spiritual and their treatment in education (Best, 1996), a religious tradition – particularly one that is ready to engage with the prevailing 'post-Christian' culture we now inhabit – is well placed to engage such people in dialogue. The word 'dialogue' is of vital importance in this context in that in the exchange between people of different convictions several stances are possible on the part of one who believes that (s)he has something important to share with others. These stances include at least the following:

1) *Declamation,* in which the tone is judgmental, the manner aggressive and the content definite.
2) *Declaration,* in which an assured conviction is proclaimed as true and the hearers are called to accept it.
3) *Debate,* in which contrary points of view are acknowledged for the sole purpose of undermining them and establishing one's own.
4) *Discussion,* where the issues on which people disagree are focussed for the sake of pursuing understanding of the matter being discussed.

5) *Dialogue,* the meeting of people, each seeking to help the other to recognise the true import of her own and the other person's convictions.

Acknowledging the unsatisfactory brevity of these descriptions, they may be sufficiently recognisable in general terms for the following claim to be understandable, whether or not it is accepted. In the present climate, in which the reasonableness of a view is considered a precondition of its intelligent acceptance, options 1 and 2 will have little, if any, place within the context of education. Options 3 and 4 will figure more prominently in the educational process in areas concerning convictions and values. Option 5 will come into its own in those situations where it is considered legitimate and proper for the learner and the teacher to acknowledge explicitly the personal element which, though it is present to some extent in every human exchange (however formal), affords an appropriate – and perhaps the only possible – methodology for gaining accurate insight into what is itself irreducibly personal.

While this discussion concerns only a part of the issue, it is peculiarly the part which provides the interface between people of different persuasions in their efforts to advance mutual understanding. Some such approach is crucial to the advancement of understanding in a way which neither traduces the deepest convictions of others; nor waters down one's own; nor seeks to impose an orthodoxy as a precondition of mutual support on the common journey towards human fulfilment. Elaboration of this point might, in another context, offer helpful guidance to teachers of religious education (or other convictional matters) in terms of the stances and approaches likely to provide the greatest congruence between values, intentions and methods used.

Not everyone, however, would agree with the contention that education *of* the spirit is more likely to be effective where the form of faith which is accepted by those who teach *in* this spirit is applied to relationships both within and without the community. Nonetheless, this education is to be offered, rather than required, as a stance to be considered by the learner; and offered with the concomitant invitation that it be used heuristically. This means that it should be adopted as though true in order to find out the actual congruence between it and other well-accredited knowledge and personal experience, through testing it, in practice, against experience. Thus it is to be employed as a tool of enquiry rather than uncritically accepted as an act of faith. A final requirement must be added: that this stance for living and learning be demonstrated in its practical implications and outworking in the life of the community whose faith it embodies. In this it is clear that, although aspects of this will occur primarily in the context of religious education, the vast bulk of it will take place pervasively throughout the school; in its life and relationships; its systems and structures, its events and interactions; its curriculum and all its external dealings.

A contribution worth making

The key is catholicity. Our society as a whole needs to find more effective terms for conducting its internal conversation in a way which will enable it to move beyond its present internal contradictions – and to do so in honest response to the external challenges facing it. This dialogue, like any other, will be one in which it is discovered that the participants and their relationship of mutual attention, appreciation and challenge are more important than the specific agendas with which they come or, for that matter, the particular positions which they adopt. For dialogue, by its own nature, challenges those who participate in it to face the call to risk their fixed positions, to be open to 'alien' truths, to become vulnerable to the meanings of outsiders; in short, to face the call to transcendence in response to what can only be discovered on this risky path. A part of this leaving behind of our given situation will be the discovery in the other, through openness to the other, of aspects of ourselves which we have dissociated, repressed and denied – individually and communally. This is not *per se* the task of schools. But it is an essential preparation of the ground for the work that can only be done in schools. Much harm is done to successive generations of young people as a direct result of the failure of the adult generation to address these issues.

Within those Roman Catholic schools influenced by such a clear sense of the contribution which they might make to the wider society, the religious and the educational leaders will work together to bring into real existence a place which is faithfully responsible by seeking to live its faith responsively. For this to happen, the religious leaders must move generously and confidently into neglected rooms within the Church's treasure store of 'things old', and the educators more courageously and expectantly hold alongside these the 'new things' that they and their colleagues are discovering about each other and about faith in the contemporary world. There can then be a collective good stewardship of the education of young people for living out of ageless truth, but firmly in the modern world.

Internal tensions

Reflection on 'the potential relationship between Catholic education and public moral education and civic morality' provokes considerations of various kinds. Despite the ambiguities referred to above, it is clear that one of the central aims of Roman Catholic education concerns the formation of the learner within and for the community. This entails the socialising of the pupil into a tradition and a way of life. The process may be envisaged at the level of a mere shaping of patterns of thinking, dispositional responses and habits of action. More important, however, and more central to the intentions of the educator, is that the learner should come to live within a whole awareness of the world and human beings, in their relation to God, and also to live out of this awareness in every part of her life. In other words, it encompasses a form of life, a way of being. One of the crucial current tensions within the Roman Catholic community pivots around this issue. It is not merely that some are primarily concerned for the socialisation process as a means of perpetuating the Catholic community, whereas others have a central concern for the welfare of our society as a whole, though that is probably true. There is a correspondingly radical difference within the leadership of that community between two competing paradigms of education.

The latter outlook sees education as being for autonomy and personal responsibility, understood as freedom's way of responding in openness to the perceived will of God. The former favours a more controlled and controlling education, calling for obedience to the authorised custodians of knowledge about God and God's will. It is, thankfully, not often that either of these views is pursued in isolation from the other. The debate and its consequences for practice swing between the two poles as these are emphasised by different Catholics, or the same ones, at the same or different times.

In Scotland and since the mid-twentieth century, the Roman Catholic hierarchy has, under political and social pressures of different kinds, emphasised authority and education for membership. Yet, since at least the time of the Education (Scotland) Act of 1872, the universal spread of education has led to profound and important changes in the relationships between laity and clergy, rooted in education's inherent tendency to free the learner from heteronomous authority by offering personal and direct access to the sources of human knowledge and the means of its validation and testing. The objection that this is not the whole truth, especially in matters concerning a revealed faith, has a fair claim to be heard. But, whatever its validity in relation to the fundamental teachings of the faith, it can scarcely justify claims to authority in matters which are open to human enquiry, except on the basis of mastery of the canons and criteria of knowledge and judgement which arise from the subject matter itself (Hirst & Peters, 1970). This is far from being a new – or even a peculiarly modern – problem. Yet, in every age, faith must grapple with it in its contemporary form.

In recent decades, then, the resistance to authority as a given, taken for granted and unquestioned source of decision has greatly increased. In some cases, to be sure, this has very normal human tendencies as its explanation. And it obviously has much to do with the forces unleashed in society after the Second World War. The advance of education itself increased the willingness and competence of growing numbers in society to adopt a more critical and less compliant attitude to the deliverances of authorities of all kinds. The Second Vatican Council reinforced many of these tendencies and produced ferment within Roman Catholicism. There was a greater freedom felt by educated Catholics, particularly in the professions, to question – even to challenge and resist – what they judged as misconceived deliverances and policies affecting their own areas of expertise. David Lodge's *How Far Can You Go?* (1981) may be notable for its directness, but it is far from being an isolated expression of this 'new' mood.

Allowing for the radical direction set by Vatican II, a question has to be placed over the extent to which its pronouncements relating to the issue of the laity's role have been implemented in the Scottish Churches. The power of the clergy, specifically the roles and activities of priests in relation to education – in education committees and their decisions and appointments, in schools and the details of their daily arrangements (including curriculum), in specific decisions and judgements affecting individual teachers and their career opportunities – seems strangely dated. My point here is not to question the good faith or effectiveness of many priests in these areas of activity, but to point to the fundamental incongruity of giving to people, most of whom lack the appropriate training or experience in education, the authority to overrule the judgement of Roman Catholics who have these requisite qualifications in abundance. It would be surprising if this did not sometimes result in unwise decisions, or lead many priests, who feel themselves miscast as educational experts of any kind, to devote themselves assiduously to the political side of education, where they are more adept. That such a situation seems not to give rise to significant questions for the Church authorities is not reassuring.

No systematic study of this kind of disaffection exists, making it difficult to gauge how widespread it actually is. Nevertheless, it is to be encountered in conversations with committed Catholic colleagues in a wide variety of circumstances. It certainly includes Roman Catholic teachers in training who determine not to teach in Roman Catholic schools as a result of a perception of injustice that a person's appointment or promotion has been blocked by a private word which is nowhere recorded and for which no one is accountable – and according to what seem to be variable, even idiosyncratic criteria. It also includes frustration in some head teachers that they do not feel free to do the job to which they have been appointed without constant reference to the priest whose influence in their school is disproportionate to the amount of time he spends there, and dwarfs the extent of his real involvement in the school's educational life and work.

What role, then, for the Catholic school?

The views of Roman Catholic education referred to above have different implications for the role of the Roman Catholic school within an open society, which may be construed in a variety of ways. In terms of emphasis, it might be asked whether the appropriate role for the Catholic school at the present time is best construed mainly as, to be an instrument of priestly authority, to exercise a prophetic ministry or to be a witnessing community. The situation is complex and easily misunderstood by an observer. So the following reflections are intended more by way of raising questions than presuming to offer advice.

1) *Priestly* – Is the Catholic school placed, by its obligation to both the religious and the State authorities, in a position which may, in some circumstances, result in a conflict of loyalties and responsibilities in the school's leaders? Do these conflicts arise when a person, Catholic or not, judged on educational and other grounds to be the most suitable person to occupy a post of authority in the school, is debarred by the Church's decision from being appointed to it? Or when the curriculum guidelines prepared by Scottish teachers, including Roman Catholic teachers, are modified at the Church's insistence? Or when the pastoral responsibilities of the school, simply as a school, impinge upon the local Church's pastoral interest in a pupil?

How realistic is it, where the Catholic school has a significant proportion of pupils from homes of other denominations, faiths or of no religious background, to regard that school as a worshipping faith community within the Roman Catholic tradition?

It is important to raise such questions because they are matters of concern at the present time for people who, for a variety of reasons, send their children to Catholic schools; and, likewise, for Catholic parents who choose not to.

2) *Prophetic* – Is it more appropriate – and likely to be more effective – to regard the school's role as prophetic, at least in part? By this is meant the explicit recognition of the role of lay Catholics within the school as best placed to exercise the ministry of reminding pupils of and recalling them to the faith which the school espouses. Is this not likely to happen more effectively within the whole life of the school, through the teaching of subjects and caring for pupils carried out by teachers whose own faith is alive and lived out in their work place, than it is through the specifically 'religious' elements which many of the pupils will, in any case, have abandoned? The words of such teachers and support staff may still carry influence. Given such a context, will not even the overtly religious activities of the school seem more credible?

While there is little doubt that such arrangements are already working in many situations, the implications of a general and genuine shift of emphasis more towards such a prophetic ministry are likely to be far reaching, probably in direct proportion to the degree to which this is an expression of agreement and cooperation between the school and the Church authorities. One role of the prophet is to hold before those who are members of a faith community their unceasing obligation to live by that faith consistently in a context which is constantly changing. Rather than an articulated code to be obeyed, the prophet points to the rootedness of the life of the community of faith in given ground (its core insights and spiritual values) and its responsiveness to its variable environment (its living expression of these insights and values in response to changing circumstance).

The prophet speaks specifically into the community; his appeal is to a loyalty already pledged. The prophet and the prophet's hearers share the same vocation to let the faith be seen in action by all those who observe them from beyond the community's bounds. They are also called, that is, to witness.

3) *Witnessing* – A witness is someone who can speak from first-hand personal experience to others who depend, for their information, on his or her testimony. Where such witness concerns convictions – the beliefs by which a person lives – the credibility of the witness that is borne is inseparably linked with the congruence between what the person says and what he or she is known to be in daily life. Every Christian within a school community is, in that sense, consciously or otherwise, a witness to his or her faith before the community's other members.

It is possible, in this way, to see the Catholic school also as a witnessing community. As a school which is publicly acknowledged as representing a specific faith, it will be expected to demonstrate this in its way of being a school. This can, of course, mean a number of different things. The view sketched here holds a balance between the alternatives of either regarding the whole school as a single faith community (which, usually, it is not), or regarding the school as a community with no specific faith commitment (which, equally, it is not). The faith community, considered realistically, will be a community within the school community – not in any exclusive sense; rather, in a representative sense, so that the whole community may be considered as a community which is identified and defined in its self-understanding by that faith.

What this might entail was well expressed by a Latin American colleague of conservative evangelical persuasion, referring to a school of which he was a board member. This school originated as a Scottish Presbyterian foundation in the nineteenth century, though its constituency is now predominantly Argentine and mainly Roman Catholic, with significant numbers of pupils of other Christian denominations and other – religious and non-religious – persuasions. Looking for a solution to the conflicting requirements of the present situation of that school, he suggested that they 'must be a confessing, but not a confessional school'.

Such a stance would provide the possibility of holding together a necessary faithfulness to a fixed reference point and an essential flexibility in response to a changing environment. It would help to establish a clear and living sense of school identity, justifying an expectation on the part of the school's leaders that the school's faith will be the faith commended for use, in an exploratory and heuristic way, by its community of learners – pupils and staff alike.

One inevitable consequence of such a willingness, were it to be present, would be the dismantling of many of the defences which have been erected around Roman Catholic institutional – specifically ecclesiastical – interests. This is always and inescapably an ambiguous and contentious issue. Yet it seems clear to many that only an institution which is separated from the source of its life can refuse to respond to the obligations which that source lays upon it. The institution which becomes self-serving (even in the name of serving its Master) is suffering from goal-displacement which, however successful it may be in achieving its self-chosen goals, will vitiate the credibility of its efforts to bring in its Master's kingdom.

Conclusion

It will be clear from the foregoing that I do not believe that the major contribution of the denominational schools to the wider community is likely to be anything specifically and exclusively Roman Catholic. That specific contribution is more likely to be potent within the context of a more generously humane recognition of faith's engagement with the society of which its members are citizens. For I see no possibility in the twenty-first century that Christians of any kind are likely to have significant influence within society without embracing their membership of it more wholeheartedly than some appear to.

This could be seen as a faithless call to be of the world, as well as to be in it. It is not intended in that way. It is important, however, to identify those assumptions and values which Christians share with the rest of society if we are to engage in its internal dialogue and influence its future. Many of our society's values are Christian and have been shaped by Christian influence within its institutions over centuries. A more radically faithful witness to these values – equally espoused by professing Christians and the majority of others within our society – might be the most effective witness that Christians can make in terms of the call to be salt and light and leaven within the world. But this does not require (in fact it forbids) the claim to be the only true exemplars of these values – or even to be wholly faithful exemplars of them! Effective witness is, in my view, more likely to be borne by a 'Catholic education' which, while it seeks to influence the wider society of which it is part, accepts that genuine commitment to that goal will entail consequent changes within itself.

CATHOLIC LEADERSHIP:
SIMILAR OR DIFFERENT?

Douglas McCreath

'It is a fearful thing to fall into the power of the living God.'

In these words of D. H. Lawrence is perhaps encapsulated the central leadership challenge for staff of educational institutions which have a religious foundation – whether Christian in general or Catholic in particular. The challenge, implicit in Lawrence's words, is the awesome responsibility it places upon its institutional members; a challenge which also provides a clear point of separation between them and their counterparts in secular educational institutions. Not only must routine organisational arrangements be such that the goals of the school, college or university are realised efficiently and effectively, but these arrangements must also afford the possibility of the continuing Christian development of all of its community members. Of course, this rhetoric is now almost universally represented in mission statements and planning documents. But it is in highlighting the necessary pervasiveness of the challenge that Lawrence's words make their mark.

Mission statement rhetoric notwithstanding, in operational terms how many Catholic or Christian schools actively succeed in supporting the capacity of individuals to exalt the Lord in their day-to-day activities and interactions? Indeed, how many may be reluctant or even embarrassed to use such language. And yet, if this purpose is not actively planned for, will the necessary and visible witness of adults (as teachers) be diminished, and so too the educative impact on the pupils or students? Crucially, are the lived experiences of pupils and staff in Catholic schools and colleges qualitatively any different from those of their non-religiously-based counterparts? If a confident and affirmative response can be given to this question, then clearly there is no problem. But if not, what does this mean for the leadership and management of these institutions? Could it mean that formal leaders, through no fault of their own, may have been insufficiently supported through sustained and intellectually challenging opportunities, pre- and post-appointment, to develop a personal and guiding theoretical perspective? In this, are the conventional conceptual frameworks of school leadership and management, in general, sufficient or appropriate for schools in the millennium? If not, what needs to be done to develop them? In Scotland at present, given the development of a Scottish Qualification for Headship, the question has particular significance. This qualification, part of the pre-appointment process, will serve a gate-keeping function on the path to headship. Its emergence has provided a stimulus to the ongoing debate about the nature of the distinctiveness of Catholic school leadership and management, and to the best means of leadership development.

Leadership – an elusive concept?

One of the potential dangers for the unwary in this well-intentioned debate is a too-ready assumption of consensus on the meaning of leadership. A number of authors outline the general complexities surrounding its meaning (Boles & Davenport, 1983; Korac-Kakabadse & Korac-Kakabadse, 1997). Paisey (1984), in a review of trends in educational leadership thought, asserts that 'discussion about leadership is confused because the word is used ambiguously' and that 'many different assumptions are made about it…'. Bryman (1986), in a detailed and critical examination of the literature, concludes that 'the concept of leadership is an elusive one. Not only are there difficulties attached to distinguishing it from neighbouring ideas and concepts, but research designs so frequently fail to capture its distinctiveness'. Gronn (1996), in mapping contemporary thinking on its theory and practice, notes the growing interest in leadership matters – 'with Bass's (1990) *Handbook* now in its third edition, and over 7,500 references listed in it, there is no better evidence of people's abiding concern with what it means to lead and what it means to follow'. This escalation, notwithstanding, he concludes that 'the issues which have been in contention for so long (e.g. what leadership means; whether it is the same thing as management or something different; whether or not it really does make a difference, and so on) remain matters which continue to divide scholars'. Fidler (1997) selectively highlights some key ideas on school leadership for practitioners and researchers. He claims to have done this for two reasons

> Firstly, to help practitioners and others to increase their range of conceptualisations and theoretical insights into leadership in order to aid their understanding of school leadership and their ability to formulate plans for action. Secondly, to encourage researchers to use theoretical models in their studies of practice and to increase the interaction between theoretical formulations of leadership and empirical investigation.

He offers five perspectives on leadership (situational; four frames of leadership; leading professional and chief executive; moral leadership; curricular leadership) in the belief that:

> no one theory nor any one approach can subsume the complexities of leadership and, indeed, that a search for such an all-encompassing theory may be illusory. It is, therefore, a matter of choosing one or more conceptualisations of leadership which appear appropriate in order to understand a particular situation, and, using these, to formulate actions.

It is precisely this activity, in rigorous, intellectual form, which has traditionally informed all educational leadership programmes. It is a dimension which must be retained and reinforced because, as Gronn (1996) notes, the contemporary

> emphasis on cultural transformation in schooling is a direct consequence of the emergence of a wider enterprise culture in education as part of the new managerialism.... For individual schools, accountability-driven school-based management entails evaluation of their performance in attaining outcomes measured against predetermined indicators of quality. School managers, as a result, are judged on the extent to which they secure and sustain quality in the so-called 'core technology' of teaching and learning.

Fidler's discussion (1997) of the 'Moral Leadership' perspective is illuminating by way of contrast. In observing the recently increasing attention being paid to ethical principles in management, he notes that 'organisational culture is not only a reflection of "how we do things around here" but also the more value-laden "how we think it right to do things here".' For all schools, but especially for Catholic schools, this has a particular resonance. The tension between the 'new managerialism' and 'Christian democracy' embodies a fundamental challenge both for school leaders and for the design and delivery of developmental courses for aspiring school leaders. This tension, with its practical day-to-day action implications, resides in a line management lexicon of customers, service delivery, marketing, target setting, value for money and quality assurance on the one hand; and, on the other, a valorising vocabulary based on the dignity of the person, personal autonomy and responsibility, authentic relationships and a theology of community.

The Scottish leadership policy agenda

Scotland has developed a distinctive approach to quality improvement in education, known as the Quality Initiative in Scottish Schools. This school-based reform programme has two major interrelated strands:

- Improving school effectiveness.
- Enhancing the professional capability of all staff.

The publication in 1984 by Her Majesty's Inspectorate of Schools of *Learning and Teaching in Scottish Secondary Schools: School Management* was a watershed in school management matters. Its publication marked official recognition of the need for head teachers to exercise 'high level management skills'. In order to exemplify and encourage the then official view of good practice the Inspectorate published two further documents – *Effective Secondary Schools* (1988) and *Effective Primary Schools* (1989). Around the same time, in September 1988, the Scottish Education Department launched a major national management initiative, *Management Training for Headteachers* with the aim of providing a structure within which the training of head teachers of primary, secondary and special schools could take place. A set of nine modules intended to address what were perceived to be the main issues of management were developed. Since then, management training courses have been provided for large numbers of senior managers in nursery, primary, secondary and special schools; a central feature of the provision being partnership arrangements between higher education institutions and local authorities. During the 1990s subsequent developments have included:

- The issuing of national policy guidelines to local authorities for the introduction of staff development and appraisal (1990).
- The publication of *The Role of School Development Plans in*

Managing School Effectiveness (1991).
• The publication of *Using Ethos Indicators in Secondary School Self-Evaluation: Taking Account of the Views of Pupils, Parents and Teachers* (1992).
• The issue of guidelines for local schemes of devolved school management (1993).
• The publication of *How Good is Our School? Using Performance Indicators for Self-Evaluation* (1996).

Casteel *et. al.* (1997), who were commissioned by the SOEID to design 'A Framework for Leadership and Management Development in Scottish Schools', note that:

> The overall effect of these initiatives was to increase the range of duties and responsibilities of school leaders and managers. They were to be responsible for the planning which underpinned the quality of the service their schools provided, the staff development which was necessary for the implementation of these plans, and the effective deployment of a large part of the budget to meet school targets.

And from this they conclude that with such an increased range of duties and powers, the need for high-quality leadership and management (and management training) is now more vital than ever before. It is against such a background that the Framework has been developed.

A Framework for Leadership and Management Development in Scottish Schools

Within the Framework, the *key purpose* of school leadership and management is 'to create, maintain, develop and review the conditions which enable teachers and learners to achieve effective learning within national and local authority policies'. Further, it 'defines three elements of practice in school leadership and management which must be used in order to achieve the key purpose'. They are:

- The actions taken by competent leaders and managers (The Management Function).
- The professional attitudes, understandings and knowledge which underpin these actions (The Professional Qualities).
- The personal abilities which are used to carry them out effectively.

The Four Management Functions are subdivided into ten *Core Activities*, from which in turn are derived *Key Tasks*. For example:

- Key Function – (A) Manage policy and planning.
- Core Activity – (A1) Review, develop and present school aims, policies and plans.
- Key Task – (A1 iv) Review and update school or department aims, policies and plans so they are consistent and further the stated values of the school.

In June 1998, based on the work of Casteel's team, the Standard for Headship in Scotland' was published:

The Standard for Headship sets out the key aspects of professionalism and expertise which the Scottish education system requires of those who are entrusted with the leadership and management of its schools. It defines the level of competence required of effective head teachers in the early years of their headship. It serves, therefore, as the template against which those aspiring to be head teachers may be assessed in order to determine their strength and development needs.

Some concerns? Buyer beware!

It is acknowledged that the Framework's aetiology owes much to the work of the Management Charter Initiative (MCI), modified by a consortium of local authorities in England, School Management South (SMS). This group adapted the MCI functions to apply specifically to schools by undertaking a functional analysis of the work of effective school managers. Following revision and piloting in Scottish schools, the SMS standards were the subject of extensive consultation. This in turn provided the structure for the Scottish Framework – a framework intended for all schools, denominational and non-denominational alike. However, a number of management gurus would challenge the fundamental assumptions of this approach. Bennis (1989), in a general commentary on leadership and management in America, offers a cautionary note regarding such a strategy – despite, in this case, its avowed and well-intentioned school improvement aim. He argues that life on our turbulent, complex planet is no longer linear and sequential; rather it is spontaneous, contrary, unexpected and ambiguous:

> Things do not happen according to plan, and they are not reducible to tidy models. We persist in grasping at neat, simple answers, when we should be questioning everything.... And though the context is highly volatile, it's not apt to change in any fundamental way as long as the principal players are driven by it, are swimming through it like fish blind to the water. To put it another way, the current climate is self-perpetuating because it has created an entire generation of managers in its own image (p. 25).

The need for a new mind-set is also echoed by Tribus:

> The growth of world populations, the depletion of natural resources, the degradation of the environment, the demands for a higher standard of living by an increasing number of

people, the spread of information by satellites, the creation of a worldwide economic system (in which money travels at the speed of light) and the proliferation of weapons of mass destruction... these forces have produced an era of rapid change. These forces now challenge our abilities to *manage* our institutions and to learn collectively. We need to *learn* to adapt to new and ever-changing conditions (1996, p.93).

If these analyses are valid, a major issue may be seen to surround the emerging Scottish Qualification for Headship – an issue of equal significance for denominational and non-denominational schools alike. Namely, is its framework capable of supporting searching professional debate about the very nature of schools and schooling? Or, in the present educational policy agenda context, depicted by Apple (1998, pp. 3-17) as a period of 'conservative restoration', will the process simply promote a narrow and self-perpetuating management orthodoxy? By contrast, if the framework can embrace the proposition of Aronowitz and Giroux (1991) that head teachers 'ought to provide models of leadership that offer the promise of reforming schools as part of a revitalisation of public life', then a different challenge is offered to the Qualification, its processes and surrounding discourse. If the task is, in the terminology of Wagner (1998), the reinvention of schools, then this 'requires a kind of leadership which is very different from what one finds in most education systems today'.

On a broader front, on the assumption that their core activities are conceptually different, the question may be asked if it is possible, within the defined 'standard', to provide management and leadership training simultaneously. Kotter (1996) draws a clear distinction between management and leadership and claims that management has been given much greater prominence than leadership in development programmes because it is easier to teach. For Kotter (p. 25), 'Management is a set of processes that can keep a complicated system of people and technology running smoothly... Leadership is a set of processes that creates organisations in the first place or adapts them to significantly changing circumstances....'

Others such as Shea (1990) offer a model which shows that management and leadership functions overlap, though requiring different capabilities, and Kerry and Murdoch (1993) in reviewing the relationship between management and leadership conclude that:

> Education leadership is... that part of the management function which provides progress towards new goals in a time of change. This progress can take place only where the leader, through collaborative team work and on the basis of smooth organisation ('sound management structures'), achieves such progress. The lone leader is increasingly being recognised as not only deadening to the spirit but also ineffective.

These perspectives again have a particular bearing on any discussion of the role of leadership in Scotland's Catholic schools. Given their *raison d'être*, the gospel imperative clearly cannot be considered a new goal (in Kerry and Murdoch's terms). Rather the leadership demand, as adumbrated by Kotter, is much more likely to be that of adaptation to significantly different circumstances. In a world where Western or European Christianity is experiencing a dramatic downturn in active membership, the Catholic school can sometimes be perceived as the key evangelising organ of the Church. If this agenda is limited simply to the numbers game, with ambitions little beyond cynical institutional survival, its purposes, and indeed the very existence of the schools themselves, must be cast in doubt. However, if its purpose is focused on human dignity and the liberation of the spirit of all members of its community, adult and child alike, then the justification is clear and unequivocal. It is this transformational task, firmly founded on the virtues of its unique anthropology, which makes the challenge of Catholic school leadership distinctive. It is also this which lends it its awesome dimension. In this context, defining what is a 'reasonable' expectation of schools, within the wider faith community, is vital, for on this hinges the expectations likely to be placed upon school leaders. The importance of this definitional task is that it will also help illuminate the nature of the leadership task in Catholic schools, and the extent to which it is similar or different from that of school leadership generally.

The dual character of leadership and management?

Kerry and Murdoch's negative reference to the 'lone leader' is meaningful in the distinction it makes between organisational effectiveness and the impact of organisational activities on the spiritual well-being of its members. Duignan and Bhindi (1997, pp. 195-209), in offering a radical critique of current practices, note that 'despite a new rhetoric of paradigm shifts based on post-positivist views of the world and claims for an improved morality and ethics in management behaviour, it would seem that leadership and management practices, especially at top levels, often belie this rhetoric'. They cite a number of reasons for this state of affairs, most especially the following:

- Most leaders have insufficient understanding of the dynamics and complexities of organisations and cling to a fixed mind-set, viewing them as linear, deterministic and mechanistic systems.

- Structures of 'domination' prevail in organisations which produce unjust and depersonalising relationships among individuals and groups. (The dominant individuals or groups assume an entitlement to ownership of ideas, processes and property and an entitlement to be served by and receive deference from others.)

• The existence of a 'culture of artifice' in many organisations where truth, honesty and spiritual experiences are the exception.

As a response to such a situation, Duignan and Bhindi offer a new, embryonic though potentially challenging paradigm – 'authentic leadership':

> The emerging paradigm of authentic leadership, as leadership praxis linking theory, practice and ethics of leadership, responds to many of the concerns about honesty and integrity in leadership and is an antidote to the artifice and deception prevalent in leadership in many modern organisations.

> Authentic leadership links assumptions, beliefs about, and actions related to, authentic self, relationships, learning, governance and organisation, through significant human values, to leadership and management practices that are ethically and morally uplifting.

Sadly, the power of this analysis lies in its ready identification by many individuals with their lived experiences – in both Catholic and non-Catholic institutions alike. Duignan and Bhindi's explanation of the mismatch between the rhetoric and reality of management practice (insufficient understanding of the dynamics and complexities of organisations, structures of domination and cultures of artifice) might be attributed to an absence of universal management training or limitations in orthodox provisions – especially in relation to the beliefs and assumptions which underlie it. If leadership is, as perceived by Chatterjee (1998), 'a state of relationship between the leader and led', then institutional processes need to be understood from a different perspective to that of traditional, hierarchical command-control.

Sjöstrand (1997) contends that there is a significant gap between management theories and practical organisational realities. He challenges both the 'myth of managerial rationality' and classical Western rationality more generally and, in so doing, proposes a duality in the managerial task – involving both 'rational' aspects (i.e. activities associated with cognition and habit) and so-called 'irrational' aspects (i.e. the behaviour associated with emotions, intuitions and aesthetics). The implication of Sjöstrand's position is that a reluctance to recognise this duality may contribute to the institutional pathologies depicted by Duignan and Bhindi. An ever-increasing leadership literature, however, parallels their analysis and places the 'wholeness' of the individual explicitly at its centre, for example, 'principle-centred leadership' (Covey, 1992); 'heart leadership' (Gilley, 1997); 'sacred leadership' (Shipka, 1997); and 'total leadership' (Barrett, 1998). Shipka succinctly summarises the thread common to these different though conceptually related approaches.

> ...under the current structures and strictures of business organisations, most of us do not believe we should bring all of what we know or can do to our working environments. At present there are rules and taboos about what we can legitimately bring into our workplaces. The result is that many of us believe we are supposed to check our deepest personal selves – our inner lives , our soul's development – at the door of our workplaces. This assumption prevents us from bringing some of the most powerful and creative parts of ourselves to our jobs.

Such perspectives which resonate with, for example, the seminal work of Greenfield (1993) in the realm of values in educational management are surely worthy of inclusion in activities which purport to support educational leadership development; for as Starratt (1993) states:

Leadership in the post-modern world is desperately needed. It must be a new kind of leadership, however, a leadership grounded in the sober understandings and memories gained at such cost in human lives and suffering. We need a leadership, therefore, able to critique the shortcomings, and the myths that support, the status quo. It has to be a leadership grounded in the new anthropology, an understanding of the human condition as both feminine and masculine, as multicultural, as both crazy and heroic, violent and saintly, and as embedded in and responsible to nature.

Without such a commitment to encourage leaders and potential leaders to reframe and re-evaluate their personal and organisational experiences, then the warning by Harrison (1995) of the 'tyranny of fixed ideas' remains – the potential danger that the imposition of fixed ideas 'by government or other power groups can reduce human enterprise to the calculus of mechanics and a one-level ontology'. It is within these wider parameters that the future value of the Scottish Qualification as preparation of the next generations of head teachers must be judged. For the Catholic school of tomorrow the Qualification must also be capable of supporting the dual academic and spiritual role of the Catholic school leader.

The concept of Catholic leadership as a distinctive form

Given the praxis-based, developmental perspective provided by the SQH there is cause for cautious optimism that the framework does in fact offer a realistic means of both supporting management and leadership development in Scotland and contributing more generally to international discourse on Catholic leadership formation. The alternative, to develop a separate set of competences for Catholic school leadership, would be to separate and distance the debate from the mainstream, and thus deny the system as a whole a valuable opportunity for interaction, both professional and conceptual. Engagement in the mainstream programme might strengthen the process overall by adding the spiritual to what might otherwise remain a secular debate. It would also encourage a more generous recognition of the Catholic school as an important and significant institution in our society.

Leadership and management development, however, must be seen as part of a lifelong process of professional development; potential participants having engaged in a range of prior professional opportunities appropriate to the stage in their career and holding an expectation of continuing post-appointment support. From the perspective of Catholic school leadership, the proposed framework appears to have equal validity, especially in the context of a lifelong development pathway linking initial teacher training and continuing professional development.

The distinctiveness of Catholic schools based on a theology of community has, of course, to be recognised. In this regard, it may be illuminating to speculate on the extent to which the following extract from The Secondary Education Report of the Advisory Council on Education in Scotland (1947) could act as a guiding template for Catholic schools (substituting Catholic for Christian).

> For Christian education means much more than finding a place in the curriculum for religious and moral instruction. It involves acceptance of a doctrine of human nature which courageously applied will determine priority of aim in education, better still reconcile seemingly conflicting aims; it must enter into all debate on the content of schooling; and above all, it decisively establishes the child as an end in himself, requiring an approach to him which is patient, persuasive and at every point respectful of his growth toward personality.

If there is congruence of purpose (and the means of its achievement), does this suggest that the claim for the existence of a distinct form of leadership that is Catholic has to give sway to the view explored in recent internet conversations (Australian Catholic University, 1998) that it is simply the cultural/anthropological context which is Catholic? Bryant (1998, pp. 7-20) notes that in studies of educational leadership, culture has been a missing variable and accepts that much remains to be learned about cultural understandings of leadership. He accepts the assertion of Hofstede (1991) that culture is 'the collective programming of the mind which distinguishes the members of one group or category of people from another' and adds 'it should be equally obvious that leadership is also rooted in culture'. However, the question remains: given the distinctiveness of the Catholic tradition and its manifestation in schools by a particular ethos, is it possible to define in unique terms what constitutes Catholic leadership, as well as leadership behaviours?

Sergiovanni (1984) – cited in Caldwell and Spinks (1988) – suggests the existence of five leadership 'forces', each of which 'can be thought of as the means available to administrators, supervisors and teachers to bring about or preserve changes needed to improve schooling':

1) *Technical leadership* – concerned with sound management techniques.

2) *Human leadership* – involved with harnessing and engaging staff.

3) *Educational leadership* – involving the use of expert knowledge about education and schooling.

4) *Symbolic leadership* – involved in 'institutionalising' the vision for the school by focusing the attention of others on matters of importance to it.

5) *Cultural leadership* – which involves the building of a unique, strong school culture marked by frequent public references to the characteristics of the school and its mission in the community.

Sergiovanni suggests that these five leadership forces can be arranged in a hierarchy. Technical and human leadership forces are important but alone are insufficient for the achievement of excellence. Adding educational leadership achieves more but it is only with the addition of the symbolic and cultural that a school can achieve excellence. Given that examples of cultural leadership offered include frequent public reference to the characteristics of the school and its mission in the community, the socialisation of new members, telling stories, maintaining myths and rewarding those who reflect the culture, this 'force' has particular significance in the present discussion. It reflects O'Keefe's (1998) description of the 'school as a community of memory' with its implicit challenge for leadership and leadership development. O'Keefe argues that in confronting the challenges of the present, Catholic educators can turn to the past to find elements of a creative response to the present:

> Catholicism honors a tradition that is centuries old. In a world plagued by *anomie* students must learn the stories told in a way that is compelling for the present. Students should be exposed to Catholic culture: literature, history, music and art. Likewise students should learn the rich and complex history of the church, read developmentally appropriate original sources in theology and philosophy and learn about the controversies and councils that chronicle a pilgrim church, a community. Education is the passing of sacred stories from one generation to the next.

It is this capacity to understand and guide the anthropological exposure that differentiates the Catholic and non-Catholic school leader. The 'technical', 'human' and 'educational' forces or means (with certain exceptions in the latter case) are likely to be common to all schools – if they are genuinely educational in intent. It is in the realms of the 'symbolic' and 'cultural that the main differences may be found and where the awesome challenge lies. To be judged successful, the Catholic school leader must integrate gospel values and moral ethics not only in the curriculum but in the policies and very life of the school. Collaborative planning is consequently justified not simply on grounds of institutional efficiency but equally, and perhaps more importantly, as the means of ensuring that the underlying gospel values provide the life-blood of all of the school's activities. It is in this more than anything else that the distinctiveness of Catholic leadership may be located.

Conclusion

The emerging Scottish Qualification for Headship has been used as a context within which to explore some aspects of the nature of school leadership in general and Catholic school leadership in particular. It has been argued that for the most part the processes (means) of leadership and management are largely similar. As such the proposed Scottish Qualification for Headship, as one element in a continuing professional development pathway, provides a route equally valid for denominational and non-denominational aspirants alike. It is within the specifics of an inherited tradition and anthropology, with its distinctive moral and ethical understanding, that the action set for Catholic school leaders and aspiring school leaders is framed. What may be necessary, however, is an additional pre-entry, 'Catholic Anthropology' module. Ciriello (1994) identifies four broad areas of responsibility of which it might comprise:

1) *Faith development,* including supporting consistent practices of Christian service.
2) *Building a Christian community,* including fostering collaboration between the parish, parents and the school.
3) *Moral and ethical development,* especially the integration of gospel values.
4) *History and philosophy of the Catholic school* and its unique character.

Whether this module is depicted in pre-entry terms for SQH or whether it may be more usefully regarded as a module necessary for all staff is a matter for debate; a debate predicated on the literature on leadership/followership behaviours. Given the research findings of Posner and Schmidt (1993) that 'people who had the greatest clarity about both personal and organisational values had the highest commitment to the organisation', there is perhaps a prima facie case for the latter. In the final analysis, educational leadership within the context of a life-enhancing tradition is never likely to be easy and likely to demand high order commitment from those endowed with such responsibility. It is a moot point whether such leadership could, in principle, be exercised by members of other Christian faith communities. Within the context of the present discussion, the answer could only be in the affirmative if the individual were able to demonstrate a capability and commitment, where capability is conceptualised as function of knowledge and/or skills gained through all elements of the developmental programme.

EPILOGUE

Bartholomew J. McGettrick

Introduction

This collection of essays has offered a diverse range of perspectives on issues of concern to Catholic education. Despite this diversity they share a range of important features in so far as they attempt to give expression to what Catholic education has to offer both the Catholic community and the wider polity. In this epilogue I wish to suggest a number of themes which the ongoing conversation about Catholic education will need to take to heart.

Recent years have given an increased prominence to the place of citizenship in education and while this may differ from country to country it tends to include a concern with political literacy, personal development, social education and cultural transmission. Given that Catholic education must continue to be in the world while not necessarily *of* it, the promotion of 'citizenship' must be as much part of the life and mission of Catholic education as it is of any other public or private institution of higher education.

The concept of citizenship is an elusive one. It does not consist merely in ensuring a society which conforms to state norms and legal obligations; nor a society which unthinkingly follows political ideologies; nor, indeed, one which tolerates all values without thought or reflection. Given these beliefs Catholics ought to expect their education to promote values and ideals which bring justice to all, and dismiss action which allows injustice, and silences the gospel message. These values are, in turn, concrete derivatives of faith, hope and love which are the essential expression of the Catholic institution. The issue for Catholic education, as a system, may not be unqualified conformity to the State, but if its concern for these issues as they relate to all is incontrovertible then it certainly implies a full participation in the life and work of the State.

For some, 'citizenship' might imply a form of conformity to the State. This needs to be questioned since there are some aspects of legal frameworks which run contrary to Catholic thought; for example, the position of many governments in relation to abortion. Additionally, there are some citizens who might feel a certain political tension with the State. For example, to be fully Scottish at present is to seek a degree of autonomy from the British Government. While this does not imply civil disobedience it does imply a 'tension'. The same may be true of the Basques, Flemish, and many peoples of Eastern Europe.

Put like this it gives an impression that Catholic education is simply concerned to offer the social teaching of the Church – perhaps at a high level of abstraction. Such a construction is to miss the point that an essential purpose is to assist the personal formation of women and men who can discuss, negotiate, persuade and inspire others to follow God's will by the power of rational argument, charismatic leadership and personal witness. The development of solutions consistent with the gospel message must be the hallmark of our Christian impact of service to society. Offering these together with a robust critique is the work of the fully integrated and not the 'half-hearted' citizen.

Contemporary understandings of citizenship will include, at a minimum, appropriate political tolerance, legitimate religious freedom, social equity and equality. To be an effective Catholic citizen is not to be introspective about our skills, processes and practices, but to use them in the service of others. There is an imperative placed on Catholic educators to enhance and develop these features of citizenship. Without this the very notion of Catholic education is incomplete and ineffective.

It is through the influence of teachers who authentically hold these beliefs about their role that students learn how to express more adequately the gospel message and learn to be people who can transform our society. Catholic education must seek to be an agent of transformation and change while recognising the ongoing challenge of holding together the concerns of both this life and the 'beyond'. Just as 'The Kingdom of God' is not easily formed within a political state, so 'a theology of citizenship' is a slightly awkward juxtaposition of ideals. Are we the citizens of twin cities – the State and the Church?

In looking forward to the evolution of Catholic education it is just as important to recognise that 'the spiritual Kingdom' transforms 'the temporal State', as it is to see the temporal State as influencing our spiritual thinking and formation. Our spiritual formation is set in a time and place. While the 'theology of place' is more visibly a motive force in places such as contemporary Palestine, or Northern Ireland, it is increasingly a feature of all our lives. In reflecting upon place and time, Catholic educators can begin to shape a view of education that is proactive, dynamic and responsive.

So, how then is Catholic education to move this agenda forward? Certainly the increasing interest in 'citizenship education' offers new opportunities for involving Catholic education in a wider debate with civic society at large. The content of citizenship in courses is most frequently dealt with in the fields of social sciences, humanities, and philosophical enquiry. There are of course vital items relating to citizenship which occur in fields of science, technology, and matters related to communication. Indeed, it might be thought appropriate that citizenship is an underlying theme in all aspects of education. Citizenship need not be confined to these disciplines if the broad concepts of negotiation, compromise and social action lie at the heart of the objectives of citizenship, as they do with education more generally. Catholic education may wish to consider whether undertaking appropriate programmes in citizenship should be a core requirement for all its students; in so doing it might also wish to reflect on the content of these.

Both the internal and external dimensions of Catholic education are equally important in promoting citizenship. In the case of the former it is imperative that the culture and climate created in Catholic institutions is sufficiently dynamic so as to be responsive to the needs of its students. Equally, in the case of the latter, Catholic education cannot exist in a state of isolation or at a remove from its social and external relationships. It is the role of Catholic education to try to act as 'an institutional evamngelist' for the society which it serves. This feature of our educational offering is integral to a developed notion of citizenship, since no citizen can function successfully if not part of a fully developed community.

It is also important that Catholic institutions regard themselves as part of an international community of education and scholarship. The development of increasingly sophisticated technologies for communication should be harnessed to this end. In their turn these offer the possibility of increased personal contact and the evolution of genuinely Catholic perspectives on both Catholic education and on being Catholic in the world. It is the long cherished internationalism enjoyed by European Catholic institutions which continues to nurture such visions and we must ensure that Catholic schools derive real benefit from this.

In all of this, negotiation, debate, conversation and listening must lie at the heart of the processes, and the gospel values at the soul of our endeavours in Catholic education. It is for these reasons that I welcome this volume, which draws upon the insights of a wide range of scholars who offer their, sometimes very different, perspectives as part of both a serious conversation between Catholics and between Catholics and others.

THE CONTRIBUTORS

John Brick is Head of Department for Educational Foundations at the Australian Catholic University's Melbourne Campus where he is also co-editor of the interdisciplinary journal *Interlogue*. He has lectured throughout Australasia and was a visiting lecturer at St Andrew's College, Glasgow in 1997. John is a leading figure in ACU's Educational Leadership Network and works extensively in professional development programmes for senior staff in schools.

David Carr is Reader in Education at the University of Edinburgh. For many years he has been one of the most respected and widely read philosophers of education. A prolific author, David has published articles in almost every major philosophy journal in the English language, on topics ranging from the philosophy of art to the logic of religious education. He is Secretary to the Scottish Branch of the Philosophy of Education Society of Great Britain. An Aristotelian by instinct and conviction his most recent book is *Educating the Virtues* (Routledge). As a Catholic scholar he has a concern to see clarity brought to bear on our reflections on Catholic education.

James C. Conroy is Director of Religious Education and Pastoral Care at St Andrew's College, Glasgow. Prior to this he lectured in Religious Education and Philosophy of Religion at St Mary's College, Strawberry Hill and taught in schools in London and Bristol. He has a long-standing interest in moral education and leadership in Catholic education, having written and published widely in the field. He has recently written a handbook for primary schools entitled *Foundations* (GCF, St Andrew's College) and a training manual (with Douglas McCreath) for *Leadership in Catholic Schools* (Strathclyde Regional Council). He also directs a

Development Project in Values Education. Jim is currently secretary/treasurer of the Values Education Council for the UK, a member of the Boards of the Association for Moral Education and the *Journal of Moral Education*.

Robert A. Davis is Director of Inservice Education and sometime lecturer in the Department of Language and Literature at St Andrew's College, Glasgow. Prior to this he held teaching positions in Glasgow, Falkirk and Dundee. He is well known, in both literary and education circles, for his scholarly and incisive approach to issues of contemporary culture, having written widely on topics ranging from the work of Robert Graves to children's spirituality, including the recent 'Children and Spirituality in the Context of a Traditional Festival' in *The International Journal of Children's Spirituality*. Together with Jim Conroy he has published a number of papers in the field of moral education, most recently, *Teacher's Authenticity* and *The Future of Moral Education*, in Leicester *et al.* (Falmer).

James M. Day is Professor of Psychology and Religious Development at the University of Louvain-La-Neuve. He has been a visiting scholar at Cambridge, Columbia and Princeton and has lectured extensively in America and Europe. He serves on the boards of a number of scholarly journals and book series, including the *Journal of Moral Education*. He is a prolific and insightful scholar in the fields of moral and religious experience and development, having written three books and a host of articles. In addition to his academic researches and teaching he is also a clinician working in a variety of therapeutic contexts. An American Lutheran by background, James has worked for many years with Catholic educationalists and is actively involved in lay ministry in the Anglican Communion. He has been recently appointed Associate Dean for Academic and Student Affairs in the Faculty of Psychology and Educational Sciences at Louvain.

Vincent J. Duminuco SJ is a member of the Society of Jesus and has held a wide range of posts, including Principal, in schools and colleges. He has also been President of the Jesuit Secondary Education Association and a senior figure in the Society's Generalate where, until 1997, he held the position of Director of the International Jesuit Secretariat for Education. He is currently based at the Jesuit Centre for Refugees in New York and teaches at the Gregorian University in Rome. He has published many articles and monographs on Catholic education including *The Role of Catholic Higher Education in the Light of the Development of Christian Social Teaching in Ankara University* (Human Rights Centre Publications,1993).

John J. Haldane is Professor of Philosophy at the University of St Andrew's and Director of the Centre for Philosophy and Public Affairs. He has an international reputation as one of Britain's most incisive philosophers and has published widely in metaphysics, philosophy of mind, social philosophy and, most recently, the philosophy of religion, where he has co-authored a new volume with J. J. C. Smart, *Atheism & Theism* (Blackwell). An art teacher at an earlier stage in his career, John has maintained a long-standing interest in Catholic education and has written a number of articles in the field. Keen on popularising clear thinking, he is a regular broadcaster and correspondent in the Press, with a regular 'Credo' column in *The Times*.

John M. Hull is undoubtedly the most famous and respected name of his generation in the field of religious education. He holds a professorship in Religious Education at the University of Birmingham, the first such professorship anywhere in Britain. His name is synonymous with scholarship and inventiveness in the field where he has led religious educators for over twenty years. John has written countless books and articles in addition to having been the editor of the *British Journal for Religious Education* for many years. He has also had a long-standing interest in Christian education and, as a non-conformist Australian, brings very particular insights which may be used by Catholic educators. *Touching the Rock* is a moving and refreshing autobiographical account of his blindness and was first broadcast as a play by Radio 4 in 1996.

Malcolm L. MacKenzie is Senior Lecturer in Education at the University of Glasgow. Having supervised and tutored a whole generation of senior Scottish educationalists he is held in high esteem in Scottish educational and political circles. He has a developed research interest in educational policy and management and has published a large number of studies in the field of education, most recently, as editor with Humes, of *The Management of Educational Policy: Scottish Perspectives* (Longman). He is a member of the Boards of the Scottish Further Education Unit and the General Teaching Council for Scotland. A regular broadcaster and a member of the Church of Scotland, Malcolm has had a long-standing phenomenological interest in the nature and position of Catholic education in Scottish culture.

James MacMillan studied music at the Universities of Edinburgh and Durham. He subsequently taught at the University of Manchester and currently teaches composition at The Royal Scottish Academy of Music and Drama and is visiting Professor at Strathclyde University. He is one of Britain's most acclaimed composers, having had a season at the Barbican in 1997 on his work *Raising Sparks*. He draws inspiration from the Christian story and his most recent CD release (BIS, February 1999) is entitled *Tridiuum*. It comprises 3 pieces, 'The World's Ransoming', 'Cello Concerto' and 'Symphony: Vigil'. His latest composition, *Quickening,* will be premiered at the BBC Proms in 1999. Rooted in the Catholic tradition, James' children are 'consumers' of Catholic education.

Douglas McCreath was until recently Assistant Principal at St Andrew's College where he was previously the Head of the Department of Educational Studies. Chair of the Scottish Educational Management Association, he has written extensively on management issues in education, his most recent book being co-edited with Alastair MacBooth (Falmer, 1996). As a member of the Church of Scotland who has spent much of his career working in a Catholic college, Douglas is interested in exploring the distinctive qualities of management and leadership which obtain in Catholic institutions.

Bartholomew J. McGettrick is Principal of St Andrew's College, Glasgow. He has held a number of prominent positions in Scottish education including Vice-Chair of the Scottish Consultative Council on the Curriculum. He is currently chair of a number of important bodies including boards of governors of schools and other educational foundations. He has also been a leading figure in the development of ASCICE (The European Association of Catholic Faculties of Education) and is, at this time, President. In recent years he has played an important role in the development of a public conversation about values in education.

Terence H. McLaughlin is university Lecturer in Education and Fellow of St Edmund's College, Cambridge. Before this he held senior posts in schools. His background is in the philosophy of education with a particular emphasis on morality in education. Among his many publications is the important study of Catholic education co-edited with Joe O'Keefe and Bernadette O'Keefe, *The Contemporary Catholic School: Context, Identity, Diversity* (Falmer, 1996). Terry is also in much international demand as an entertaining and insightful scholar and lecturer in education. His concern for Catholic education is evident in the extensive work he conducts in Eastern Europe.

Joseph J. O'Keeffe SJ is well known to Catholic educationalists throughout the English-speaking world as a thoughtful and challenging proponent of Catholic education. He is currently Associate Professor of Education in the School of Education at Boston College, where he also directs the Centre for Leadership in Catholic Higher Education. Having taught in schools, Joe continues to take an active as well as theoretical interest in their management as trustee of a number of Catholic schools. Widely published, his most recent works include *The Contemporary Catholic School: Context, Identity, Diversity,* co-edited with T. H. McLaughlin and B. O'Keeffe (Falmer, 1996), and *Conversations in Excellence: Providing for the Diverse Needs of Youth and their Families,* co-edited with Haney 1998, (NCEA).

Albert Price spent a career in education in England. He has in turn been a classroom teacher, head of department and head teacher before being appointed to Her Majesty's Inspectorate of Schools. He was recruited from the Inspectorate to be Director of the Catholic Education Service for England and Wales at what must be seen as the most difficult and turbulent time for the management of the Catholic education system since 1870. He retired from the post in 1995 and became a freelance adviser to schools in Britain and elsewhere, taking a special and continuing interest in schools which are experiencing difficulties.

Alex Rodger recently retired from the post of Director of Professional Development for the Post-graduate Certificate Programmes and Head of Religious Education at the Northern College of Education. He continues as Director of the Values Education Project housed there and his work in both religious education and moral education has made him one of the most important figures in Scottish education. From the publication of his ground-breaking work, *Religious Education in an Open Society* (Handsel, 1982), through his participation in a wide range of national initiatives, to his current work in moral education, Alex has established a national and international reputation as a scholar of generosity and insight. As an ordained minister in the Baptist Church he provides an interesting and challenging perspective on the work of Catholic education. His most recent publications have included *Developing Moral Community in a Pluralist School Setting* (Gordon Cook Foundation, 1996).

BIBLIOGRAPHY

Introduction

Hirst, P., *Moral Education in a Secular Society* (London: University of London Press/National Children's Homes, 1974).

Hornsby-Smith, M. P. and Lee, R., *Roman Catholic Opinion: A Study of Roman Catholics in England and Wales in the 1970s* (Guilford: University of Surrey, 1979).

Nichols, K., *Orientations: Six Essays on Theology and Education* (Slough: St Paul Publications, 1979).

Nichols, K., *Voices of the Hidden Waterfall: Essays on Religious Education* (Slough: St Paul Publications, 1980).

Roman Catholic Bishops' Conference of England and Wales, *Signposts and Homecomings: The Educative Task of the Catholic Community* (Slough: St Paul Publications, 1980).

Chapter 1: Visionary Leadership in Catholic Schools

Barth, R. S., *Improving Schools from Within* (San Francisco: Jossey-Bass, 1990).

Bellah, R. N., Madsen, R., Sullivan, W. M., Swidler, A. and Tipton, S., *Habits of the Heart: Individualism and Commitment in American Life* (New York: Harper & Row, 1985).

Bellah, R. N., *The Good Society* (New York: Knopf 1991).

Bolman, L. and Deal, T., *Reframing Organizations: Artistry, Choice and Leadership* (2nd Edition) (San Francisco: Jossey-Bass, 1997).

Bowman, T., 'Religious and cultural variety: Gift to Catholic schools', in Kelly, F. D. (ed), *The Non-Catholic in Catholic Schools* (Washington: National Catholic Educational Association, 1984).

Bridges, D. and McLaughlin, T. (eds), *Education and the Market Place* (London: Falmer, 1994).

Bryk, A. S., 'Lessons from Catholic high schools on renewing our educational institutions', in McLaughlin, T., O'Keefe, J. and O'Keeffe, B. (eds), *The Contemporary Catholic School: Context, Identity and Diversity* (Washington DC: Falmer, 1996).

Catechism of the Catholic Church (Dublin: Veritas Publications, 1994).

Commission on Research and Development of the Jesuit Secondary Education Association, *Profile of the Graduate of a Jesuit High School* (Washington DC: Jesuit Secondary Education Association, 1992).

Coontz, S. *The Way We Never Were: American Families and the Nostalgia Trap* (Washington DC: Basic Books, 1992).

D'Antonio, W. V., Davidson, J. D., Hoge, D. R. and Wallace R. A., *Laity, American and Catholic: Transforming the Church* (Kansas City: Sheed & Ward, 1996).

Daloz, L. A. P., Keen, C. H., Keen, J. P. and Parks, S. D., *Common Fire: Lives of Commitment in a Complex World* (Boston: Beacon 1996).

Davis, C., 'Catholic African Americans: A historical summary', in Committee on African American Catholics of the National Catholic Conference of Bishops (eds), *Keep Your Hand on the Plow: The African American presence in the Catholic Church* (Washington: United States Catholic Conference, 1996).

Dellatre, R., 'The Culture of procurement: Reflections on addiction and the dynamics of American culture', in Reynold, C. and Norman, C. (eds), *Community in America: The Challenge of Habits of the Heart* (Berkeley: University of California Press, 1988).

Documents of Vatican II., *Gaudium et Spes: Pastoral Constitution on the Church in the Modern World* http://listserv.american.edu/catholic (1965); *Gravissimum educationis: Declaration on Christian education*, (1965), http://listserv.american.edu/catholic.

Elshtain, M. B., 'Catholic social thought, the city, and liberal America', in *Catholicism and Liberalism: Contributions to*

American Public Philosophy (New York: Cambridge University Press, 1994).

Elshtain, M. B., *Democracy on Trial* (New York: Basic Books, 1995).

Galbraith, J. K., *The Culture of Contentment* (Boston: Houghton-Mifflin, 1992).

Gibson, D., 'Black Catholics in America: A Documentation Overview', in Committee on African American Catholics of the National Catholic Conference of Bishops (eds), *Keep Your Hand on the Plow,* op. cit.

Grace, G., 'Leadership in Catholic schools', in McLaughlin, T., O'Keefe, J. and O'Keeffe, B. (eds), *The Contemporary Catholic School: Context, Identity and Diversity,* op. cit.

Groome, T. H., Educating for Life: *A Spiritual Vision for Every Teacher and Parent* (Allen, TX: Thomas More Press, 1998).

Hollenbach, D., 'The common good, pluralism and Catholic education', in McLaughlin, T., O'Keefe, J. and O'Keeffe, B. (eds), *The Contemporary Catholic School: Context, Identity and Diversity,* op.cit.

International Commission on the Apostolate of Jesuit Education, 'Ignatian pedagogy: A practical approach', in Meirose, C. E. (ed), *Foundations* (Washington DC: Jesuit Secondary Education Association, 1994).

Lasch, C., *The Culture of Narcissism: American Life in an Age of Diminishing Expectations* (New York: W. W. Norton, 1979).

Lasch, C., *The True and Only Heaven: Progress and its Critics* (New York: W. W. Norton, 1991).

Lasch, C., *The Revolt of the Elites* (New York: W. W. Norton, 1995).

Morris, C. R., *American Catholic* (New York: Random House, 1997).

National Catholic Conference of Bishops, *Brothers and Sisters to Us* (Washington DC: United States Catholic Conference, 1979).

National Catholic Conference of Bishops, *The Hispanic Presence: Challenge and Commitment* (Washington DC: United States

Catholic Conference, 1983).

Perkins, D., Borden, L. and Hogue, T., 'Standards of practice for community-based educational collaborations', in Haney, R. and O'Keefe, J. (eds), *Conversations in Excellence: Providing for the Diverse Needs of Youth and Families in Catholic Schools* (Washington DC: National Catholic Educational Association, 1998).

Pontifical Commission for Justice and Peace, *The Church and Racism: Toward a More Fraternal Society* (Washington DC: United States Catholic Conference, 1988).

Pontifical Council for the Pastoral Care of Migrants and Itinerant People, Refugees: *A Challenge to Solidarity* (Vatican City: Libreria Editrice Vaticana, 1992).

Pope John Paul II, *Solicitudo rei socialis: Encyclical on social concern* http://listserv.american.edu/catholic (1987); *Ut unum sint: Encyclical on ecumenism,* http://listserv.american.edu/catholic (1995).

Purpel, D., *The Moral and Spiritual Crisis in Education* (New York: Bergin and Garvey, 1989).

Synod of Roman Catholic Bishops, *Justice in the World,* http://www.mcgill.pvt.k12.al.us/jerryd/synodjw.htm. (1971).

Walch, T., Parish School: *American Catholic Parochial Education from Colonial Times to the Present* (New York: Crossroad, 1996).

Wallis, J., *The Soul of Politics: Beyond religious right and secular left* (San Diego: Harcourt Brace, 1995).

Walsh, M. E., Buckley, M. A. and Howard, K. A., 'Critical collaboration: School, family and community', in Haney, R. and O'Keefe, J. (eds), *Conversations in Excellence,* op. cit.

Chapter 2: 'The Long Johns' and Catholic Education

Aquinas, T., *The Summa Theologia,* Q168; art 1-4 (trans) Fathers of the English Dominican Province (London, Burns and Oates: 1921).

Arthur, J., *The Ebbing Tide: Policy and Principles of Catholic*

Education (Leominster: Gracewing, 1995).

Bainton, R. H., *Erasmus of Christendom* (New York and London: Charles Scribner and Collins, 1969).

Beresford, P., 'Gizz a real job' in *The Guardian*, 4 June 1997, p. 26.

Berlin, I., *The Sense of Reality: Studies in Ideas and their History* (ed) Hardy, H. (London, Chatto and Windus, 1996).

Bossy, J., *The English Catholic Community* 1570-1850 (London: Darton, Longman and Todd, 1975).

Catholic Bishops' Conference of England and Wales, *The Common Good and the Catholic Church's Social Teaching* (London: Catholic Bishops' Conference, 1996).

Conroy, J. and Davis, R., 'Teachers, authenticity and the future of moral education' in Leicester, M., Mogdil, C. and Mogdil, S.(eds), *Values Education and Cultural Diversity*, vol. 2 (London: Falmer, 1998).

Conroy, J., 'Political aspirations, moral education and the literary imagination' in *Interlogue: Promoting An Interdisciplinary Approach to Community Issues* (December 1997).

Conroy, J., 'Poetry and human growth' in *The Journal of Moral Education* (to be published November 1999).

Critchley, S., Deconstruction and pragmatism: Is Derrida a private ironist or a public liberal?, in Van Haute, P. and Birmingham, P. (eds), *Dissensus Communis: Between Ethics and Politics* (Kampen: Kok Pharos, 1995).

Davis, A., 'The Limits of Educational Assessment', in *Journal of Philosophy of Education*: Special Issue vol. 32:1 (1998).

Department for Catholic Education and Formation of the Catholic Bishops' Conference of England and Wales, *A Struggle for Excellence: Catholic Secondary Schools in Urban Poverty Areas* (London: Catholic Education Service, 1997).

Eco, U., *The Name of The Rose* (London, Harcourt Brace Jovanovich Inc; Secker and Warburg; Pan Books Ltd, 1983 and 1984).

Erasmus of Rotterdam, *Praise of Folly* and *Letter to Martin Dorp* (trans) Radice, B. and (Introduction and Notes) Levi, A. H. T. (London: Penguin, 1971).

Fukuyama, F., 'The end of history' in *The National Interest* (summer, 1989).

Gallagher, D. and Gallagher, I. (eds), *The Education of Man: The Educational Philosophy of Jacques Maritain* (Indiana: Notre Dame Press, 1962).

Gray, J., *Post-Liberalism: Studies in Political Thought* (London: Routledge, 1993 and 1996).

Gray, J., 'Hague's road to legal heroin' in *The Guardian*, 18 October 1997, p.21.

Hegel, G. W. F., 'Vorlesungen über die Philosophie der Weltgeschichte', 1, 45 Hoffmeister, (ed.), cited in Crites, S. (1966), 'The Gospel according to Hegel' in *The Journal of Religion* XLVI (April 1955).

Hirst, P., *Moral Education in a Secular Society* (London: Hodder and Stoughton, 1974).

HM Inspectors of Schools, *A Curriculum Framework for Children in their Pre-school Year* (Edinburgh: The Scottish Office, September 1997).

Hornsby Smith, M., *Roman Catholics in England* (Cambridge: Cambridge University Press, 1987).

The Industrial Society, *2020 Vision* (London: Industrial Society, 1998).

Little, T., 'Peer calls for end to State cash for Catholic schools' in *The Scotsman*, 4 February 1998, p.1.

McCann, J., 'A system of morals that gets a result' in *The Scotsman*, 4 February 1998.

Morson, G. S. and Emerson, C., *Mikhail Bakhtin: Creation of a Prosaics* (Stanford, CA: Stanford University Press, 1990).

Morris, A., 'By their fruits you will know them: distinctive features of Catholic education' in *Research Papers in Education* (13(1): pp. 87-112, 1998).

Munro, N., 'Enterprise culture to be central to Schools', in *The*

Times Educational Supplement (Scotland) 14 November 1997, p.1.

Murray, D. (Bp), *A Special Concern: The Philosophy of Education: A Christian Perspective* (Dublin: Veritas Publications, 1991).

Oakshott, M., 'Learning and teaching' in Peters, R. S. (ed), *The Concept of Education* (London: Routledge and Kegan Paul, 1967).

O'Keefe, J., *Visionary Leadership in Catholic Schools* (Glasgow: St Andrew's College, 1998).

Pilkington, E., 'Good year for an opt out leader' in *The Guardian*, 23 July 1991, p.21.

Pius X, *Rappresentanti In Terra* @ www.http: listserv.American.edu/catholic/church/papal/pius.xi. (1929).

Qualifications and Curriculum Authority, Advisory Group on Education for Citizenship and the Teaching of Democracy in Schools: *Initial Report* (London: QCA, 1998).

Rahner, H., *Man at Play or Did You Ever Practice Eutrapelia?* (trans) Battershaw, B. and Quinn, E. (London: Burns and Oates, 1963 and 1965).

Rorty, R., *Contingency, Irony and Solidarity* (Cambridge: Cambridge University Press, 1989).

Royal Society for the Encouragement of Arts, Manufactures and Commerce, *Redefining Work* (London: Royal Society, 1998).

Rupp, E. G., Marlow, A. N., Watson, P. S. and Drewery, M. A. (eds and trans), *The Library of Christian Classics, Vol XVII, Luther and Erasmus: Free Will and Salvation* (London: SCM Press, 1969).

Sawicki, N., *The Gospel in History: Portrait of a Teaching Church: The Origins of Christian Education* (New York; Paulist Press, 1988).

Scottish Office Education and Industry Department, *A Curriculum Framework for Children in their Pre-school Year,* op. cit.

Screech, M., *Laughter at the Foot of the Cross* (London: Allen Lane, The Penguin Press, 1997).

Theissen, E., *Teaching for Commitment: Liberal Education, Indoctrination and Christian Nurture* (Montreal and Leominster: McGill University Press and Gracewing, 1993).

Times Education Supplement (Scotland), 'Assembly avoids clash over religious schools', in *The Times Education Supplement (Scotland)*, 29 May 1998, p.4.

Todd, J. M., *Martin Luther: A Biographical Study* (London: Burns and Oates, 1964).

Zwart, H., *Ethical Consensus and the Truth of Laughter: the Structure of Moral Transformations* (Kampen: Kok Pharos, 1996).

Wilson, B., Values in Government, A public address to The Scottish Parents Consultative Forum, 23 May, held at St Andrew's College, Glasgow, 1998.

Chapter 3: Distinctiveness and the Catholic School: Balanced Judgement and the Temptations of Commonality

Astley, J. and Francis, L. J. (eds), *Critical Perspectives on Christian Education. A reader on the aims, principles and philosophy of Christian education* (Leominster: Gracewing, 1994).

Arthur, J., *The Ebbing Tide. Policy and Principles of Catholic Education* (Leominster: Gracewing, 1995).

Bishops' Conference of England and Wales *Religious Education: Curriculum Directory for Catholic Schools* (London: Catholic Education Service, 1996a).

Bishops' Conference of England and Wales *The Common Good and the Catholic Church's Social Teaching* (London: Bishops' Conference of England and Wales, 1996b).

Bishops' Conference of England and Wales *A Struggle for Excellence: Catholic Secondary Schools in Urban Poverty Areas* (London: Bishops' Conference of England and Wales, 1997a).

Bishops' Conference of England and Wales *Catholic Schools and Other Faiths* (London: Bishops' Conference of England and Wales, 1997b).

Bryk A. S., Lee, V. E. and Holland, P. B., *Catholic Schools and the*

Common Good (Cambridge MA: Harvard University Press, 1993).

Canavan, K., 'The Quiet Revolution in Catholic Schooling in Australia' in *Catholic Education: A Journal of Inquiry and Practice,* vol 2, no. 1., pp. 46-54 (1998).

Carr, W., For Education: *Towards Critical Educational Inquiry* (Buckingham: Open University Press, 1995).

Catechism of the Catholic Church (London: Geoffrey Chapman; Dublin: Veritas, 1994).

Catholic Education Service, *Quality of Education in Catholic Secondary Schools. A review of inspection reports on Catholic secondary schools* (London: Catholic Education Service, 1994).

Catholic Education Service, *Learning from OFSTED and Diocesan Inspections. The distinctive nature of education in Catholic primary and secondary schools* (London: Catholic Education Service, 1995).

Catholic Education Service, *Education in Catholic Schools and Colleges: Principles, Practices and Concerns. A statement from the Catholic Bishops of England and Wales* (London: Catholic Education Service, 1996a).

Catholic Education Service, *The Common Good in Education. A commentary on the implications of the Church's social teaching for the work of Catholic schools and colleges* (London: Catholic Education Service, 1997).

Catholic Education Service and *Briefing, Partners in Mission. A collection of talks by Bishops on issues affecting Catholic education* (London: Catholic Education Service and *Briefing,* 1997).

Congregation for Catholic Education, 'The Catholic school on the threshold of the third millenium', reprinted in *Catholic Education: A Journal of Inquiry and Practice,* vol 2, no. 1., pp. 4-14 (1998).

Congregation for the Clergy, *General Directory for Catechesis* (London: Catholic Truth Society, 1997).

Crawford, M. and Rossiter, G., *Missionaries to a Teenage Culture. Religious Education in a Time of Rapid Change* (Sydney:

Christian Brothers Province Resource Group, 1988).

Dunne, J., *Back to the Rough Ground: 'Phronesis' and 'Techne' in Modern Philosophy and in Aristotle* (Notre Dame IN: University of Notre Dame Press, 1993).

Feheney, J. M., 'The Future of the Catholic School: An Irish Perspective' in Feheney, J. M. (ed), *From Ideal to Action. The Inner Nature of a Catholic School Today* (Dublin: Veritas, 1998).

Gallagher, J., 'The Catholic School and Religious Education: Meeting a Variety of Needs' in McLaughlin, T. H., O'Keefe J. and O'Keeffe, B., (eds) *The Contemporary Catholic School: Context, Identity and Diversity* (London: The Falmer Press, 1996).

Gallagher, M. P., 'New Forms of Cultural Unbelief' in Hogan, P. and Williams, K., (eds) *The Future of Religion in Irish Education* (Dublin: Veritas, 1997).

Greeley, A. M., 'Catholic Schools at the Crossroads: An American Perspective' in Feheney, J. M., (ed) *From Ideal to Action. The Inner Nature of a Catholic School Today* (Dublin: Veritas, 1998).

Hirst, P. H., 'The Theory-Practice Relationship in Teacher Training' in Booth, M., Furlong, J. and Wilkin, M. (eds), *Partnership in Initial Teacher Training* (London: Cassell, 1990).

McBrien, R. P., *Catholicism,* Third edition (London: Geoffrey Chapman, 1994).

McLaughlin, T. H., 'Values, Coherence and the School' in *Cambridge Journal of Education,* vol 24, no. 3., pp. 453-470 (1994).

McLaughlin, T. H., 'The Distinctiveness of Catholic Education' in McLaughlin T. H., O'Keefe, J. and O'Keeffe, B. (eds), *The Contemporary Catholic School. Context, Identity and Diversity* (London: The Falmer Press, 1996).

McLaughlin, T. H., 'Beyond the Reflective Teacher' in *Educational Philosophy and Theory,* vol 31, no. 1., (1999).

Morris, A. B., 'Catholic and other secondary schools: and analysis of OFSTED inspection reports, 1993-95' in *Educational Research* vol 40, no. 2., pp. 181-190 (1998a).

Morris, A. B., 'So Far, So Good: levels of academic achievement in

Catholic Schools' in *Educational Studies* vol 24, no. 1., pp. 83-94 (1998b).

Morris, A. B., 'By their fruits you will know them: distinctive features of Catholic education' Research Papers in *Education* vol 13, no. 1., pp. 87-112 (1998c).

Nichols, K., *Refracting the Light. Learning the Languages of Faith* (Dublin: Veritas, 1997).

O'Donoghue, T. A., 'Addressing Some Misconceptions in the Cultural Inheritance in Catholic Education' in McMahon, J., Neidhart, H. and Chapman, J. (eds), *Leading the Catholic School* (Victoria, Australia: Spectrum Publications, 1997).

O'Keefe, J., 'No Margin, No Mission' in McLaughlin, T. H., O'Keefe, J. and O'Keeffe, B. (eds), *The Contemporary Catholic School*, op. cit.

Pendlebury, S., 'Practical Reasoning and Situational Appreciation in Teaching' in *Educational Theory* vol 40, pp. 171-179 (1990)

Rawls, J., *Political Liberalism* (New York: Columbia University Press, 1993).

Robinson, G., *Travels in Sacred Places*, (Blackburn, Australia: Harper Collins, 1997).

Smith, R., 'Judgement Day' in Smith, R. and Standish, P. (eds), *Teaching Right and Wrong: moral education in the balance* (Stoke on Trent: Trentham Books, 1997).

Sullivan, J. W., 'Catholic Education: Distinctive and Inclusive Unpublished PhD thesis', (Institute of Education, University of London, 1998).

Wrenn, M. J., *Catechisms and Controversies. Religious Education in the Postconciliar Years* (San Francisco: Ignatius Press, 1991).

Chapter 4: The Catholic School is as Good as its Ethos

Abbott, W.M., *Documents of Vatican II* (New York: Corpus Books, 1966).

Bernier, P., *Ministry in the Church* (Conn: Twenty-Third Publications, 1992).

Brennan, G., 'Catholic Education' in Fraser, M. (ed), *Australian Catholics* (Richmond: Jesuit Publications, 1996).

The Congregation for Catholic Education, *The Religious Dimension of Education in a Catholic School* (Dublin: Veritas Publications, 1988).

Conroy, J. & Davis, R., 'Values and the curriculum', in *The Times Educational Supplement (Scotland)*, 22 November 1996.

Didion, J., *Slouching towards Bethlehem* (NewYork: Noonday Press, 1969).

Drucker, P., *The Leader of the Future* (New York: The Peter F. Drucker Foundation, 1996).

Duignan, P. & Macpherson, R.J.S. (eds.), *Educative Leadership: a practical theory for new administrators and managers* (London: Falmer, 1992).

Dulles, A., *Models of the Church* (New York: Image, 1978).

Gray, T., 'Ode On a Distant Prospect of Eton College' (1750) and 'Elegy Written in a Country Churchyard' in Smith, D. N. (ed), *The Oxford Book of Eighteenth-century Verse* (Oxford: Clarendon Press, 1926).

Greenleaf, R., *Servant Leadership* (New Jersey: The Paulist Press, 1977).

Handy, C., *The Empty Raincoat* (London: Hutchinson, 1994).

Hardy, T., *Tess of the D'Urbervilles* (Harmondsworth: Penguin, 1981).

Klinger, K., *A Pope Laughs* (London: Collins, 1964).

Lepani, B. 'Education in the information society' in Kennedy, K. (ed), *New challenges for civics and citizenship education* (Canberra: The Australian Curriculum Studies Association, 1996).

Muggeridge, M., *The Thirties* (London: The Quality Book Club. 1967).

Padavano, A., *The Estranged God* (New York: Sheed and Ward, 1966).

Spears, L. (ed.), *Reflections on Leadership* (New York: John Wiley, 1995).

Sacred Congregation for Catholic Education, *The Catholic School* (New York: St Paul, 1977).

Starratt, R., *Transforming Educational Administration* (New York: McGraw-Hill, 1996).

Scottish Consultative Council for the Curriculum, *The Heart of the Matter* (Dundee: SCCC, 1995).

Wickens, P., *The Ascendant Organisation* (London: Macmillan, 1995).

Wojtyla, K. (Cardinal), *The Acting Person* (trans) Potocki, A. (Dordrecht: D. Reidel Publishing Company, 1979).

Chapter 5: Turbulent Times – A Challenge to Catholic Education in Britain Today

Bishops' Conference of England and Wales, *Developing a Mission Statement* (London: CCIEA, 1990).

Bishops' Conference of England and Wales, *A Struggle for Excellence* (London: Catholic Education Service, 1997).

Buber, M., *Between Man and Man*, (trans) Smith, R. G. (Glasgow: Collins, 1947).

Department of Education and Science, *Better Schools* (London: HMSO, 1985).

Eliot, T. S., *Notes Towards a Definition of Culture* (London: Faber & Faber, 1948).

Flannery, A., The Conciliar and Post-Conciliar Documents, *Gravissimum Educationis; Declaration on Christian Education* (Dublin: Costello, 1975).

Gardner, H., *Intelligence: Multiple Perspectives* (New York: Harcourt, Brace, Jovanovich, 1996).

Great Britain, Laws and Statutes, Children Act (London: HMSO, 1989); Education Act (London: HMSO, 1994); Education (Scotland) Act (London: HMSO, 1996a); Children (Scotland) Act, (London: HMSO, 1995); Education Act (London: HMSO, 1996b).

Hume, B. (Card.), 'The Moral and the Spiritual in Education' in *Briefing*, vol. 22, 7 (1992).

OFSTED, *Access and Achievement in Urban Education* (London: HMSO, 1993).

Treston, K., 'The school as an agent of evangelisation', in Feeney, J. M. (ed), *From Ideal to Action: The Inner Nature of a Catholic School Today* (Dublin: Veritas Publications, 1998), pp. 57-71.

Patten, J., 'The education debate: A lifeline to literacy' in *The Guardian*, 16 November 1993, p.2.

Chapter 6: Towards the Millennium – Catholic Education: Identity, Context, Pedagogy

Arupe, P., *Men for Others* (Rome: International Centre for Jesuit Education, 1973).

Barker, D. *et al.*, *The European Values Study: 1981-1990* (Aberdeen: Gordon Cook Foundation/European Values Group, 1992).

Dickens, C., *A Tale of Two Cities* (New York: The Heritage Press, 1938).

Flannery, A., *Vatican II: The Conciliar and Post-Conciliar Documents, Gaudium et Spes* (Dublin: Costello Publishing, 1975).

Flynn, M., *Catholic Schools and the Communication of Faith* (Homebush, NSW: Society of St Paul, 1979.)

Flynn, M., *The Effectiveness of Catholic Schools* (Homebush, NSW: St Paul Publications, 1985.)

Flynn, M., *The Culture of Catholic Schools* (Homebush, NSW: St Paul Publications, 1993.)

Grimmitt, M., *Religious Education and Human Development* (Great Wakering, McCrimmons, 1987).

O'Malley, W.J., *Becoming a Catechist* (New York: Paulist Press, 1992).

O'Malley, W.J., *Origins* (Vol. 5: No.29, January, 1976).

Pope Paul VI, *Evangelii nuntiandi* (London: CTS, 1976).

Pope John Paul II, *Christifdeles laici* (London; CTS, 1989).

Society of Jesus, *Ignatian Pedagogy: A Practical Approach* (Rome: International Center for Jesuit Education; 1993).

Steiner, G., *Bluebeard's Castle: Some Notes on the New Definition of Culture* (Yale: Yale University Press, 1974).

Tarkington, B., *Seventeen* (New York: Buccaneer Books 1981).

Chapter 7: Catholic Faith and Religious Truth

Ayer, A. J., *Language, Truth and Logic* (London: Gollancz, 1967).

Carr, D., 'Education and values', in *British Journal of Educational Studies* vol. 39, 3, pp. 244-59 (1991).

Carr, D., 'Moral and religious education' 5-14, in *Scottish Educational Review* vol. 24, no. 2, pp. 111-17 (1992).

Hare, R. M., *The Language of Morals* (Oxford: Oxford University Press, 1972). For criticism, see Geach, P., *Logic Matters* (Oxford: Blackwell, Part 8, 1952).

Hume, D., *A Treatise of Human Nature*, Possner, E. C. (ed), (Harmondsworth: Penguin, 1969).

Kant, I., *Groundwork of the Metaphysic of Morals* (London: Hutchinson, 1948 (trans) Paton, H. J. – under the title of *The Moral Law*).

MacIntyre, A. C., *After Virtue* (Notre Dame, Indiana: Notre Dame Press, 1981).

MacIntyre, A. C., *Whose Justice, Which Rationality?* (Notre Dame, Indiana: Notre Dame Press, 1987).

MacIntyre, A. C., *Three Rival Versions of Moral Enquiry* (Notre Dame, Indiana: Notre Dame Press, 1992).

McLaughlin, T. H., O'Keefe, J., and O'Keeffe, B. (eds), *The Contemporary Catholic School: Context, Identity and Diversity* (Falmer Press: London, 1996).

Office for Standards in Education, *Spiritual, Moral, Social and Cultural Development: An OFSTED Discussion Paper* (London: Office for Standards in Education, 1994).

Pope John Paul II, *Crossing the Threshold of Hope* (London: Jonathan Cape, 1994).

Quine, W. V. O., *From a Logical Point of View* (New York: Harper and Row, 1952).

Rorty, R., *Contingency, Irony and Solidarity* (Cambridge: Cambridge University Press, 1989).

Rorty, R., *Philosophy and the Mirror of Nature* (Oxford: Blackwell 1981).

Scottish Office Education Department, *Religious and Moral Education*: 5-14 (Edinburgh: HMSO, 1992).

Smart, J. J. C. and Haldane, J. J., *Atheism and Theism* (Oxford: Blackwell, 1996).

Taylor, C., *Sources of the Self: The Making of the Modern Identity* (Cambridge: Cambridge University Press, 1989).

Wittgenstein, L., 'A lecture on ethics', in *Philosophical Review* vol. 74 (1965).

Chapter 8: The Need of Spirituality in Catholic Education

Chesterton, G. K., *What's Wrong with the World?* (London: Cassell, 1910).

Chesterton, G. K., 'The Revival of Philosophy' in *The Common Man* (London: Sheed and Ward, 1950).

De Caussade, J. P., *On Prayer* (ed. and trans) Thorold, A. (London: Burns, Oates and Washbourne, 1939).

Gardner and MacKenzie, *The Poems of Gerard Manley Hopkins* (Oxford: Oxford University Press, 1970).

Groeschel, B., *Stumbling Blocks or Stepping Stones* (New York: Paulist Press, 1987).

Haldane, J., 'Catholic education and Catholic identity' in McLaughlin, T., O'Keefe, B. and O'Keefe, J. (eds), *The Contemporary Catholic School*, op.cit.

McLaughlin, T., O'Keeffe, B and O'Keeffe, J. (eds), *The Contemporary Catholic School*, op. cit.

Smart, J. J. C. and Haldane, J. J., *Atheism and Theism* (Oxford: Blackwell, 1996).

Wicker, B., 'Adult Education' in *The Tablet*, 24 February 1979.

Chapter 9: Can there be a Catholic Curriculum?

Adamson, J. W., 'Education' in Crump, C. G. and Jacobs, E. F. (eds), *The Legacy of the Middle Ages* (Oxford: Clarendon, 1926).

Alliez, E., *Capital Times: Tales from the Conquest of Time* (trans) Van Den Abbeele, G. (Minneapolis: University of Minnesota Press, 1996).

Arthur, J., *The Ebbing Tide* (Leominster: Gracewing Publications, 1995).

Bloom, B. S., *A Taxonomy of Educational Objectives* (London: Longmans, Green and Co, 1964).

Blumenberg, H., *The Legitimacy of the Modern Age* (trans) Wallace, R. M. (Cambridge: Mass, MIT Press, 1983).

Bryk, A. S., Lee, V. E. and Holland, P. B., *Catholic Schools and the Common Good* (Harvard: Harvard University Press, 1993).

Burnside, J., *The Myth of the Twin* (London: Cape, 1994).

Cassirer, E., *The Individual and the Cosmos in Renaissance Philosophy* (New York: Harper Torchbooks, 1964).

Clark, S., *How to Think About the Earth* (London: Mowbray, 1993).

Carruthers, M., *The Book of Memory: A Study of Memory in Medieval Culture* (Cambridge: Cambridge University Press, 1990).

Dawkins, R., *River Out of Eden* (London: Weidenfeld and Nicolson, 1995).

Eagleton, T., 'Catholic education and commitment', in *Catholic Education Today* 1, January/February 1967.

Fletcher, R., *The Conversion of Europe: From Paganism to Christianity 371-1386AD* (London: Harper Collins, 1997).

Funkenstein, A., *Theology and the Scientific Imagination from the Middle Ages to the Seventeenth Century* (Princeton, NJ: Princeton University Press, 1986).

Gay, P., *The Enlightenment: The Rise of Modern Paganism* (London: Weidenfeld and Nicolson, 1967).

Gleason, P., *Contending with Modernity: Catholic Higher Education in the Twentieth Century* (Oxford: Oxford University Press, 1995).

Groome, T., 'What makes a school Catholic?', in McLaughlin, T., O'Keefe, J. and O'Keeffe, B. (eds), *The Contemporary Catholic School*, op. cit.

Hamlyn, D. W., *Experience and the Growth of Understanding* (London: Routledge and Kegan Paul, 1978).

Harries, R., *Art and the Beauty of God* (London: Mowbray, 1993).

Hickman, M. J., *Religion, Class and Identity: The State, the Catholic Church and the Education of the Irish in Britain* (Aldershot: Avebury, 1995).

Hirst, P., *Knowledge and the Curriculum* (London: Routledge and Kegan Paul, 1974).

Hull, J. M., *New Directions in Religious Education* (London: Falmer, 1982).

Humes, W. M., 'Science, religion and education: A study in cultural interaction' in Humes, W. M. and Paterson, H. (eds), *Scottish Culture and Scottish Education 1800-1980* (Edinburgh: John Donald, 1980).

James, E., *An Essay on the Content of Education* (London: Harrap, 1949).

Kennedy, P., *The Rise and Fall of the Great Powers: Economic Change and Military Conflict from 1500 to 2000* (London: Unwin Hyman, 1988).

Kristeller, P. O., *Renaissance Concepts of Man* (New York: Harper Torchbooks, 1972).

Le Goff, J., *Medieval Civilization* (trans.) Barrow, J. (Oxford: Blackwell, 1988).

Lyotard, J. F., *The Postmodern Condition: A Report on Knowledge* (trans.) Bennington, G. and B.Massumi (Manchester: Manchester University Press, 1984).

McLaren, P., *Schooling as a Ritual Performance* (London: Routledge and Kegan Paul, 1986).

McLaughlin, T., O'Keefe, J. and O'Keeffe, B. (eds), *The*

Contemporary Catholic School, op. cit.

O'Leary, D., *Religious Education and Young Adults* (Slough: St Paul Publications, 1983).

Ong, W., *Rhetoric, Romance and Technology* (Ithaca: Cornell University Press, 1971).

Peters, R. S., *The Concept of Education* (London: Routledge and Kegan Paul, 1967).

Peters, R. S., *The Philosophy of Education* (London: Routledge and Kegan Paul, 1973).

Pickstock, C., *After Writing: On the Liturgical Consummation of Philosophy* (Oxford: Blackwell, 1998).

Scaglione, A., *The Liberal Arts and the Jesuit College System* (Amsterdam: John Benjamins Publishing, 1986).

Schama, S., *Citizens: A Chronicle of the French Revolution* (London: Viking, 1989).

Schofield, H., *The Philosophy of Education: An Introduction* (London: George Allen and Unwin, 1980).

Scottish Consultative Council on the Curriculum, *The Heart of the Matter: A Paper for Discussion and Development* (Dundee: SCCC, 1995).

Scruton, R., 'The philosopher on Dover Beach' in *The Philosopher on Dover Beach: Essays* (Manchester: Carcanet, 1990).

Seigel, J. E., *Rhetoric and Philosophy in Renaissance Humanism,* (Princeton NJ: Princeton University Press, 1968).

Sheed, F. J., *Ground Plan for Catholic Reading* (London: Sheed and Ward, 1954).

Toulmin, S., Cosmopolis: *The Hidden Agenda of Modernity* (Chicago: University of Chicago Press, 1990).

Ullmann, Walter, *Medieval Foundations of Renaissance Humanism* (London: Elek, 1977).

Von Balthasar, H. U., *In the Fullness of Faith: On the Centrality of the Distinctively Catholic* (San Francisco: Ignatius Press, 1988).

Walsh, P., 'The Church secondary school and its curriculum', in O'Leary, D. (ed), *Religious Education and Young Adults* (Slough:

St Paul Publications, 1983).

Woodward, W. H., *Vittorino da Feltre and Other Humanist Educators* (New York: Columbia University, 1963).

Chapter 10: Inspiration, Transformation and the Holy Spirit

Buber, M., *I and Thou* (trans. and notes) Kaufmann, W. (Edinburgh: T. & T. Clark, 1970).

Burns, S. and Lamont, G., Values and Visions: *A Handbook for Spiritual Development and Global Awareness* (London: Hodder and Stoughton, 1995).

The Dorset Education Authority, *Reaction, Reflection, Response: The Dorset Agreed Syllabus for Religious Education* (Dorchester: Dorset County Council, 1992).

MacMillan, J., *Adam's Rib: For Bass Quintet* (London: Boosey and Hawkes, 1994/95).

McDade, J., 'A deathless song' in *The Month*, January 1994.

Markus, G., 'The potency of God the Father', in *Spirituality* no. 3, November/December 1995.

Swanick, K., *A Basis for Music Education* (Slough: NFER, 1980).

Williams, R., *Open to Judgement: Sermons and Addresses* (London: Darton, Longman and Todd, 1994).

Taylor, J., *From Festival Hymns on the Annunciation of the Blessed Virgin Mary.* The Manuscript reprinted in Heber, Bp. (1822), *The Collected Works of Jeremy Taylor*, vol. 15, 1665.

Chapter 11: Catholic Education in Scotland: A Phenomenological Approach

Accounts Commission, *Room for Learning, Managing Surplus Capacity in School Buildings* (Edinburgh: HMSO, September 1995).

Bacharach, S. B. and Mundell, B. (eds), *Images of Schools, Structures and Roles in Organizational Behaviour* (California: Corwin Press, 1995).

Benn, C. and Chitty, C., *Thirty Years On, Is Comprehensive*

Education Alive and Well or Struggling to Survive? (London: Penguin Books, 1997).

Briault, E. and Smith, F., *Falling Rolls in Secondary Schools* (Slough: NFER, 1980).

Brown, A, McCrone, D. and Paterson, L., *Politics and Society in Scotland* (London: Macmillan, 1996).

Bush, T., *Theories of Educational Management* (Second Edition), (London: Paul Chapman, 1995).

Casteell, V., *A Framework for Leadership and Management Development in Scottish Schools* (Edinburgh: SOEID, 1997).

Campbell, J., 'Roll Decline and Educational Policy. A Study of "Adapting to Change"', An Attempted Rationalisation of Educational Provision in Strathclyde Region' (unpublished PhD thesis: University of Edinburgh, 1996).

Connor, S., *Postmodernist Culture: An Introduction to Theories of the Contemporary* (Second Edition) (Oxford: Blackwell, 1997).

Deal, T. E., 'Schools as Cultural Arenas. Symbols and Symbolic Activity', in Bacharach, S. B. and Mundell, B. (eds), *Images of Schools, Structures and Roles in Organizational Behaviour* (California: Corwin Press, 1995).

Great Britain, Laws and Statutes, Scotland Bill (Edinburgh: HMSO, 1997).

Greenfield, T., 'Theory about organization. A new perspective and its implications for schools' in Hughes, M. (ed), *Administering Education, International Challenge* (London: The Athlone Press of the University of London, 1975).

Greenfield, T. and Ribbins, P. (eds), *Greenfield on Educational Administration, Towards a Humane Science* (London: Routledge and Kegan Paul, 1993).

Hall, S. and du Gay, P. (eds), *Questions of Cultural Identity* (London: Sage Publications, 1996).

Hall, S., 'Who needs identity?' in Hall, S. and du Gay, P. (eds), *Questions of Cultural Identity* (Sage Publications: London, 1996).

Halsey, A. H. Lauder, H., Brown, P. and Wells, S. A., *EDUCATION: Culture, Economy, Society* (Oxford: Oxford University Press, 1997).

Harvey, D., *The Condition of Postmodernity* (Oxford: Blackwell, 1990).

Herrnstein, R. J. and Murrray, C., *The Bell Curve, Intelligence and Class Structure in American Life* (New York: The Free Press, 1994).

Humes, W. M. and MacKenzie, M. L. (eds), *The Management of Educational Policy: Scottish Perspectives* (Harlow: Longman, 1994).

Jones, P., 'Education' in Linklater, M. and Denniston, R. (eds), *Anatomy of Scotland* (Edinburgh: W. & R. Chambers, 1992).

Kellas, J. G., *The Scottish Political System* (Cambridge: Cambridge University Press, 1973).

Lindsay, C., *School and Community* (London: Pergamon, 1969).

MacFadyen, I. and McMillan, F., *The Management of Change at a Time of Falling School Rolls* (Edinburgh: Scottish Council for Research in Education, 1984).

McGettrick, B., 'Management and values', in Humes, W. M. and MacKenzie, M.L. (eds), *The Management of Educational Policy: Scottish Perspectives,* op. cit.

McIntosh, J. P., *The Devolution of Power* (London: Penguin Books, 1968).

MacKenzie, M. L., 'The road to the circulars: A study of the evolution of Labour Party policy with regard to the comprehensive school', in *Scottish Educational Studies I,* No. 1, pp. 25-33 (1967).

Morgan, G., *Images of Organization* (London: Sage Publications, 1997).

Murray, C., *The Emerging British Underclass* (London: IEA Health and Welfare Unit, 1990).

O'Keefe, J. M., *Visionary Leadership in Catholic Schools* (Occasional Papers in Education: No. 6, Glasgow, St Andrew's College 1998).

Palmer, P. J., *The Company of Strangers, Christians and the Renewal of America's Public Life* (New York: Crossroad, 1990).

Peters, T., *Thriving on Chaos* (London: Pan Books, 1987).

Scottish Education Department, *Secondary Education, A Report of the Advisory Council on Education in Scotland* (Edinburgh: HMSO, 1947).

Scottish Office Education Department, *Higher Still: Opportunity for All* (Edinburgh: HMSO, 1994).

Scottish Office Education and Industry Department, *Consultation Paper on a Scottish Qualification for Headteachers* (Edinburgh: SOEID, 1997).

Shane, H. G., *Curriculum Change Toward the 21st Century* (Washington DC: National Education Association of the United States, 1977).

Strathclyde Regional Council, *Adapting to Change. Report of the Working Group on the Implications of Falling School Rolls* (Glasgow: SRC, 1986).

Wicklow, C., *Integrated Education in Northern Ireland, The Lagan Experience* (University of Glasgow: Unpublished M Ed Dissertation, 1997).

Williams, R., *Culture and Society 1780-1950 (London, Chatto and Windus, 1958).*

Chapter 12: The Primacy of Relationship: A Meditation on Education, Faith and the Dialogical Self

Belenky, M., Clincy, B., Goldberger, N., Tarule, J., *Women's Ways of Knowing: The Development of Self, Voice, and Mind* (New York: Basic Books, 1986).

Brown, L. & Gilligan, C., *Meeting at the Crossroads: Women's Psychology and Girls' Development* (Cambridge, MA: Harvard University Press, 1992).

Bruner, J., *Actual Minds, Possible Worlds* (Cambridge, MA: Harvard University Press, 1986).

Bryk, A. *et al., Catholic Schools and the Common Good* (Cambridge,

MA: Harvard University Press, 1993).

Carroll, M., 'Visions of the Virgin Mary: the effects of family structure on Marian apparitions', in *Journal for the Scientific Study of Religion* 22, pp. 205-21 (1983).

Carroll, M., 'The Virgin Mary at La Salette and Lourdes: Whom did the children see?', in *Journal for the Scientific Study of Religion* 24, pp. 56-74 (1985).

Cupitt, D., *What is a Story?* (London: SCM Press, 1991).

Cupitt, D., *The Time Being* (London: SCM Press, 1992).

Day, J., 'Recognition and responsivity: Unlearning the pedagogy of estrangement for a Catholic moral education', in McLaughlin, T., O'Keeffe, B. and O'Keefe, J (eds), *The Contemporary Catholic School: Context, Identity and Diversity* (London: Falmer, 1996).

Day, J., 'Speaking of belief: Language, performance, and narrative in the psychology of religion' in *The International Journal for the Psychology of Religion* 3(4), pp. 214-31, 1993a.

Day, J., *Desire, Risk, and the Yearning for Reception: Regulating Vocabularies in Moral and Religious Development* (Paper given at the 'Inquiries in Social Construction' Conference, Durham, New Hampshire, United States, 1993b).

Day, J., *Religious Development: Concepts and Consequences* (Paper delivered at the Colloquium on 'Religiosität bei psychosomatischen Patienten: Methodische und inhaltliche Aspekte'[Bad Kreuznach: Germany, 1993c].

Day, J., 'The moral audience: On the narrative mediation of moral "judgment" and moral "action"', in Tappan, M. & Packer, M. (eds), 'Narrative and Storytelling: Implications for Understanding Moral Development' in *New Directions for Child Development* 54, pp. 27-43 (1991a).

Day, J., 'Role-taking reconsidered: Narrative and cognitive-developmental interpretations of moral growth', in *The Journal of Moral Education* 20, pp. 305-17 (1991b).

Day, J., Naedts, M. and Saroglou, V., 'Reading interview texts for gender, self, and religious voice', in *International Journal for the Psychology of Religion* (in press).

Day, J. and Tappan, M., 'From the epistemic subject to dialogical selves: The narrative approach to moral development', in *Human Development* 39, 2, pp. 67-82 (1996).

Dolan, J., *The American Catholic Experience* (Garden City, N. Y: Doubleday, 1985).

Greeley, A., *The Mary Myth: On the Femininity of God* (Seabury, New York, 1977)

Greeley, A., 'Evidence that a maternal image of God correlates with liberal politics. Sociology and Social' in *Research* 72, pp. 150-54 (1988).

Greeley, A., *The Catholic Myth: The Behavior and Beliefs of American Catholics* (New York: Scribner's, 1990).

McBrien, R., *Catholicism* (2 vols.) (Minneapolis: Winston, 1980).

Rohr, R. and Martos, J., *Why be a Catholic? Understanding our Experience and Tradition* (Cincinnati: St Anthony Messenger Press, 1989).

Schreck, A., *Catholic and Christian: An explanation of Commonly Misunderstood Catholic Beliefs* (Ann Arbor, Servant Books, 1984).

Stanford, R., *Fatima Prophecy* (New York: Ballantine Books, 1988).

Tappan, M., 'Narrative, authorship, and the development of moral authority', in M. Tappan & M. Packer (eds.), Narrative and Storytelling: Implications for Understanding Moral Development, in *New Directions for Child Development* 54, pp. 5-27 (1991).

Tappan, M. and Brown, L., 'Stories told and lessons learned: Toward a narrative approach to moral development and moral education', in Harvard Educational Review 59, pp. 182-205.

Tracy, D., *The Analogical Imagination* (New York: Crossroad, 1982).

Wertsch, J., *Voices of the Mind: A Sociocultural Approach to Mediated Action* (Cambridge, MA: Harvard University Press, 1991).

Witherell, C. and Noddings, N. (eds), *Stories Lives Tell: Narrative and Dialogue in Education* (New York: Teachers College Press/ Columbia University Press, 1991).

Zimdars-Swartz, S., *Encountering MARY: From La Salette to Medjugorje* (Princeton University Press: Princeton, 1991).

Chapter 13: Spiritual Education, Religion and the Money Culture

Bauxrillard, J., *The Mirror of Production* (St Louis: Telos Press, 1975).

Bellah, R. M., *Beyond Belief: Essays on Religion in a Post-traditional World* (London: Harper and Row, 1970).

Berger, P. L., *The Heretical Imperative, Contemporary Possibilities of Religious Affirmation* (New York: Doubleday Anchor Press, 1979).

Chopp, R. S., *The Praxis of Suffering, An Interpretation of Liberation and Political Theologies* (Maryknoll, New York: Orbis Books, 1986).

Christian Aid, *The Gospel, The Poor and The Churches* (London: Christian Aid, 1994).

Davis, C., *Body as Spirit, The Nature of Religious Feeling* (London: Hodder and Stoughton, 1976).

Elster, J., *Sour Grapes: Studies in the Subversion of Rationality* (Cambridge: Cambridge University Press, 1983).

Erikson, E. H., *Identity, Youth and Crisis* (London: W. W. Norton, 1968).

Fingarette, H., *Self-Deception* (London, Routledge and Kegan Paul, 1969).

Habermas, J., *Legitimation Crisis* (Boston: Beacon Press, 1975).

Hartsock, N., *Money, Sex and Power, Towards a Feminist Historical Materialism* (New York: Longman, 1983).

Haug, W. F., *Critique of Commodity Aesthetics, Appearance, Sexuality and Advertising in Capitalist Society* (Cambridge: Polity Press, 1986).

Huczynski, A., *Encyclopedia of Organizational Change Methods* (Aldershot: Gower, 1987).

Hull, J. M., 'Religionism and Religious Education', in O'Maolain, C. (ed), *Religion and Conflict* (Centre for Research and Documentation: Belfast, 1995a).

Hull, J. M., *The Holy Trinity and Christian Education in a Pluralist World* (London: National Society, 1995b).

Hull, J. M., 'Christian Education in a Capitalist Society, Money and God' in Ford , D. and Stamps, D. L. (eds), *Essentials of Christian Community, Essays in Honour of Daniel W Hardy* (Edinburgh: T. & T. Clark, 1996a).

Hull, J. M., 'The ambiguity of spirituality' in Halstead, M. and Taylor, M. J. (eds), *Values in Education and Education in Values* (London: Falmer, 1996b).

Lamb, M. L., *Solidarity with Victims: Toward a Theology of Social Transformation* (London: Crossroad, 1982).

Marx, K., *Capital: A Critique of Political Economy*, 3rd vol. (Harmondsworth: Penguin, 1976).

McLaughlin, B. P. and Rorty, A. O. (eds), *Perspectives on Self-Deception* (London: University of California Press, 1988).

National Curriculum Council, *Education for Economic and Industrial Understanding* [Curriculum Guidance 4] (NCC: York, 1990).

Rossiter, G. and Crawford, M., *The Secular Spirituality of Youth* (unpublished paper delivered to the Religious Education Research Seminar in the University of Birmingham on 6 October, 1994).

Simmel, G., *The Philosophy of Money* [1901] (London: Routledge and Kegan Paul, 1990).

Slee, N., 'Spirituality in education, an annotated bibliography', in *Journal of Beliefs and Values* vol. 13, no. 2, 1992.

Sohn-Rethel, A., *Intellectual and Manual Labour: A Critique of Epistemology* (London: Macmillan, 1978).

Thompson, G., *The First Philosophers* [Studies in Ancient Greek

Society, vol. 2] (London: Lawrence and Wishart, 1961).

Via, D. Q., *Self-Deception and Wholeness in Paul and Matthew* (Minneapolis: Fortress Press, 1990).

Vilar, P., *A History of Gold and Money 1450-1920* (London: NLB, 1976).

Wolf, E. R., *Europe and the People without History* (London: University of California Press, 1982).

Chapter 14: Catholic Education: Authority and Engagement

Best, R. (ed), *Education, Spirituality and the Whole Child* (London: Cassell, 1996).

Congregation For Catholic Education, *The Religious Dimension of Education In A Catholic School* (London: Catholic Truth Society, 1988).

O'Brien, C.C. (*The Observer*, 1974)

Fowler, J., Nipkow, K. E. and Schweitzer, F., *Stages of Faith and Religious Development: Implications for Church, Education and Society* (London: SCM, 1992).

Gillis, C., *Pluralism: A New Paradigm for Theology* (Louvain: Peeters Press/W. B. Eerdmans, 1993).

Haldane, J., *The Need of Spirituality in Catholic Education* (Glasgow: St Andrew's College, 1997).

Hirst, P. & Peters, R. S., *The Logic of Education* (London: Routledge and Kegan Paul, 1970).

Lodge, D., *How Far Can you Go?* (London: Penguin, 1981).

McPhail, P., Ungoed-Thomas, J.R. and Chapman, H., *Moral Education in the Secondary School* (London: Longman, 1972).

Price, A., *Turbulent Times* (Glasgow: St Andrew's College, 1993).

Macquarrie, J. and Taylor, J. V., *Invitation to Faith* (Ridgefield CT: Morehouse, 1995).

Rodger, A., *Education and Faith in an Open Society* (Edinburgh: Handsel, 1982).

Scottish Office Education Department, *Curriculum and Assessment in Scotland: National Guidelines: Religious and Moral Education.*

5-14 (Edinburgh: SOED, 1992).

Wittgenstein, L., *Lectures and Conversations on Aesthetics, Psychology and Religious Belief* (ed) Barrett, C. (Oxford: Blackwell, 1938).

Chapter 15: Catholic Leadership: Similar or Different?

Australian Catholic University, acu-conversations @acu.edu.au. 1998.

Apple M. W., 'How the conservative restoration is justified: leadership and subordination in educational policy', in *International Journal of Leadership in Education* 1 (1, 1989).

Aronowitz, S and Giroux, H. A., *Post Modern Education: Politics, Culture and Social Criticism* (Minneapolis: University of Minnesota Press, 1991).

Barrett, J., *Total Leadership: How to Inspire and Motivate for Personal and Team Effectiveness* (London: Kogan Page, 1998).

Bennis, W., *On Becoming a Leader* (Massachusetts: Addison-Wesley, 1989).

Boles, H.W. and Davenport, J. A., *Introduction to Educational Leadership* (Revised Edition) (Lanham: University Press of America, 1983).

Bryant, M. T., 'Cross-cultural understandings of leadership: Themes from Native American interviews' in *Educational Management and Administration* 26, 1 (1998).

Bryman, A., *Leadership and Organisations* (London: Routledge and Kegan Paul, 1986).

Caldwell, B.J. and Spinks, J. M., *The Self-managing School* (London: Falmer, 1988).

Casteell, V., Forde, C. and Reeves, J., *A Framework for Leadership and Management Development in Scottish Schools* (Edinburgh: SOEID, 1997).

Chatterjee, D., *Leading Consciously: A Pilgrimage Towards Self-Mastery* (Boston: Butterworth-Heinemann, 1998).

Ciriello, M. J. (ed), *Formation and Development For Catholic School*

Leaders vol. II, The Principal as Spiritual Leader (Washington: United State Catholic Conference, 1994).

Connock, S. and JOHNS, T., *Ethical Leadership* (London: IPD, 1995).

Covey, S., *Principle-Centred Leadership* (London: Simon and Schuster, 1992).

Davies, B. and Ellison, L., *School Leadership for the 21st Century: A Competency and Knowledge Approach* (London: Routledge, 1997).

Duigan, P. A. and Bhindi, N., 'Authenticity in leadership: an emerging perspective', in *Journal of Educational Administration* 35, 3 (1997).

Fidler, B., 'School leadership: some key ideas', in *School Leadership and Management* 17, 1, pp. 23-37 (1997).

Gilley, K., *Leading from the Heart: Choosing Courage over Fear in the Workplace* (Boston: Butterworth-Heinemann, 1997).

Greenfield, T. and Ribbins, P. (eds), *Greenfield on Educational Administration: Towards a Humane Science* (London: Routledge, 1993).

Gronn, P., 'From transactions to transformations: A New World Order in the study of leadership', in *Educational Management and Administration* 24, 1, pp. 7-30 (1996).

Harrison, B. T., 'Revaluing leadership and service in educational management', in Bell, J. and Jarrospm, B. T., *Vision and Values in Managing Education: Successful Leadership Principles and Practice* (London: David Fulton, 1995).

Hofsstede, G., *Culture and Organisations: Software of the Mind* (New York: McGraw-Hill, 1991).

Kerry, T. and Murdoch, A., 'Education managers as leaders: Some thoughts on the context of the changing nature of schools', in *School Organisation* 13, 3, pp. 221-30 (1993).

Korac-Kakabadse, A. and Korac-Kakabadse, N., 'Best practice in the Australian Public Service (APS): an examination of discretionary leadership' in *Journal of Managerial Psychology* 12, 7, pp. 433-491 (1997).

Kotter, J. P., *Leading Change* (Boston: Harvard Business School Press, 1996).

O'Keefe, J. M., *Visionary Leadership in Catholic Schools* (Glasgow: St Andrew's College, 1998).

Paisey, A., 'Trends in educational leadership' in Harling, P. (ed), *New Directions in Educational Leadership* (London: Falmer, 1984).

Posner, B. Z. and Schmidt, W. H., 'Values congruence and differences between the interplay of personal and organisational value systems', in *Journal of Business Ethics* 12 (1993).

Senge, P. M., *The Fifth Discipline: The Art and Practice of The Learning Organization* (New York: Doubleday, 1990).

Shea, M., *Leadership Rules* (London: Century, 1990).

Shipka, B., *Leadership in a Challenging World: A Sacred Journey* (Boston: Butterworth-Heinemann, 1997).

Starratt, R. J., *Building an Ethical School* (London: Falmer, 1994).

Sjostrand, S. E., *The Two Faces of Management: The Janus Factor* (London: International Thomson Business Press, 1997).

Tribus, M., 'Quality in Education According to the Teachings of Denning and Feuerstein' in *School Psychology International* 17, pp. 93-112, (1996).

Wagner, T., 'Change as collaborative inquiry: A "Constructivist" methodology for reinventing schools' in *Phi Delta Kappan* 79, 7, pp. 512-17 (1998).